PRIMITIVE MAGIC

THE PSYCHIC POWERS OF SHAMANS AND SORCERERS

ERNESTO DE MARTINO

PRISM · UNITY

Originally published in the English Language 1972 by
Bay Books Pty. Ltd., N.S.W. Australia

This edition published in Great Britain 1988 by:
PRISM PRESS
Bridport, Dorset

and distributed by:
CARDINAL BOOKS
Metro House
Northgate
Chichester
West Sussex
PO19 1BE
U.K.

ISBN 1 85327 021 0

Reprinted 1990
Reprinted 1999

Printed and bound in the Channel Islands
by The Guernsey Press Company Limited

PREFACE

'There is no such thing as unreality; there are only various forms of reality' wrote Eugene Ionesco. The Western world is inclined to believe that only *its* concept of reality is valid, and that our frame of reference—the distinction between real and unreal that has developed throughout centuries of Western civilization—is applicable to all civilizations at all times. If ethnology itself, in all its wisdom and experience, has failed to see the subjectivity of such an attitude, it is not surprising that the 'average' man's reaction to magic and magical phenomena reflects an *a priori* rejection and disbelief; magic is for eccentrics and fakes, or for unenlightened savages.

De Martino points out the error of this line of thought. What is 'real' for us is not necessarily real for other civilizations, whether they be ancient, primitive, or contemporary with our own. It is Western man's conviction that his own world view is finally the only valid one that leads him to make presumptuous judgements upon phenomena that play no part in his own set of culturally-conditioned concepts. Whatever he fails to understand, or can make no use of, he rejects, automatically, as 'superstition'.

Many of our attitudes are based upon a series of what tradition has come to accept as 'granted facts'. Whatever lies beyond this framework of 'truths' is considered as 'unreal' or 'non-existent'. A fundamental principle, one that we all accept unquestioningly, is our own identity and autonomy as individuals, our participation in a world of ordered rapports and relationships. We cannot comprehend the possibility of an identity that is not decided from the moment of birth, one that might be very much 'hanging in the balance'. Nor can we understand a culture that sees the establishment of one's presence in the world as a task to be accomplished, and that presence as always fragile and liable to slip out of one's grasp, be undermined by outside influences, or even stolen away.

De Martino sees magical beliefs and institutions as the expression of this striving towards personal identity in a world of fragile and uncertain relationships between men, objects and natural phenomena. Magic, for those who practise it, is a system of compensations, guarantees and protections, a vital form of self-preservation. We may resort to drugs, or to the psychiatrist's couch, when we feel our sanity is endangered; the 'primitive' will consult his witch-doctor who may prescribe the temporary observance of some taboo.

If one considers the basic tenets of Christianity, the ideas of sin (taboo), expiation and forgiveness (exorcism), public worship (seance), etc., then the analogy between the loss of one's soul and the loss of one's 'presence' needs no explicit formulation. Yet how important is the acceptance of 'facts' on faith alone in the Christian religions? Upon how many 'established truths' do we base our beliefs? Why are we not as ready to apply the word 'superstition' to these, as we are to other cultural institutions? To see an analogy between Christ and the witch-doctor as redeemers of mankind can no longer be regarded as blasphemous, but rather as the vindication of the validity of two separate cultural truths.

In any debate about the reality of magical phenomena we must ask: what precisely do we mean by 'reality'? Do we mean only those things that are real for us? Or is something that is real for any one individual *ipso facto* a reality? Or does it all depend upon effectiveness? The pointing of a bone is most unlikely to cause us any discomfort, yet it can, and has, caused death among Australian tribal aborigines. Does our greater imperviousness to suggestion make the effectiveness of such a practice any less real in its own milieu?

Whether or not one accepts De Martino's thesis, the comprehensive ethnological and psychological documentation of this work must encourage any reader to revise at least some of his attitudes towards the 'scandalous' subject of magic, and make him more aware of the insularity of many aspects of the Western mind. Even this minor achievement would be a major step in humanism.

Paul Saye White

CONTENTS

Preface

PART I
The Problem of Magical Powers   1

PART II
The Historical Drama of the Magic World   65

PART III
The Problem of Magical Powers in the
History of Ethnology   155

PART I

The Problem of Magical Powers

The first barrier to our penetrating the secrets of the world of magic is prejudice. Prejudice, particularly, against the idea of magical powers.

It is usually perfunctorily and automatically supposed that magicians' claims are clearly false or misguided and that magical phenomena are at best illusions, and at worst, fakes.

Of course, against this point of view it is fruitless to try to argue a case for considering the facts. The sceptics are more likely to feel it more profitable to examine the origins and incidence of magic and try to explain how it survives despite the evident flimsiness of its claims. But such glib assumptions give no answer to many problems—problems that are glossed over or camouflaged out of sheer intellectual laziness or dishonesty.

We must begin our exploration by testing the supposedly self-evident claim that magical powers are non-existent. Here, a new difficulty presents itself and complicates what seemed, at first glance, to be a simple question of fact.

In investigating the reality of magic powers, there is a temptation to demand as evidence what must be comprehended through *reality* as if there was a concept which the mind apprehends as a self-evident truth; a concept which the investigator must apply or not, as if a predicate to the subject on which a judgment is to be formulated.

But sooner or later there must be some consideration given to the fact that this problem involves not just the quality of magic powers, but also our concept of reality. The research embraces not just the subject under dispute (magic powers), but the very criterion of judgment (the concept of reality).

So we must reject all presuppositions that cannot be justified by pure reasoning. Our own judgment on the concept of reality will be the result of active thought—thought that will allow no obstruction by preconceived notions.

The best way to get our enquiry under way and initiate support of our argument is to examine a series of ethnological documents that deal with apparently *existent* magical powers. Shirokogoroff writes as follows:

'In the state of great concentration the shamans and other people may come into communication with other shamans and ordinary people. Among all Tungus groups this is done quite consciously for practical needs, especially in urgent cases. What is the mechanism of this process may now be only hypothetically supposed. For practical use to achieve such a communication, the person must think about another person and formulate the desire, e.g. "please, come here" (to a given locality). This must be repeated until one "sees" the person called or until one "knows" that the person perceives the call. One can "see" the person called as a physical person in the natural surroundings. Afterwards when the person called is met he may be asked to confirm the surroundings and location at the moment of call. The person may also reply in the form of a bird or animal which would speak with the person's voice. The same animals cannot do it in their ordinary state. So these animals are not understood as physical animals. The Tungus who are connected by close relations, e.g. the children and parents, friendship, and mutual understanding (e.g. the fighting shamans may be hostile one to another but they would understand each other), may communicate easier than the people who do not know each other. Yet, some people cannot do it at all. About such a people the Tungus would say "they do not know how to do it", but they would not be able to explain how they do it themselves. The shamans use this method in their common practice when they want to meet some people or other shamans. Sometimes they do not realize the motive as to why they leave one place and go to another where they meet the person who called them—they go because they feel they must go. The best period for such a call is calm weather and night. V. K. Arseniev related to me a case in Maritime Gov., when under his observation a shaman invited the other two shamans from distant places on an accidental occasion (sudden illness of a young man) and they arrived within such a period that they could not have physically done it if invited by a messenger. The Tungus speak about such cases as a common thing, and do it when they have no time for sending a messenger.

This series of observations is interpreted in the sense that there is an element which exteriorates as an immaterial substance—the soul—which communicates with the souls of other persons. In the same group of evidences of the existence of the soul, the Tungus include the cases of "vision on distance" the mechanism of which is perhaps the same as that of "telepathy". According to the Birarcen, the soul of a dying man enters into the body of one of the young near-relatives. The young person may feel this. In addition to the above enumerated evidences confirming the existence of the soul, there must also be included a large number of coincidences. In fact distant communication may sometimes be only the mutual desire of meeting on the part of two people connected by common interest, especially when the periods of relative freedom are short which greatly increases the chance that two persons will think about the matter and dream about it at the same time. Such coincidence would be, of course, interpreted as an evidence of the activity of the soul.

This point of view is still more supported by the fact of the soul's travelling, according to the will of the bearers of the soul. In fact, before falling asleep the Tungus express their desire of seeing distant places and people. If the dream occurs the fact is interpreted as a voluntary direction of the soul. The practice of conscious loss of consciousness practised by the shamans and candidates to become shamans gives hundreds of facts which confirm the hypothesis of the existence of soul. In the same line are found all cases of hypnotic actions.

Some illustrations given by the Tungus are that in general when some misfortune to the people occurs, one may know it at a distance by a peculiar feeling perceived by the heart. On the third day after the grandfather of my communicator arrived, a nephew (or brother) had committed suicide by hanging himself. The grandfather had not been able to stay away for he had felt an uneasiness which compelled him to return. He was not surprised at the suicide. When people die the young members of the clan may know it and relate what has happened and the circumstances of the death. The Birarcen say that this is also true among the Manchus and the Dahurs'.

This further passage by the same author will show just how widespread is the use of seemingly abnormal psychic powers among the Tungus:

'The following occurrence may be taken as proof: a small boy "saw" his uncle commit patricide and he predicted that the murderer would return three days later with the antlers of a deer that had been killed by the father. The man returned as foreseen and was led immediately in front of the boy who repeated his accusation. The man confessed and was condemned to death.'[1]

Apart from the common methods such as reasoning and intuition, the Shaman has special ways of intensifying his perception and understanding — by thought-reading, communication at a distance and autosuggestion through dreams and states of frenzy. All these methods are used to varying degrees by ordinary members of the community, but for the Shaman they form a vital part of his art. The possibility of transmitting thoughts is a phenomenon not based on conclusions gleaned from given facts but, to the contrary, seems to result from direct communication. In many cases it may be explained as a simple 'intuition' or as a coincidence of thoughts between two individuals. Not all the Shamans possess this power; some are able to use it to a very limited extent while others to a far greater degree; but all of them make attempts in this direction. The Shamans use different methods when they communicate at a distance; they are able to achieve this in their dreams, in a state of ecstasy or even in a 'normal' state by concentrating intently on a wish. In each case they are 'sending out their soul' during a communication. Night-time is more conducive to this particularly as darkness enables the Shaman to induce a state of ecstasy far more easily. Communication at a distance often occurs in the form of animals which transmit the message to the recipient. These animals—bears, dogs, snakes—appear either in a dream during normal sleep or in hallucinatory visions (among the Birarcen). Sometimes the communication occurs in the form of voices being heard. Sometimes perception may not be brought into play at all, and the communication is received unconsciously, followed by the actions indicated in the message. It is extremely difficult to analyze these cases because it is hard to judge whether or not the communication at a distance has been effective. There are other cases where two persons (of whom one may be a Shaman, or both) do not know one another or exactly when a particular communication has taken place, as in urgent cases when a Shaman requires the help of another.[2]

1. S. M. Shirokogoroff, *The Psychomental Complex of the Tungus.* London, 1935, pp. 117 ff., 118 note.
2 Shirokogoroff: op. cit. p. 361

Abnormal psychic powers are sometimes in evidence during the Shamans' seances; the author states that the Shamans can sometimes tell what people present at the seance are thinking and doing. In many cases this is easy, for the Shaman may guess the thoughts of people who have been under his influence for a long time and whom he has known for years; when those present reach an ecstatic state the whole thing may be explained quite simply as the result of the Shaman's own powers of suggestion. But other cases are not so simple. For example, a Shaman accused a young man at one seance of having eaten the kidney of a sacrificial animal—it was not possible that the Shaman knew who had done this . . . The Shaman ordered the youth to put back the kidney, and the latter promptly vomited it into a bowl.[3]

Trilles' book about the pygmies of equatorial Africa gives further interesting examples along these lines. A sacrifice was made before the undertaking of a tribal war:

> 'On this occasion the victim is to be an elephant, chosen in a special manner. For three to seven days, depending upon the importance of the tribe that is to be attacked, the tribal chief follows a strict fast. During this period he neither eats nor drinks . . . During one of the nights that follow this three to seven-day fast, the chief has a dream in which he sees a young elephant—this in itself is not surprising, but the amazing thing is that, upon waking, the chief is able to describe the beast, its weight and height, and the exact place where it may be found. He declares that he has seen the elephant, the clearing where it grazes, the trees that surround it and he indicates the road to take and what dangers to avoid. Everything is later verified.'[4]

On another occasion a negrillo sorcerer 'sees' the canoes carrying the men for whom Trilles is waiting in his magic mirror.

> 'One day I was talking to a negrillo witch-doctor. I was waiting for my paddlers to bring provisions and I spoke of this to the fellow while wondering aloud if they were far away and if they would bring me the things I'd asked for. "Nothing could be easier to find out!" he cried. Then he took his magic mirror and with great concentration

3. Op. cit. p. 331
4. R. G. Trilles: *Les Pygmées de la forêt équatoriale*, Paris, 1931, p. 493

pronounced some incantation. Then he said: "At this moment the men are rounding this bend in the river (it was more than a day's paddling away), the tallest man has just shot a large bird, it falls into the water and the men are paddling hard towards it. They've caught it. They're bringing you back what you asked for."

In fact everything was true; the provisions, the shooting, the bird, and, as I said, they were a day away!'[5]

This vision seems to go hand-in-hand quite often with the comprehension of foreign languages which, to all intents and purposes, are quite unknown to the person:

'During one of our voyages with Le Roy, we arrived at a village one evening and met the witch-doctor who described to us in detail the route we had taken, the stops we had made, various meetings, the food we ate and even the conversation we exchanged. Here is a typical example: On the way we came across a small tortoise and Le Roy said "There's tonight's dinner", and because we were very hungry, I added, laughing: "And if necessary we'll add the guide's head to it!" We were speaking French, so the witch-doctor could not have understood a word, yet, without budging from his village, he had seen us in his magic mirror and repeated everything we said.'[6]

The negrillo tribes are far-apart and isolated, but the unity between them is maintained by the witch-doctors, magicians and singers:

'All the pygmy tribes that we have come across are almost completely unknown to each other, unless they live quite close together or have recently branched off from a single tribe. It is possible that tribal unity and awareness could be much stronger than we think, sustained by the activities of the priests, magicians and singers who go from tribe to tribe, rediscover them, visit them, as if called in some unaccountable way—through their mysterious sciences.

On this subject we will mention the following occurrence. An old chief had just died in our region. This particular small tribe was very isolated. Two days after his death, without anyone having advised him, a young negrillo magician arrived in the village to preside over the burial of the old man. When I asked him how he had known,

5. Trilles: op. cit. p. 181
6. Trilles: op. cit. p. 180. Trilles adds to this: 'And how many other cases we could mention!'

he replied: "I know that you are our friend. Silege mfunga
wa lur—ask the wind that passes by." His answer was
given in all seriousness. He had no wish to make fun of
me.'[7]

Ethnology has at its disposal D. Leslie's document concerning paragnostic attitudes among the Zulus. The author,
who was himself an observer, tells how one day he had to
cross Zulu territory in order to meet up with his Kafir
hunters. There was no sign of the Kafirs at the appointed
meeting-place. A porter then advised Leslie to consult a
clairvoyant and the explorer welcomed the suggestion. This
is how the clairvoyant 'opened up the doors of distance':

'The doctor then made eight little fires—that being the
number of my hunters; on each he cast some roots,
which emitted a curious sickly odor and thick smoke;
into each he cast a small stone, shouting, as he did so, the
name to which the stone was dedicated; then he ate some
"medicine", and fell over in what appeared to be a trance
for about ten minutes, during all which time his limbs kept
moving. Then he seemed to wake, went to one of the fires,
raked the ashes about, looked at the stone attentively,
described the man faithfully, and said: "This man has died
of the fever, and your gun is lost."

To the next fire as before: "This man" (correctly
described) "has killed four elephants," and then he described
the tusks. The next: "This man" (again describing him)
"has been killed by an elephant, but your gun is coming
home," and so on through the whole, the men being
minutely and correctly described; their success or non-
success being equally so. I was told where the survivors
were, and what they were doing, and that in three months
they would come out, but as they would not expect to find
me waiting on them there so long after the time appointed,
they would not pass that way.

I took a particular note of all this information at the
time, and to my utter amazement it turned out correct in
every particular.

It was scarcely within the bounds of possibility that this
man could have had ordinary intelligence of the hunters;

7. Trilles: op. cit. p. 144. We note that Trilles seems to be very interested
in the problem of magical powers as discovered among the tribes he
explored. Vide op. cit. pp. 162, 173 ff.

they were scattered about in a country two hundred miles away.'[8]

Reference is made in some ethnological documents to strange 'physical' powers which appear to be able to control matter; powers that are able to 'suspend' or inhibit known natural laws. The natives of the Fiji islands cook and eat the ripe 'masawe' root. The actual cooking of the root is a ceremony in itself, called the 'vilavilareivo' which means 'he who enters the furnace'. The small tribe of the Na Ivilankatas who live on the island of Mbenga prepare a ditch full of burning-hot stones in which the masawe roots will be cooked, but before doing this they themselves walk over the burning stones and suffer no ill-effects. Only the members of the Na Ivilankata tribe have the power to resist the burning quality of fire, a privilege that has been passed down to them by their mythical ancestor, Tui Nkualita, who received it himself from Tui Na Moliwai, chief of the Miliwai tribe.

We will examine some of the documents that describe this rite, beginning with an extract from B. Thomson's *South Sea Yarns*:

'We found a shallow pit, nineteen feet wide, dug in the sandy soil, a stone's throw from high-water mark, in a small clearing among coconut trees . . .
The ditch extended from the coast to the deep forest behind. It was full of large burning logs and round stones about the size of a human head . . .
When we were at last summoned, the fire had been burning for more than four hours. The pit was filled with a white-hot mass shooting out little tongues of white flames, and throwing out a heat beside which the scorching sun was a pleasant relief.'[9]

After the unburnt pieces of wood had been taken away there remained only the heap of glowing stones in the middle of the ditch, and these were carefully smoothed out. Thomson comments: 'any doubt as to the heat of the stones at the

---

8. D. Leslie: *Among the Zulu and Amatongos*, Edinburgh 1875, quoted by A. Lang, *The Making of Religion*, 1909, pp. 68 ff.
9. Basil Thomson, *South Sea Yarns*, Edinburgh-London, 1894, pp. 196, 202 ff.

end was set at rest by tongues of flame that played continually among them.'[10] Then the ceremony began:

'All eyes are fixed expectant on the dense bush behind the clearing, whence the Shadrachs, Meshachs, and Abednegos of the Pacific are to emerge. There is a cry of "Vutu! Vutu!" and forth from the bush, two and two, march fifteen men, dressed in garlands and fringes. They tramp straight to the brink of the pit. The leading pair show something like fear in their faces, but do not pause, perhaps because the rest would force them to move forward. They step down upon the stones and continue their march round the pit, planting their feet squarely and firmly on each stone. Then the natives throw leaves into the ditch; the participants return and trample down the leaves, surrounded by a dense smoke . . . The furnace was now ready for the cooking of the masawe roots.

Before the actual ceremony, a stone was taken from the furnace and one of the Europeans placed a handkerchief on it. He allowed it to remain there from the time the first man entered the ditch until the last one left it—a period of fifteen to twenty seconds. All the folds of the handkerchief that were in direct contact with the stone were carbonized and the other parts were badly scorched. The feet of four or five of the participants were examined: "they were quite unmarked and showed no signs of having been burnt; and the ankle ornaments, made from dried fern-leaves, were also unburnt." This, according to one of the influential members of the tribe, was part of the "miracle" because "dried fern-leaves burn like cotton-waste, and there were flames shooting up between the stones." According to this native, the handkerchief would not have burned if, instead of it having been placed on a single stone, it had been thrown into the middle of the ditch, because "as linen is made by the human hand, it would have become part of this power that has been granted by god to man." An outsider could also be invested with the same power, but only if one of the privileged tribe went with him when he crossed the stones.'[11]

Some years later the same fire-crossing ceremony at Mbenga was described in detail by T. M. Ocken[12]:

10. Op. cit. p. 203
11. Basil Thomson, *South Sea Yarns*, Edin., London, 1894, p. 203 ff.
12. Dr. T. M. Ocken, F.S.L. *An Account of The Fiji Fire Ceremony*, Transactions of The New Zealand Institute, XXXI, 1898

He tells how it took the natives three days to make their preparations—to dig the pit, line it with stones and heat it with burning logs (this took thirty-six to forty hours). Ocken and his friends spent the three days gathering information from witnesses concerning the firewalk, but without very encouraging results. Various explanations were given as to how the participants made their feet immune to fire with 'secret products', etc. When the time arrived for the actual ceremony, the photographers and other witnesses were placed at vantage points around the pit or 'lovo'. This was round, with a diameter of twenty-five to thirty feet. The flat bottom was covered with red-hot stones, and around the edges, the temperature was 114°F. Before the actual walk began, the pit was cleared of the burning logs by a number of natives who kept up a continuous rhythmic chant. Then the burning stones were uncovered, revealing tongues of flame, and were spread out over the bottom of the pit. Ocken had his thermometer suspended over the pit and it registered 282°, but it had to be withdrawn because the intense heat was causing the instrument to melt. Finally the descendants of Na Galita arrived, six or eight of them, amid wild acclamation from the audience. They entered the pit without hesitation, in single-file and, walking neither quickly nor slowly, they crossed the pit and then turned around and left it the way they had entered, their leader remaining a little longer than the others. After the walk, heaps of hibiscus leaves were thrown into the pit, causing clouds of steam. Ocken took the opportunity, before the ceremony, to examine some of the participants' feet, but he saw no evidence of any preparation, nor any unusual hardness. Not even charms were used any longer. He examined the feet again, afterwards, and found nothing unusual. The natives considered that only the few could work the 'miracle', but that anyone, if held by the hand. could walk, unharmed, in the pit.

According to these accounts the Fiji islanders believe that anyone may walk unharmed on the burning stones, provided he is accompanied by a member of the privileged tribe. This 'belief' was closely observed by the ethnologist, Gudgeon, at the Umu-Ti ceremony at Rarotonga (Cook Archipelago), the ceremony being similar to the 'Vilavilareivo' at Mbenga.

Gudgeon, on this occasion, crossed the stones unharmed, as well as his friends, with the exception of one who was seriously burnt. He writes of it as follows:

'I must tell you that I have seen and gone through the fire ceremony of the Umu-Ti.

The oven was lit at about dawn on the 20th of January, and I noticed that the stones were very large, as also were the logs that had been used in the oven for heating purposes.

About 2 p.m. we went to the oven and there found the tohunga (a Raiatea man) getting matters ready, and I told him that, as my feet were naturally tender, the stones should be levelled down a bit. He assented to this, and evidently he had intended to do so, for shortly after, the men with very long poles that had hooks, began to level the stones flat in the oven, which was some twelve feet in diameter. He then went with his disciple and pointed to two stones that were not hot, and instructed him the reason was that they had been taken from a marae, or sacred place.

He then unwound two bundles, which proved to be branches of a large-leaved Ti (or Dracana) plucked, it is said, from two of these trees standing close together, and it is said that the initiated can on such occasions see the shadow of a woman with long hair, called te varua kino (evil spirit), standing between the trees. The right hand branch is the first plucked, and it is said that the branches bend down to be plucked.

So much for the Shamanism, and now for the facts.

The tohunga (priest) and his tauira (pupil) walked each to the oven, and then halting, the prophet spoke a few words, and then each struck the edge of the oven with the ti branches. This was three times repeated, and then they walked slowly and deliberately over the two fathoms of hot stones. When this was done, the tohunga came to us, and his disciple handed his ti branch to Mr. Goodwin, at whose place the ceremony came off, and they went through the ceremony. Then the tohunga said to Mr. Goodwin, "I hand my mana (power) over to you; lead your friends across." Now, there were four Europeans—Dr. W. Craig, Dr. George Craig, Mr. Goodwin, and myself—and I can only say that we stepped out boldly. I got across unscathed, and only one of the party was badly burned; and he, it is said, was spoken to, but like Lot's wife looked behind him —a thing against all rules.

I can hardly give you my sensations, but I can say this —that I knew quite well I was walking on red hot stones and could feel the heat, yet I was not burned. I felt something resembling slight electric shocks, both at the time and afterwards, but that is all. I do not know that I should recommend everyone to try it. A man must have mana to do it; if he has not, it will be too late when he is on the hot stone of Tama-ahi-roa.

I cannot say that I should have performed this wizard trick had I not been one of the fathers of the Polynesian Society, and bound to support the superiority of the New Zealander all over Polynesia—indeed all over the world. I would not have missed the performance for anything.

To show you the heat of the stones, quite half an hour afterwards someone remarked to the priest that the stones would not be hot enough to cook the ti. His only answer was to throw his green branch on the oven, and in a quarter of a minute it was blazing. As I have eaten a fair share of the ti cooked in the oven, I am in a position to say that it was hot enough to cook it well.

I walked with bare feet, and after we had done so about 200 Maoris followed. No one, so far as I saw, went through with boots on. I did not walk quickly across the oven, but with deliberation, because I feared that I should tread on a sharp point of the stones and fall. My feet also were very tender. I did not mention the fact, but my impression as I crossed the oven was that the skin would all peel off my feet. Yet all I really felt when the task was accomplished was a tingling sensation not unlike slight electric shocks on the soles of my feet, and this continued for seven hours or more. The really funny thing is that, though the stones were hot enough an hour afterwards to burn up green branches of the ti, the very tender skin of my feet was not even hardened by the fire.

Many of the Maoris thought they were burned, but they were not, at any rate not severely.

Do not suppose that the man who directed this business was an old tohunga. He is a young man, but of the Raiatea family, who are hereditary fire-walkers.

I can only tell you it is mana—mana tangata and mana atua.'[13]

The documents are sufficient proof for the introduction of the problem of reality, in that they invite one to make a definite decision. The first reaction is often to withdraw from the argument by stating flatly that magic powers are 'a priori' impossible; at the most, some people will admit curiosity as to how primitive tribes and even some Europeans are so effectively convinced that the illusions are real. But whatever the attitude, it cannot be denied that ethnological documents do show that the problem of reality or illusion *does* exist. However strange and puzzling the subject may appear, the existence of such documents as these must activate the mind and direct it towards a path that must be followed to the very end. Shirokogoroff contributes to the discussion when he states that:

'there are ways of approaching a problem for the purpose of research which were not even possible a few years ago. The gathering and publication of facts have long been retarded by a scepticism that is the result of both ignorance and prejudice. In fact, until recent years, anyone who dared to discuss these questions or publish their findings would have met all sorts of opposition from the 'men of science" for whom the entire subject is but part of "superstition" or "folklore". He would have been accused of lacking a "critical approach" whilst his critics themselves deal in hypotheses and theories that they accept as "truths". In actual fact, the reaction of these scientists is itself of considerable ethnological interest and contains at least as much "folklore" as the attitudes found among the Tungus.'[14]

Admittedly ethnological documentation that deals with the reality of magical powers is often devoid of any guarantee of authenticity. The reports are sometimes even contradictory, so that one is unable to discern the claims which may be the result of illusions or hallucinations, those which are the

13. W. E. Gudgeon: *The Umu-Ti or Fire-Walking Ceremony* in The Journal of the Polynesian Society V.iii, 1899. For another account of a European's participation in such a ceremony, see Miss Teuiraw Henry: *Fire-Walking in Tonga* in The Journal of the Polynesian Society II, 1893, p. 2.
14. Shirokogoroff: Op. cit. p. 118 note.

product of witch-doctors' tricks and those which are simple coincidences promoted into the realm of the miraculous.

We recall that Trilles was present when, with the help of a magic mirror, a thief was correctly identified. E. Schebesta, who was also among the Negrillos, observed a similar case in which a different technique was used:

> 'All the pygmies had crowded into the hut and inside one could hear the beating of drums and monotonous chanting. The pygmy who had the magic powers, with arms outstretched held an antelope horn that was "anointed" with wax and which contained some magic "medicine". Without saying a word, the pygmy crouched down and stared ahead, his pupils dilated. Minutes went by until his arm began to tremble, slightly at first and then more violently. The man became unconscious, fell into a trance, struggled frantically, howled and sighed, gesticulated, thrashed about to the point of exhaustion and made wild threats. The other participants pushed him violently outside the hut where he fell and rolled about on the ground, the antelope horn still gripped firmly in his hand. He called out the name of the village, cried out inarticulate sounds and sometimes phrases, but did not give the name of the thief.'[15]

Apparently the attempt was a failure, so another witch-doctor intervened and snatched the antelope horn from his colleague who was meanwhile regaining consciousness. The second one then entered a trance:

> 'This trance was characterized by a twitching that was more violent than the first attempt . . . the same howling and struggling occurred and, after he had been ejected forcibly from the hut he rushed off into the dark forest. He ran through the forest for about four kilometers until he reached the neighboring village. He battered down the door of one of the huts and searched about inside, but without finding the stolen object, which, he indicated, had been taken away. Then he said that 'the thieves were the owners of the hut and that a pygmy woman had left the camping area the day before. The witch-doctor was still in a frenzy and had to be restrained by the others who

15. E. Schebesta: *Der Urwald ruft wieder. Salzburg-Leipzig* 1936, pp. 45-47

snatched the horn away from him, after which he regained consciousness . . .'16

Obviously one would not consider such a document as proof of paragnostic powers among peoples who live in a so-called 'natural state'. Were the accused really the guilty ones? Schebesta mentions other similar occurrences, but dismisses them all, including the example cited, as 'hallucinations'. Why does he reject them, a priori, as false, without troubling to make a systematic analysis of the subject?

In a report by M. Gusinde we are told:

'On the 23 March, 1923, in the company of some other people, Masemikens said to me quite distinctly: "I can see a long canoe approaching, with some 'touwisiwa'" (Phalacrocorax olivaceus); Accordingly, the next day, a dense flock of these birds was seen; it is extremely rare to see them cross a stretch of water in so great a number.'17

We see here a kind of precognition. But one may also claim that the native 'sensed' the birds' approach in which case it would be an example of hyperaesthesis or, on the other hand, and this is unlikely, he may simply have made an induction based on signs that he had observed on previous occasions, in which case it would be the result of a normal thinking process.

In other cases of 'foresight' among the Yamana, we are left with a feeling of uncertainty:

'(on one occasion) Emily, staring at the ocean, cried out: "The sea is turning white, it is frothing and foaming!" The surface of the water was as smooth as glass, so we were astonished at her words. But the next day some bad weather rose up in the east and caused high waves and we remembered what had happened on the previous day. It was noon when Emily had foreseen the change.'18

'In winter the families gather together in their dwellings for some time . . . If a snow-storm persists and the people become worried, the "yekamus" promises: "Calm down and be content. We will have good weather tomorrow (or the day after tomorrow)." The small children remain quiet and

16. E. Schebesta: op. cit., loc. cit.
17. M. Gusinde: *Die Feuerland-Indianer* II ('Die Yamana'), Modling, 1937, pp. 1422 ff.
18. M. Gusinde: op., cit. p. 1423

the adults wait, full of hope. Accordingly, on the predicted day, the storm dies down and there may even be a clear sky. On one rainy day I heard: "Tomorrow 'Uxapu' (the constellation, Jacob's Staff) will appear." And on another winter's day a Yekamus assured me: "Tomorrow we shall see the 'Yoalox Tarnuxipa' (the Aldebaran star)." Each time the prediction came true.'[19]

Gusinde is guarded in his comments: 'I am unable to say whether or not these Yekamus are guided by a knowledge that arises from experience and precise observation.'[20] But the same author comments move openly on the Selk'nam witch-doctors: 'When the witch-doctors predict bad weather, one must not assume that they base this on their experience of nature or on lengthy observation, without their realizing that this is precisely what they *are* doing'.[21]

Gusinde admits later to being unable to explain exactly which everyday experiences are used by the witch-doctor in his 'professional' activities. In any case it is more likely to be an unconscious 'Einfuhlen' or intuitive perception than a skilful manipulation of his knowledge of nature, and he doubtless mixes native perception with a considerable amount of private fantasy.

K. Rasmussen also reports a similar somewhat confusing incident. One evening, the Iglulik Shaman, Padloq, was using his art to enquire about the fate of his adopted son, Qahitsoh. The latter was a poor, emaciated creature whose health caused much concern and who eventually died. Padloq was standing with his eyes closed, chanting some magic incantation. After searching for an hour in the depths of his mind, he believed that he had found what he was looking for: during the previous summer his son had gone out in a boat, using a sail which had belonged to a dead man. A breath of wind from the land of the dead had swept over the child and caused his sickness. Qahitsoh was waiting for his time to pass into the land of the dead. Rasmussen's story continues:

'We settled down then all together on the bench, waiting for the meal that was cooking. It was midwinter, the days

19. Gusinde: op. cit. pp. 1421 ff.
20. ibid.
21. Gusinde: op. cit. I 'Die Selk'nam' p. 772

were short, and the evenings long. A blubber lamp was used for the cooking, the pot being hung over it by a thong from a harpoon stuck into the wall. Suddenly the pot gave a jump, and rocked to and fro, as if someone had knocked it. The heat had melted the snow at the spot where the harpoon was fixed, the harpoon had slipped down a little, jerking the thong, and making the lumps of meat hop in their soup. Padloq, still under the influence of his trance, leapt up from his place and declared that we must at once shift camp, and move up on to the firm old winter ice; for our hut here was built among some pressure ridges forming a fringe between the old ice and the open sea. We had taken up this position in order better to observe the movements of the walrus, but Padloq now asserted that we were too near the open sea, and were filling the feeding grounds of the walrus with our own undesirable emanations. They did not like the smell. of us. And the sea spirit Takanakapsaluk was annoyed, and had just shown her resentment by making our meat come alive in the pot. This is said to be a sign often given to people out near the fringe of the ice, and we were obliged to accept it. But the rest of us were not at all inclined to turn out just at that moment, all in the dark, and shift camp. It would be several hours before we got into new quarters, and hours again before we got anything to eat. Therefore, despite Padloq's protest, we stayed where we were, and when we had eaten our fill, crept into our sleeping bags. None of us dreamed how nearly Padloq had been right until next morning, when to our horror we found a crack right across the floor. It was only a narrow one, but wide enough for the salt water to come gurgling up through it now and again. The roof of the hut was all awry over by the entrance, and on knocking out a block of snow, we saw the black waters of the open sea right in front of us. The young ice on which the snow hut was built had broken away, but instead of being carried out to sea, it had drifted in at the last moment among some high pressure ridges kept in place by a small island.

After that I was obliged to promise Padloq that I would in future have more respect for his predictions as a Shaman.'[22]

22. K. Rasmussen. *Intellectual Culture of the Iglulik Eskimos,* in 'Report of the 5th Thule Expedition', 1921-24, VII, No. 1 (Copenhagen, 1929, pp. 34 ff.).

Once again it is impossible to say whether or not this is a case of precognition. Or is it just a normal induction proceeding from more or less consciously registered signs? Or is it an 'Einfuhlen' or intuitive perception of one's surroundings? Or perhaps just pure coincidence? The document is too ambiguous and imprecise for us to answer.

Father Trilles, in his work on the Pygmies of equatorial Africa, reports what is apparently an incident of vision into the future, but, once again, this document cannot be used as an ethnological demonstration of an act of precognition. A negrillo witch-doctor, when consulted about a suitable time for beginning an elephant hunt, reacts in the following manner:

> 'The witch-doctor becomes more and more excited; chanting all the time and turning in circles, he bends backwards and strikes the ground violently with his head; then he takes great leaps into the air; he approaches a psychic state which is somewhere between consciousness and trance: his divining powers increase; he goes through the actions of a hunter and mimes the quarry and the various phases of the hunt in the most life-like way . . .'[23]

The witch-doctor plays out the entire drama of the hunt; the attack, the retreat, the man who flees, the one who is seized by the maddened beast, and finally the victory of the bravest.

> 'The seance came to an end and the tribe was satisfied to know that the hunters would kill eight elephants, of which six would be males; they were also informed that one of the hunters would be killed.
> The hunters made their last preparations and left for the hunt in a state of elation. The most amazing thing was that all of Akhor's predictions proved to be entirely correct.'[24]

It is certainly impossible to treat this as a lucky coincidence, or as hyperaesthesis, or as the usual kind of foresight. Even clairvoyance and telepathy must be excluded from consideration, as no prior knowledge could have given rise to such a complex prediction. Naturally, one could claim that the witch-doctor might have guessed the place where the

23. R. G. Trilles; *Les Pygmées de la forêt équatoriale*. Paris, 1932, pp. 189 ff.
24. ibid. pp. 193 ff.

hunt would take place. Then there is the possible hypothesis of the power of suggestion; the coincidence between the prediction and the actual result of the hunt could be explained by claiming that the huntsmen, under the influence of suggestion, *played out* what they *believed* must happen. But this theory becomes complicated when one remembers that, for all the events to unfold as predicted, a certain type of behavior from the elephants was essential, and this, of course, was completely divorced from any amount of willing or wish on the part of the hunters. It still appears, at this stage, that ethnological documents are unable to clarify the problems surrounding powers of precognition.

What is sometimes thought to be precognition may, in fact, be pure coincidence, or else a belief or conviction which may influence a person's actions through suggestion. It may be the usual kind of foresight, based on observation and a perspicacious nature, or it may be a simple premonition of death or illness brought about by a vague awareness of changes that are taking place in the organism. Furthermore, many presages are nothing more than unaccomplished acts (Freud's *Fehlleistungen*) that are being unconsciously stimulated. These stimuli may act on a future occasion and thus determine the future so that it conforms to the original presage, and so produce what appears to be a true precognition. In the same manner, many dreams that are interpreted as prophecies and which eventually come true, may be explained by psychoanalysis. Certain unconscious complexes become active in dreams and can condition actions in the waking state, thus making reality conform to the content of the dream. Besides this, even if one accepts the existence of clairvoyant and telepathic powers, there still remains the possibility that the clairvoyant, when consulted about the course of future events, simply reads between the lines and discovers the unconscious wishes of his client. Even if the client remains quite uninfluenced by any power of suggestion that may emanate from the clairvoyant's prophecy, his unfulfilled desires may themselves determine his actual conduct, so that he acts in the way indicated by the 'fortune-teller'—and this, of course, will induce the client to vouch for the clairvoyant's apparent powers of precognition. And finally, when the witch-doctor predicts that 'such and such a person will arrive tomorrow', and that person does arrive, one should not jump to the conclusion that the absence of normal channels of information must make this a straight-forward case of precognition; it could be that the person had been 'seen' coming, that his approach had been 'sensed' or that it was a simple case of distant thought-reading. However, as ethnological documents say nothing about these problems and possibilities, for the time being, they must remain un-solved.

We turn now to a different type of ethnological document that is also unable to solve the mystery. R. P. Callaway gives many instances in his study of the religious system of the Zulus. These are accounts related by the natives themselves, concerning their belief in paragnostic powers. Here is one of them:

'There is among black men a something which is divination within them. When anything valuable is lost, they look for it at once; when they cannot find it, each one begins to practise this inner divination, trying to feel where the thing is; for, not being able to see it, he feels internally a pointing, which tells him if he will go down to such a place it is there, and he will find it. At length it says he will find it; at length he sees it, and himself approaching it; before he begins to move from where he is, he sees it very clearly indeed, and there is an end of doubt. That sight is so clear that it is as though it was not an inner sight, but as if he saw the very thing itself, and the place where it is; so he quickly arises and goes to the place. If it is a hidden place he throws himself into it, as though there was something that impelled him to go as swiftly as the wind; and, in fact; he finds the thing, if he has not acted by mere head-guessing. If it has been done by real inner divination, he really sees it. But if it is done by mere head-guessing and knowledge that he has not gone to such a place and such a place, and that therefore it must be in such another place, he generally misses the mark.'[25]

This sort of 'interior divination' is used to ensure the metagnomic powers of the 'inyanga' or clairvoyant. When

25. R. P. Callaway: *The Religious System of the Amazula*, 'Publications of the Folk-lore Society' XV, 1884, pp. 338 ff.

the spirits enter or take hold of someone and grant him powers, an argument arises between those who are believers and those who are more sceptical:

'Some dispute and say, "No. The fellow is merely mad. There is no Itongo in him." Others say, "O, there is an Itongo in him; he is already an inyanga."

The others say, "No; he is mad. Have you ever hidden things for him to discover by his inner sight, since you say he is an inyanga?"

They say, "No; we have not done that."

They ask, "How then do you know he is an inyanga?"

They say, "We know it because he is told about medicines, which he goes to dig up."

They reply, "O! he is a mere madman. We might allow that he is an inyanga if you had concealed things for him to find, and he had discovered what you had concealed. But you tell us what is of no import, as you have not done this."[26]

Then, on the order of the village medicine-man, the test is prepared:

'They take things; one takes beads, and goes and hides them; others take picks, and go and hide them; others hide assagais; others bracelets; others hide their sticks, others their kilts, others their ornaments, others their pots; others hide baskets, and say, "Just let us see if he will find all these things or not." Others hide cobs and maize; others the ears of amabele, or sweet cane, or of ujiba, or the heads of upoko.'[27]

But the spirit, by means of a dream, informs the 'inyanga' of the discussion and of the test to which he will have to submit. The next day, before he is called, the clairvoyant goes to the place where the test is to take place:

'He says to them, "Have you then hid things for me to find?"

They deny, saying, "No; we have not hidden things for you to find."

He says, "You have."

They deny, saying, "It is not true; we have not."

He says, "Am I not able to find them?"

26. Callaway: op. cit., p. 273
27. ibid. pp. 276 ff.

They say, "No; you cannot. Have we hidden then things for you to find?"

He says, "You have."

They deny, declaring that they have not done so. But he asserts that they have.

When they persist in their denial, he starts up, shaking his head. He goes and finds the beads; he finds the picks, and the kilts, and the bracelets; he finds the cobs of maize, and the ears of the amabele and ujiba and of upoko; he finds all the things they have hidden. They see he is a great inyanga when he has found all the things they have concealed.'[28]

Callaway reports another case of a native who had lost a heifer and who went to the clairvoyant to ask him to find it. When asked the reason for his visit, the native replied that he had lost several head of cattle: he said this intentionally in order to see if the clairvoyant was able to correct the erroneous information. If this had not been done, and if the clairvoyant had spoken as if there were, in fact, several head of cattle, then the client would have known that the 'inyanga' was not a true master of the art[29]. In another case, a native named John visited the clairvoyant to find out what was causing his sister's sickness. According to the custom, he should have replied to the 'inyanga's' questions by beating the earth lightly with a rod if the answer was negative, and harder if the answer was affirmative. Having decided that he would not be tricked, John beat the ground in a mechanical manner, not following the convention. The clairvoyant became obviously embarrassed and could not extricate himself from the ruse. John said: 'Very well, my friend, as you are not capable of telling me what sort of sickness it is, give me back my shilling, and I'll find another clairvoyant.' He went to another clairvoyant who used a more reliable method—the replies to his questions were not given by the client, but by 'animated sticks'.[30] Even those who have faith in the technique that failed to convince John have,

28. Callaway: *The Religious System of the Amazulu*, 'Publications of the Folk-Lore Society' XV, 1884, pp. 278 ff. For a similar test, see pp. 320 ff.
29. Callaway: Op. cit., pp. 300 ff.
30. ibid. pp. 323-326

nevertheless, a certain critical sense, and proceed with caution, so as not to be swindled:

'Men go to the diviner that he may tell them what they wish to know. They merely go to him, and on their arrival do not tell him for what purpose they have come. They are silent. But he tells them they have come on some matter of importance. They assent by striking the ground. If they strike vehemently, they do so because they hear the diviner mention things which they know and about which they have come to him. If he mentions things unknown to them, they strike the ground slightly. If he mentions the very things they know, they strike vehemently.

If any thing is lost, an ox for instance, they go to a diviner and he tells them that if they look for it in a certain place they will find it. They go to the place he mentions, and find it. But if they do not find it where he says, they say, the diviner is false; he does not know how to divine. They then go to another, who is known to divine truly; he tells them, and they go and seek there. If they find it, they believe in that diviner, and say, he is a true diviner.'[31]

The ethnological value of such documents lies in the fact that the beliefs are expressed in the natives' own words. For our purpose, they are of little use; the study of magic powers requires the detailed, objective observation of the European, not the account of a credulous native whose findings are backed only by the crude tests that are sometimes devised by the tribe in order to 'verify' their witch-doctor's powers.

Ethnological documentation is equally deficient of proof when claims of certain 'physical' powers are investigated. The following extract by Waldemar Bogoraz deals with the skills of the Chukchee Shamans:

'The Chuckchee ventriloquists display great skill, and could with credit to themselves carry on a contest with the best artists of the kind of civilized countries. The "separate voices" of their calling come from all sides of the room, changing their place to the complete illusion of their listeners. Some voices are at first faint, as if coming from afar; as they gradually approach, they increase in volume, and at last they rush into the room, pass through

31. ibid. pp. 313 ff.

it and out, decreasing, and dying away in the remote distance. Other voices come from above, pass through the room and seem to go underground, where they are heard as if from the depths of the earth. Tricks of this kind are played also with the voices of animals and birds, and even with the howling of the tempest, producing a most weird effect.

I heard a voice which professed to be an echo. It repeated faithfully all sounds and cries which we chose to produce in its presence, including phrases in English or Russian. The foreign words were, of course, slightly mispronounced, still the reproduction proved the "spirit" to be possessed of a fine ear, catching quickly the sounds of an unknown language. The only way in which the "spirit" could imitate the clapping of our hands (another test to which we put him) was by clacking his tongue, which caused much mirth even among the native listeners. I heard also the "spirit" of a grasshopper, horsefly, and mosquito, who imitated exceedingly well the sounds produced by the real insects.

In proof of his accuracy as to the location of the sounds, the shaman Qorawge, previously spoken of, made one of his "spirits" shout, talk, and whisper directly into my ear, and the illusion was so perfect that involuntarily I put my hand to my ear to catch the "spirit". After that he made the "spirit" enter the ground under me and talk right in between my legs, etc. All the time that he is conversing with the "separate voices", the shaman beats his drum without interruption in order to prove that his force and attention are otherwise occupied.

I tried to make a phonographic record of the "separate voices" of the "spirits". For this purpose I induced the shaman Scratching-Woman to give a seance in my own house, overcoming his reluctance with a few extra presents. The performance, of course, had to be carried out in utter darkness: and I arranged my machine so as to be able to work it without any light. Scratching-Woman sat in the farthest corner of the spacious room, at a distance of twenty feet from me. When the light was put out, the "spirits", after some "bashful" hesitation, entered, in compliance with the demand of the shaman, and even began to talk into the funnel of the gramophone. The records show a very marked difference between the voice of the shaman himself, which sounds from afar, and the voices of the "spirits", who seemed to be talking directly into the funnel.

All the while, Scratching-Woman was beating the drum incessantly to show that he was in his usual place, and occupied with his usual function, that of beating the drum without interruption.'[32]

And further on:

'Tricks of various kinds break up the monotony of the performance, which may last for several hours. The "spirits" will scratch from the outside at the walls of the sleeping-room, running around it in all directions, so that the clattering of their feet is quite audible. In contrast to this, the motion of the ke'le inside of the room produces but slight noise. The rustling of their flight is similar to the buzzing of a mosquito, and the rattling of their tiny feet as they run over the surface of the drum is hardly perceptible.

Often, however, a mischievous "spirit" suddenly tugs at the skin spread in the center of the room with such force that things lying on it fly about in all directions. Therefore the housemates of the shaman usually take the precaution to remove kettles and dishes from the room. Sometimes an invisible hand seizes the whole sleeping-room by its top, and shakes it with wonderful strength, or even lifts it up high, letting in for a moment the twilight from the outer tent. This, of course, is possible only with the movable tent of the Reindeer people, where the sleeping-room is fastened none too firmly. Other invisible hands toss about lumps of snow, spill cold water and urine, and even throw blocks of wood, or stones, at the imminent risk of hurting some of the listeners.

All these things happened several times in my presence. The "spirits" would ask me, through the shamans, whether I really felt afraid; and, when I did not give a satisfactory answer, the "spirits" would try to increase my respect for them by such material manifestations. I must mention that the audience is strictly forbidden to make any attempts whatever to touch the "spirits". These latter highly resent any intrusion of this kind, and retaliate either on the shaman, whom they may kill on the spot, or on the trespassing listener, who runs the risk of having his head broken, or even a knife thrust through his ribs in the dark.

32. W. Bogoraz: *The Chukchee*, 'The Jessup North Pacific Expedition', vol. III, pp. 435 ff.

I received warnings of this kind at almost every shamanistic performance. In some cases the shaman would lay a bare knife within his own reach as an additional warning against any infringement.

The size of the sleeping-room is so small that it is really wonderful how a shaman can keep up the illusion, even under cover of the dark and with the protection of his resentful "spirits". Many times I sat so near the performer that I could almost touch him with my outstretched hand, and the warning against too great inquisitiveness on my part was of course quite necessary.

All these tricks strangely resemble the doings of modern spiritualists, and without doubt they cannot be carried out without the help of human assistants.'[33]

One day Bogoraz is present during some 'quite wonderful' demonstrations by a woman Shaman:

'After that she took a large round pebble of the size of a man's fist, set it upon the drum, and, blowing upon it from all sides, began to mumble and snort in the same ke'le-like manner. She called our attention with signs— being in the possession of the ke'le, she had lost the faculty of human speech, and then began to wring the pebble with both hands. Then a continuous row of very small pebbles began to fall from her hands. This lasted for fully five minutes, till quite a heap of small pebbles was gathered below, on the skin. The larger pebble, however, remained smooth and intact, as was quite natural that it should be. I sat quite close to the juggler, and followed attentively all her movements, and I could not discover where all these pebbles came from. She wore the usual combination-suit of women of that country, but the broad waist was thrown open together with the sleeves; and all the upper part of her body, including arms and hands, was quite naked, and accessible to inspection. After a few moments I suddenly requested U'pune to repeat the trick, meaning to try if I could not catch her unawares; but she immediately took up her stone, and without more ado wrung out of it a stream of small pebbles still larger than the first.'[34]

33. W. Bogoraz: Op. cit., pp. 438 ff.
    According to Åke Ohlmarks: *Studien zum Problem des Schamanismus*, Lund-Copenhagen 1939, p. 39, I. A. Tchakaninski reported instances of telekinesis in *Baksylyk*, Semipalatinsk 1929, pp. 79 and 83. This document was inaccessible to me.
34. W. Bogoraz: Op. cit., pp. 444 ff.

For Gusinde, the demonstrations of power given by the Selk'nam witch-doctors were 'undeniably real' and could not be dismissed as tricks:

'Having bared his arms and torso, the witch-doctor Tenenesk placed three pebbles, as big as cherries, in the open palm of his right hand. He fixed his eyes upon them and then blew violently: the pebbles disappeared, although his hand had not made the slightest movement. He repeated the trick: this time I paid more attention. I chose the three pebbles myself and placed them on his palm; once more he made them disappear. There was no possibility of conjuring or illusion.'[35]

Trilles reports a case of the transference of a patient's fever to an animal or tree:

'. . . one of the most bizarre ceremonies where it is evident the patient is calmed by a few magic gestures. He sweats profusely, then quietly falls asleep. Meanwhile the animal trembles and shudders, sinks to the ground and usually dies after a fit of convulsions followed by a sudden stiffening that causes it to topple completely. Usually it is a kid, but sometimes the favorite dog of the patient is used . . . We saw another sorcerer operate in a similar manner. One of our catechism instructors was struck by an algid fever and was gravely ill. Quinine was of no use. The witch-doctor had him carried to a "Mpala" tree, one that has particularly large leaves, then he went through his ritual, first over the sick man and then near the tree. The leaves soon began to move and then turn black and fall to the ground. The patient sweated a great deal and, the next day, was completely cured.'[36]

Trilles tells of a most complicated ritual used by the Fangs when the older medicine men admitted novices to their brotherhood. Various rituals were performed, of which the last is of particular interest to us, and was witnessed personally by Trilles. The structure that is shown in figure I is erected in a chosen place. The ceremony begins with the old men walking around the structure, clapping their hands and singing a hymn to the particular spirit they believe to be present at the ceremony. At the same time, a drum is beaten

35. Gusinde, *Die Feuerland-Indianer*, p. 777
36. Trilles, *Les Pygmées de l'Afrique équatoriale*, pp. 177-178 and note

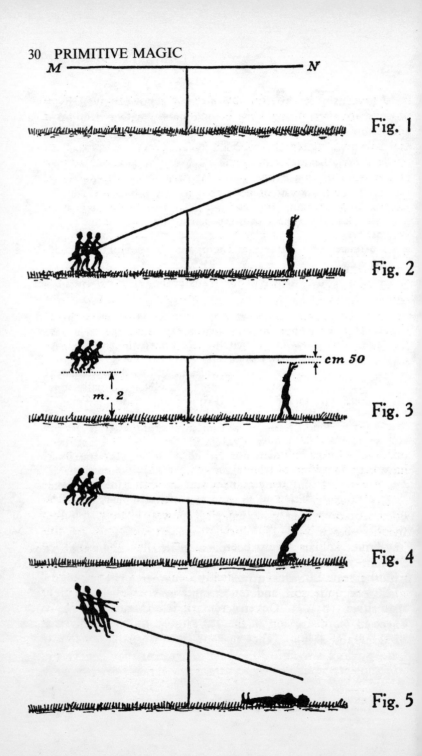

M ——————————————— N

Fig. 1

Fig. 2

cm 50
m. 2

Fig. 3

Fig. 4

Fig. 5

in a loud, regular rhythm by another medicine man. The novices are then brought in, having been prepared for their admission by a series of difficult trials. At the given signal the novices straddle the wooden beam (MN), as shown in figure 2 and the medicine man takes up his position, as seen at the right of this figure, his arms raised and the palms of his hands in the form of cups that are directed towards the nearest end (N) of the beam. Then the beam begins to descend towards his hands, slowly at first and then faster. When it reaches the horizontal position it stops, the magician's hands now being about fifty centimeters away from the end, and the novices' feet, about ten meters off the ground (fig. 3). Then those who are present circle the structure three times, still chanting. The medicine man, who is 'receiving' the novices, keeps his hands in the same position and slowly kneels (fig. 4). Then he lies on the ground, his hands on his chest, while the beam, still untouched, follows his movements (fig. 5).

He stands up and the beam returns to its horizontal position and remains there while the participants circle it once again. Finally the medicine man turns his palms downwards and the beam returns to its original position (fig. 2). The 'test' has been successful and the novices have gained their admission. At this moment the medicine man, who seems to have been in a kind of trance, falls unconscious to the ground: the others take him away and revive him with lustral water.[37]

The 'mastery of fire' is one area that enjoys a better documentation than other magical powers. Many different theories have been put forward as explanations of this 'mystery'. It has even been claimed that the so-called 'immunity' is simply the result of the participants' heavily callused feet. But Ocken explicitly denies this: 'The natives' feet were quite soft and tender and in no way leathery or insensitive' (p. 17). Ocken's remark is confirmed by R. U. Sayce in his discussion of fire-walking by Indian immigrants to the Natal region: 'Their immunity to burns is not due to

---

37. Trilles: *La sorcellerie chez les non-civilisés*, I. *Féticheurs et sorciers* in 'Semaine d'ethnologie religieuse', analytical report on the 2nd session, Louvain (Charpentier) 1914, pp. 167-186. Compare Leroy: *La Raison primitive*, Paris, Guenther 1927, where facts of this kind are used in a strong argument against Levy-Bruhl's pre-conceived notions

any particular calluses of the skin; some of them were as much used to wearing shoes as any European.'[38] Gudgeon, who actually took part in such a demonstration, claimed that his own feet were 'very delicate'. There is another theory that the feet were immunized by some sort of 'preparation'. But this obviously did not apply to Gudgeon and his friends, nor to the other trustworthy Europeans who have had a similar experience. Ocken does list various ways to bring about a certain resistance to fire, but declares that these 'by no means come within the present category.' Otto Stoll proposes 'an autosuggestive analgesia, brought about by religious ecstasy[39]': but this takes into account only the immunity to pain and ignores the fact that there is no burning. R. Fulton sees the solution to the mystery in the particular type of stones used for the ceremony[40] but this does not apply in Asia, where hot cinders or burning coals are used. Apart from this, we have already seen that the stones were hot enough to carbonize a handkerchief in fifteen to twenty seconds and to burn the rods that were used to smooth the surface.[41] The temperature in the pit was certainly more than 282°F and more likely around 400°F.

We appear to have arrived at another dead-lock. This excess of petulant doubt warns us of the mind's imminent fall into the pitiable error of Pierre Lombard, who asked the following futile questions; 'How old was Adam when he was created? Why was Eve taken from the side and not from some other part of the man? Why was she taken when the man was sleeping and not when he was awake? Why were our first parents, in their earthly Paradise, not married?' A list to which Erasmus added maliciously in his Eloge de la Folie; 'Is the following proposition possible? Would God have been able to appear in the form of a donkey or a gourd? And as for the gourd, what kind of miracles would it have performed? Would it have preached? How would it

---

38. R. U. Sayce: *Fire-Walking Ceremony in Natal*, in 'Man' XXXIII, 1931, No. 2.
39. Otto Stoll: *Suggestion und Hypnotismus in der Volkerpsychologie*, Leipzig 1904 (2nd edition) p. 71
40. Robert Fulton: *An Account of the Fiji Fire-Walking Ceremony, or Vilavilarivo, with A Probable Explanation of the Mystery*. in 'Transactions and Proceedings of the New Zealand Institute', XXXV, 1902, pp. 187-201
41. K. Roth: *The Fire-Walk in Fiji*, in 'Man' XXXIII, 1933

have been crucified?' The mind flitting from hypothesis to hypothesis, passes from doubt to certainty and again to doubt, imitating the flight of a bird. The only alternative seems to be to follow the example of research into parapsychology, a method that treads the solid ground of observation and experience. It appears that, at least in this area, we may have confidence in the facts that are presented to us and may draw decisive conclusions. Parapsychology attempts to reduce artificially the phenomena that it deals with and takes them out of their historical, spontaneous context. As a result, the human and cultural side is intentionally neglected. There is no interest in the beliefs of the participant or medium, nor in the historical origins and meaning of these beliefs. At the very most, it may be asked whether the psychological state of being confident in the success of an attempt may possibly influence the eventual result. The psychological experiment cannot elaborate on the cultural importance of clairvoyance, telepathy, pre-cognition or disembodied movement; the most it can do is to artificially reproduce the conditions that are supposedly favorable to the appearance of certain phenomena (darkness, chanting, freedom of conversation etc.) while keeping close to hand the necessary controls, such as lighting, photography, etc. There is, of course, an almost complete reduction of the historical stimulus that is at work in the purely spontaneous occurrence of such phenomena. So, in the laboratory, the drama of the dying man who appears 'in articulo mortis' to a relative or friend, is reduced to an oft-repeated experiment—one that tries to transmit to the mind of a subject the image of a playing-card, chosen at random, etc. Perhaps this is the appropriate area in which to decide, once and for all, upon the reality of magic powers. It may be here that we will discover the certainty that ethnological documents have failed to give us.

Some of the major experimental research dealing with paragnostic attitudes has been conducted by Hans Bender in the laboratories of the Psychology Institute, Bonn University. B. Rhine and his students, under the direction of McDougall, have done similar work in the Psychology department of Duke University, North Carolina.[42]

Hans Bender was motivated to make a systematic enquiry into paragnostic attitudes (examined as instances of 'clairvoyance') by the strange 'by-product' of an experiment that was quite unrelated to the subject. Among the many methods used to uncover 'psychological automatism', there is one called automatic spelling, in which a moveable object, such as a glass, is placed inside a circle of the letters of the alphabet. The subject moves the glass which, by touching certain letters, forms the answers to a list of questions. The subject remains unaware of the content of the replies. During one such experiment several of the subjects found that they were able to touch a given letter, *without being*

---

42. Hans Bender: *Zum Problem der aussersinnlichen Wahrnehmung, ein Beitrag zur Untersuchnug des 'raumlichen Hellsehens' mit Laboratoriums- methoden*, introduction by Prof. Dr. E. R. Jaensch; extract from 'Zeitschrift für Psychologie' no. 135/1935, Leipzig, J. A. Barth, 1936, pp. 1-3. Rhine's research may be read in many works, even though it was not fully developed until after 1934. We note only the following: J. B. Rhine: *Extra-Sensory Perception*, Boston, Society for Psychic Research, 1934 (reprinted by Faber and Faber, London, 1935); C. E. Stuart and J. G. Pratt: *A Handbook for Testing Extra-Sensory Perception*, New York, Farrar & Rinehart 1937; J. A. Greenwood, J. G. Pratt, J. B. Rhine, Burke M. Smith, Ch. E. Stuart: *Extra-Sensory Perception after Sixty Years*, New York, Henry Holt & Co. 1940. The rapid accumulation of material and the rapid perfecting of the study technique led to the founding of a periodical devoted to the subject, the *'Journal of Parapsychology'*. From 1937 until 1939 it was edited by W. Mcdougall, J. B. Rhine and C. E. Stuart at Duke University. After 1939 the direction was taken over by Gardner Murphy of Columbia University and Bernard E. Riess of Hunter College. A bibliography, complete until 1940, is appended to *Extra-Sensory Perception after Sixty Years* (op. cit.). Note also B. Schepish: *La esplorazione delle percezioni extrasensoriali col metodo statistico*, in 'Bollettino per i soci della Societa italiana di Metapsichica' No. 2, 1939, pp. 10-45. For more general information and earlier research on paragnostic powers, see Ch. Richet: *Traité de métapsychique*, Paris, Alcan 1922, pp. 55-509; M. R. Warcollier: *La télépathie*, Paris, Alcan 1921; E. Osty: *La connaissance supra-normale, télépathie*, Paris, Alcan 1923; R. Baerwald: *Die intellektuellen Phanomene* (in *Der Okkultismus in Urkunden*, directed by Max Dessoir, vol. II, Berlin, Ullstein 1925). Among the earlier research should be noted that of Brugmans and Heymans in the laboratory of the University of Groningen: see *Compte rendu officiel du Premier Congrés international des recherches psychiaues*, Copenhagen 1922, pp. 396-408. On the spontaneous phenomenology of so-called 'telepathic hallucinations', one may glean useful information from the old collection by E. Gurney, F. W. H. Myers and F. Podmore: *Phantasm of the Living*, 2 vols., London, Trübner and Co. 1886. Both this work and that of Mvers: *Human Personality*, contain the results of the famous inquiry made by the Society for Psychical Research. For a synthesis of the work of Rhine and Bender, see A. Winterstein: *Telepathie und Hellsehen im Lichte der modernen Forschung und wissenschaftlichen Kritik*, Amsterdam-Leipzig-Vienna, Frank Leo & Co. 1937

able to see it. This induced Bender to examine the problem without prejudice. The results of research conducted between June 1932 and June 1933 were not completely convincing in regard to the actual existence of clairvoyance;[43] however, a new series of experiments during the period May 1933 to November 1934 were more favorable. After four series of experiments conducted with a 'medium' and using a technique that had been devised to isolate any instance of clairvoyance (and exclude any telepathic interference), Bender was drawn to conclude that the subject definitely showed abilities of perception that were quite divorced from any possible knowledge through normal channels, including hyperaesthesis. There was no question of chance or trickery.

Rhine and his associates explored paragnostic attitudes using a statistical method. Schepis describes their methods:

'Given a set of twenty-five cards that represent five different symbols (five cards for each symbol), the probability of guessing a given card would be 5 out of 25, or 1 out of 5. That is: if, before guessing a card, one chooses a symbol at random, and each time the card is replaced and the pack shuffled, the average number of cards correctly guessed—i.e. whose sign corresponds to the symbol that had previously been chosen at random—would be on an average 1/5th of the total number of cards drawn. If the number of cards drawn is limited, then the results will differ notably, either less or more than this average figure; but the more cards drawn, the closer will be the number of those correctly-guessed to the established probability ratio. If, during numerous experiments that vary in time and place, the proportion of cards correctly guessed is not only superior to the 1/5th average, but even exceeds the limits between which this average should waver (according to the probability ratio), and if all outside influences (sensory, objective or subjective) have been eliminated from the experiment—then it is permissible to presume that some unknown influence has affected the results. And the first explanation would appear to lie in the subject's possession of extra-sensory faculties.'[44]

43. Hans Bender: *Psychische Automatismen zur Experimental psychologie des Unterbewussten und der aussersinnlichen Wahrnehmung.* Leipzig, J. A. Barth 1935
44. Schepis: *La esplorazionne delle percezioni extrasensoriali col metodo statistico,* p. 11.

This method has confirmed the actual existence of extra-sensory perception. The results are such, that they cannot be due to chance. Besides this, many of the tests that are devoid of the chance-factor also exclude completely any use of normal sensory means. In several cases where both the chance-factor and the normal sensory means were excluded, the conditions of the experiment were such, that they also excluded the possibility of any error in the recording of the results.[45] So we must take as proven the extra-sensory perception of objects (clairvoyance) and the mental activity of other persons (telepathy).[46] So far as the relationship between extra-sensory perception and time is concerned (that is, whether or not precognition does exist), laboratory research has had promising results through the use of the statistical method, although these results are not yet final.[47]

Paranormal psychology also seems to have arrived at positive results in the area of 'physical' powers. The first observations were made in experimental psychology, with 'hysterical' subjects. Pierre Janet, in his work *L'automatisme psychologique*, refers to psychological phenomena that have been produced through suggestion (cataleptic phenomena, actions and hallucinations that are regulated by words, actions and hallucinations when a certain reference is made, and others that are complex or else develop automatically, also general hallucinations and personality changes). He also mentions suggestions that affect the body, not the thought, of the somnambulist:

45. *Extra-Sensory Perception after Sixty Years*, p. 105.
46. Op. cit., pp. 393 ff. A special technique was necessary for this demonstration because of the difficulty in excluding clairvoyance for the purpose of isolating telepathy and vice versa. In tests dealing with pure clairvoyance, only stimuli that are completely unknown to all participants may be used (to avoid any unintentional transmission of all thought). On the other hand, telepathic tests use a range of purely subjective images that are revealed to the subject only after he has given his reply.
47. The technique used is as follows: before the pack of cards is shuffled, the subject must determine, through extra-sensory means, in what order the cards will occur àfter they have been mixed. See J. B. Rhine: *Experiments bearing on the Precognition Hypothesis, I Pre-shuffling Card Calling*, in the 'Journal of Parapsychology' II, 1938, pp. 38-54; and J. B. Rhine, B. M. Smith and J. L. Woodruff: *Experiments Bearing on the Precognition Hypothesis, II The Role of Extra-Sensory Perception in the Shuffling of Cards*, id., pp. 119-131

'All the previous suggestions, although progressively complicated, were easily understood; we refer now to far stranger occurrences that, in the light of present-day psychological studies, are extremely difficult to explain. We can only verify them. I refer to suggestions that affect the body and not the thoughts of the somnambulist (. . .) The phenomenon that interested me the most, and is the easiest to reproduce, is sinapism through suggestion. The inflammation appears slowly with Leonie but more quickly with Rose, almost under my very eyes; in a few hours the skin had become very red in the appropriate part of the body, there was swelling and all the signs of a real sinapism were present—they even lasted longer than is usually the case.

This swelling of the skin is closely connected with the somnambulist's thought; firstly, it appeared in the area of the body that had been mentioned, and not in any other; secondly, it takes on the appearance that the subject's thought gives it. One day I said to Rose, who suffered from hysterical contractions of the stomach, that I was going to cure these by placing a sinapism on this particular area. Some hours later I noticed a dark-red mark in the form of an elongated rectangle. The peculiar thing was that there were no corners, as these appeared to have been cut off. I remarked on the strange shape and she replied: "Don't you know that they always trim the Rigollot papers so that the corners won't hurt." Her pre-conceived idea of the form of the plaster had determined the shape of the inflammation. On another occasion I suggested to her that I was cutting out a sinapism in the form of a six-pointed star; the red mark had exactly this form. I ordered another one on the left side of the chest in the form of a large S . . . and my suggestion caused a large, clear S to appear on the appropriate area.'48

The origins of these phenomena are obvious:

'The formation on the skin of a red mark in the shape of a star, whether it appears after waking or in the hypnotic state (as in this case) may only be explained by a thought. It is not enough to say that the redness was caused by the excitation of a vasometer nerve, because there are no nerve-endings in the shape of a six-pointed

48. P. Janet: *L'automatisme psychologique. Essai de psychologie experimentale sur les formes inférieures de l'activité humaine*, Paris, Alcan 1889, pp. 165 ff.

star in this particular area. It is rather the partial and systematic excitation of several nerves which cannot be understood unless there has been a thought-intervention that has somehow co-ordinated these excitations. The subject directly expressed this thought while in the hypnotic state and said to us: "I was thinking of your poultice the whole time." When she had been awakened, after the suggestion, she seemed to have ceased thinking about it and was apparently quite unaware of what had happened —yet something within her must go on thinking about it, without her knowledge.'[49]

The theory of suggestion is inadequate to explain these cases of dermatography-through-suggestion; they are more likely to be the expression of an extension of the powers we have over our own body into an area that normally escapes their influence. Another similar phenomenon is suggestive tympanites:

'I suggested to Rose that we were no longer in 1888, but in 1886, in the month of April. This was done in order to examine any changes in sensitiveness that might appear. But her reaction was quite unexpected; she moaned, complained of being tired and of not being able to walk. I asked: "Well, what's wrong with you?" and she answered: "Oh nothing, but in my condition . . ." "What condition?" She replied by indicating her belly which had swelled and stretched with a sudden attack of hysterical tympanites; without knowing it, I had taken her back to a period in her life when she was pregnant.'[50]

A haemorrhage may also be provoked or stopped in a similar manner:

'Isabelle, whom I had not seen for a year, came back . . . because of a nose-bleed that had been appearing every morning for a fortnight, without her knowing the cause.

---

49. ibid. p. 267. The experiments of Schindler, Kreibich, Kohnstamm (and Pinner) Heller, Schulz, Scollosy have confirmed the possibility of provoking erythema and blisters through suggestion, and it is sometimes even possible to make them regress. The works of Bunnemann deal informatively with psychogenic dermatosis. See also H. Heyer: *Das körperlich-seelische Zusammenwirken in den Lebensvorgangen*, *Grenzfragen des Nervenund Seelenlebens* edited by Prof. Dr. Kretschmer, Munich 1925, p. 122. For the phenomena of stigmatization, see Jacobi: *Die Stigmatisierten*, *Grenzfragen etc.*, Munich, 1923, p. 114
50. Janet: op. cit., p. 160

After I had induced somnambulism, she told me that, two weeks ago, she had been involved in a street-fight—this was later verified; she had felt considerable stress and then began to bleed at the nose. Since then, she had dreamed of the fight each morning and woke up with a profuse nose-bleed. The dream was rectified and the bleeding disappeared, although no doubt it would have resisted other treatment for a long time'.[51]

This method of recall may also be used for therapeutic purposes:

'During her various hysterias, Rose suffered from pro-longed uterine bleeding. Direct suggestion, in which we simply forbade her to bleed, was unsuccessful. She mentioned, during hypnosis, that she had managed to stop the bleeding herself by drinking an ergotine solution. I replied: "Very well then, you will drink this every two hours." I then awoke her and did not mention anything about the suggestion. Consequently, Rose went through some strange motions; she closed her right hand as if holding a spoon, put it to her mouth, opened her mouth and made a rapid swallowing movement. She was asked what she was doing, but maintained that she had not moved. The most curious thing was that the bleeding had stopped.'[52]

In all the phenomena examined so far, the abnormalities have been confined to the part of the physical universe that we designate as 'the body'. But some subjects seem to possess supra-normal abilities that extend beyond their bodies and into the physical universe. Experiments have proved the existence of internal sonor vibrations, the movement of objects from a distance (telekinesis), the producing of luminous phenomena and the materialization of visible forms.[53] Among the most searching experiments are those carried out by Eugene Osty at the laboratory of the International Institute of Metapsychics, Paris, with the co-operation of the medium, Rudi Schneider. The aim was to use automatic

51. Janet: L'état mental des hystériques, Paris, Alcan 1911, 2nd edit. p. 435
52. Janet: L'automatisme psychologique, pp. 267 ff.
53. In regard to these phenomena, see: A. Von Schrenck-Notzing: Die Phanomene des Mediums Rudi Schneider, Berlin-Leipzig, W. de Gruyter & Co. 1933. Of particular interest are the seances in which an electrical controlling-apparatus was used: a luminous signal faded when the tactile contact between the medium and the control was either reduced or interrupted. During these seances, a gauze screen was used to make it practically impossible for the medium or the spectators to intervene in

photography in order to record any telekinetic phenomena that might occur in the darkness. During the seance on the 10th November, 1930, there was a quite unexpected happening, which opened up vast new horizons in this type of research. It was the first time that automatic photography was used—the equipment used invisible infra-red rays; an object was placed on the table so that if it moved into the radius of the infra-red rays, an automatic photograph of the phenomenon would be taken with a magnesium flash. At a particular moment in the seance, Olga—the 'person' whom Rudi Schneider contacted—said: 'Hold hands firmly. The force is approaching the table.' The medium had only just translated these words into French, when there was a flash. But later, when the light was turned on, the object (a handkerchief) was still in the same position on the table. The same thing occurred in the second part of the seance, but the photographs showed nothing unusual: both the people and the objects in the room were in their normal places, and the various shots only proved that no visible body had come within the radius of the infra-red rays. The equipment was examined carefully to see that it was functioning properly and that the spontaneous flash had not been caused by some fault in the mechanism. The only possible explanation seemed to be that the medium 'in his (mostly unsuccessful) efforts to raise an object through psycho-physical effort, emitted

the particular area that was reserved for the production of these paraphysical phenomena. Besides this, the medium was wearing pyjamas with luminous stripes so as to keep a strict control on his movements, despite the darkness. Under these conditions they obtained phenomena of telekinesis, the levitation of objects and the materialization of more or less clearly-defined forms. This is how Hans Driesch reports the positive results of a seance that was held on the 5th May, 1928, under the conditions described, at the Munich laboratory: 'Rudi's seance convinced me, more than anything I have yet seen, of the reality of psychical phenomena. I have repeatedly thought about what I have seen; there are really no defects. The triple controls are particularly good; luminous stripes, hands tied and electrical verification.' (Schrenck-Notzing: op. cit. p. 119). The London National Laboratory of Psychical Research later extended this electrical control to every person present, so as to guarantee the immobility of both the medium and the researchers. Positive results were also obtained under these conditions. See H. Price: *Rudi Schneider; A Scientific Examination of his Mediumship*, London, Methuen 1930. On the other hand, a new series of experiments carried out in 1932 had only partially positive results: see H. Price: *An Account of Some Further Experiments with Rudi Schneider*, London 1933. It appears that the medium's powers were declining at this stage. Nevertheless, it was still possible during the 1932 series to photograph phenomena of telekinesis at the actual moment that these occurred, and these were most probably authentic.

some substantial energy (which he called "a force") that was too subtle to be photographed, but whose presence nevertheless caused the infra-red rays to react and set off the magnesium flash.'

Some rather crude experiments have also been devised to test the reality of the 'mastery of fire' phenomenon. These were organized by the London Council for Psychical Research with the co-operation of a Kashmir Indian, Kuda Bux. They proved that the subject, through the strength of his 'faith', was able to walk in firm steps across a path of coals that had been heated to 430°F, without suffering burns. The subject affirmed explicitly that his power was due to 'faith' and before beginning his walk, he said prayers from the Koran. He also insisted upon the 'purity' of the materials used for the furnace; he maintained that if there was some impurity, such as cow-dung, he would fail. During the last test Kuda Bux refused to carry out a third crossing because the experimental controls and the instruments used had 'desecrated' the pit of coals: 'Something inside me has broken . . . I have lost my faith, and if I do it again, I shall burn myself.'[54]

Paranormal psychology seems to offer at least a partially positive solution to the problem of the reality of magic powers. But the crisis has by no means been passed. In 1893, Wilhelm Wundt made the following statement, based on the research of Charles Richet into the transmission of thoughts:

'True specialists . . . have very good reasons for not venturing into the area of paranormal phenomenology. My opinion is that these reasons are based on the results of research in parapsychology. To understand what I mean, it is enough to read one of the most detailed works in this

54. H. Price: *A Report on Two Experimental Fire-Walks*, University of London Council for Psychical Research, 'Bulletin' II, London 1936. See also Price's *Faith and Fire-Walking* in the *Encyclopaedia Britannica* 1936, supplement. Kuda Bux's exploit may be compared to that of a Moslem 'holy man' whom T. L. Pannel met among the tribes of the Afghanistan frontier. A pit had been dug and filled with coal and wood. It was lighted and the holy man walked across the coals while reciting the Moslem profession of faith. Then he invited the faithful and the brave to follow him and assured them that if they also recited the credo in all sincerity, then they would suffer no harm. The ordeal took place and some of the participants showed no traces of burning while others did: the latter were not considered as true Moslems. (Frazer: *Aftermath*, London 1936, pp. 457 ff.).

area; Richet's research into the transmission of thought and lucidity. Even if we suppose that all the experiments described in this work had positive results, so we agree with the author that magical actions at a distance have probably taken place: what then may we conclude from these results? It is obvious that the world that surrounds us is composed of two quite different worlds. On one hand there is the world of Copernicus, Newton, Leibniz and Kant; that is, the universe that is subject to immutable laws and where both big and small are unified in one harmonious whole. On the other hand, there exists, beside this grandiose and admirable universe, a small world of spirits, magicians and "mediums" which is the direct opposite of our great, sublime universe whose immutable laws are suspended for the profit of these most vulgar and frequently hysterical persons. So, we are led to believe that the laws of gravitation, the action of light and all the laws of our psychophysical organization must undergo a transformation as soon as they come before some "Madame Zara" . . . that they sleep a sort of magnetically-induced slumber, not so that she may predict some great universal catastrophe, but so that she may guess if some minor misfortune lies ahead of John Smith's small son . . . Supposing all these absurdities were in fact true, can one imagine that a psychologist or a natural scientist, who is exempt from prejudice and who has a free choice would prefer the evidence of this small world of hysterical mediums to that of our great universe, whose order depends on immutable laws?'[55]

Wundt's criticism leads us into another serious difficulty. Even if this naive faith in the absolutes of Galileo's and Newton's 'great universe' has undergone a radical transformation, and even if 'classical' physics has had to limit its perspective so that it is valid only for the macroscopic order, Wundt's judgment still retains a certain value and still merits an adequate reply. Scientific research must necessarily limit itself to a *given* universe, one which the empiricist does not always have at his disposal, and it does not matter if the epistemologist discovers a 'part of the subject' in the physical make-up of the world—the man of science, the naturalist, must remain faithful to the great precept that nature may

55. W. Wundt: *Hypnotismus und Suggestion*, in 'Philosophische Studien', 1893, pp. 6 ff.

only be mastered by being obeyed. This, of course, lies at the root of the naturalist's rejection of the possible existence of a paranormal phenomenology—this is why he cannot accept the possibility of magical powers. Indeed, the whole area of paranormal studies is characterized by the suspension of known natural laws—to the profit of empiricists just like 'Madame Zara' . . . Let us consider the mastery of fire, according to what we have seen in the related documents. According to Janet's observations, in his experiments with Leonie and Rose, it was the subjects' *imagining* of the sinapism that provoked the *real* inflammation; in the same way, the momentary suspension of the powers of combustion of fire (in the fire-walk) is related to a whole series of emotions, imaginings, beliefs and myths. Gudgeon was unharmed when he crossed the coals, but one of his friends was 'seriously burned' because he 'had looked behind him, like Lot's wife—something which is against all the rules.'[56] R. U. Sayce also vouches that the walking on the coals seems to have little or no effect on the feet. He examined several feet half an hour after the ceremony, but discovered no sign of burning . . . He was told that small blisters sometimes do appear perhaps because of insufficient faith or inadequate preparation . . . His informants also told him that of the two white men who participated in 1929, one came out with a blister, but the other, who was distracted by his friends while walking on the coals, was obliged to jump out of the ditch. His feet were seriously injured and he had to remain in bed for some time.[57] E. Foxwell, of St. John's College, Cambridge, reports a similar incident in Tokyo. The American writer, Percival Lowell, walked on the coals, but burned himself so seriously that he had to spend three weeks in bed. A Scotch engineer named Hillhouse accomplished the feat unharmed.[58] At Yucatan, fire-walking is practised to ward off calamity in an ill-omened year. The participants walk or run over the coals; some are unharmed, while others suffer more or less serious injury.[59] The French traveller, Sonnerat, described the ceremony held in honor of Darma Rajah and

56. Op. cit., pp. 6 ff.
57. Sayce: *Fire-Walk Ceremony in Natal,* loc. cit.
58. Frazer: *Balder the Beautiful* II, p. 10
59. ibid. pp. 11 ff.

his bride, Drobede, in which the participants crossed the coals at varying rates, according to their degree of religious fervor.[60] Apart from these, we have already read of how the combustibility of objects also seems to be modified by a psychic factor (the dried fern-leaf ornaments). Regarding the handkerchief that burned when placed on the stone, Thomson was told that this would not have happened had it been thrown into the middle of the furnace, because it was made by human hands, and would have been protected by the same powers granted to the fire-walkers. Such a claim was examined by William Crookes, with the co-operation of the medium, Home.[61] In this experiment, Home, in a trance, showed that he was able to pick up burning coals without suffering damage to his hands. He mentions that it is much more difficult to 'influence' an inanimate object than a part of one's body, but nevertheless indicates that he will try to prevent a burning coal from damaging the handkerchief . . . He places the coal in the handkerchief and leaves it there for about thirty seconds then removes it, with the comment that, as the 'power' was not very strong, the handkerchief would have burned if the coal had been left longer.

If the naturalist's methods are applied to paranormal phenomena, or if one attempts to prove these phenomena along the same lines as an experimental scientist when he is dealing with nature—then there appears an internal contradiction; in order to prove them, they must be considered in the same way as any 'given' phenomena, which, of course, they are not. There is no known set of laws that may be used to govern experiments in the area of paranormal phenomena. Experimental science, when dealing with nature, has the ideal of a nature that is purified of any of the psychic 'projections' that belong to the world of magic, whereas paranormal phenomena are precisely part of a nature that is made up of such 'projections'. It follows that even the mere *possibility* of paranormal phenomena is repugnant to modern scientific thought. If it was to accept such a possibility, it would mean one of two things: either it would have to create some means

60. ibid. p. 7
61. W. Crookes: *Ricerche sui fenomeni dello spiritualismo e altri scritti*, trad. Servadio. Milan (Lib. Lombarda) 1932, pp. 126 ff.; cf. pp. 125 ff.

of 'dialogue' with the magic world, and thus reject its historical origins, or else it would have to rise above its own historical background and attain a higher, more comprehensive outlook. Science was born through the gradual withdrawal of psychic elements from the natural world. The possibility of paranormal phenomena would be a complete contradiction, because the paranormal means the *reintroduction of the psychic element into nature.* And if the 'small world of hysterical mediums' joins up with the historical world of ethnological magic, then we have the paradox of a 'culturally conditioned nature', that is, one that may still be considered to be at man's disposal, one that sustains and expresses a distinct cultural drama.

We have arrived at an important stage in our research. The 'scandal' that surrounds the mere theory of the reality of magical powers, repugnance towards even an attempt to find a positive solution to the problem, the protestations of 'lack of good sense' and the doubts of even those who are trying to verify the facts in a systematic manner—all of this is due to a socio-cultural attitude that is actively anti-magic. There is evidence of the need for a less restricted outlook that will come about only when this stage in our cultural development is superseded. Only then will the present contradictions be resolved. So long as the natural scientist's 'given facts' are seen as the only possible method of approach, these contradictions will persist. But this dogmatism of the natural scientist is basically a presumption inherent in the culture. Wundt reveals the real motive that blocks the way to an uninhibited consideration of magic powers when he talks of the Western man's *preference* for the 'marvellous universe of Galileo and Newton'—that is, for a universe that lends itself to observation and to experimentation; one that may be explained rationally, within the limits of established scientific laws. This attitude is part of our present stage of cultural development and our problem takes root here because of the reaction we may expect to the question of the reality of magic powers.

In relation to what was said at the beginning of this section, the problem of magic powers involves not only the subject in dispute, but also the criterion of judgment, in this case, the criterion of *reality*. We now see that research must follow a new course because of a fundamental principle that is vital to the whole argument. But before following this new course, it is in our interest to linger a little longer on the paradoxes of a 'nature that is conditioned by culture'. We will show the essential role that magical powers play in certain cultural areas.

Among the Iglulik Eskimos, great importance is given to the Shaman's acquisition of paragnostic powers; they are even considered as fundamental to his art. The Shaman's initiation is carried out in the following manner:

'When a young man or woman wishes to become a shaman, the first thing to do is to make a present to the shaman under whom one wishes to study. Sometimes two such instructors may be employed at the same time. The present given in the first place must be something valuable, an item from among one's own possessions which has cost the owner some trouble to obtain. Among the Iglulingmiut, wood was the most expensive of all, and it was therefore customary here to pay one's instructor with a tent pole. The wing of a gull was fastened to the pole as a sign or symbol indicating that the pupil should in time acquire the power of travelling through the air to the Land of the Dead up in heaven, or down through the sea to the abode of Takanakapsaluk. The young aspirant, when applying to a shaman should always use the following formula:
"takujumagama": "I come to you because I desire to see."
The gift would then be placed outside the tent, or the house, according as it was summer or winter, and would remain there for some time as a present to the helping spirits that would in time be at the pupil's command. The shaman could have the use of the tent pole afterwards himself, there was no difficulty about that, for the spirits are creatures of air and have no use for wood; they would have the ownership of it all the same, since it had once been given them by a human being, and that was enough for the spirits.
The evening after a shaman has received and set out a gift of this nature, he must do what is called sakavea that is, invoke and interrogate his helping spirits in order to "remove all obstacles" (padzizaiᴀ·rniᴀrlugit) that is, to

eliminate from the pupil's body and mind all that might hinder him from becoming a good shaman. Then the pupil and his parents, if he have any, must confess any breach of taboo or other offence they have committed, and purify themselves by confession in face of the spirits.'[62]

To 'remove the obstacles' means, for the Shaman, to free the novice's soul from the influence of his eyes, brain and other internal organs; in doing this, the freed soul is offered to the spirits who will aid the novice so that they may familiarize themselves with his higher and more noble qualities.[63] But it is insufficient to simply 'remove the obstacles'; the novice must also receive the positive power which makes him an 'angakok'. This power is called 'gaumanek', which means *luminosity* or *illumination*, and consists of

'a mysterious light which the shaman suddenly feels in his body, inside his head, within the brain, an inexplicable searchlight, a luminous fire, which enables him to see in the dark, both literally and metaphorically speaking, for he can now, even with closed eyes, see through darkness and perceive things and coming events which are hidden from others; thus they look into the future and into the secrets of others.

The first time a young shaman experiences this light, while sitting upon the bench invoking his helping spirits, it is as if the house in which he is suddenly rises; he sees far ahead of him, through mountains, exactly as if the earth were one great plain, and his eyes could reach to the end of the earth. Nothing is hidden from him any longer; not only can he see things far, far away, but he can also discover souls, stolen souls, which are either kept concealed in far, strange lands or have been taken up or down to the Land of the Dead.'[64]

This power always intervenes through the help of some spirit (the Moon-spirit, the benevolent souls of the dead, the Mother of the Caribou etc.). But the initiation is still unfinished. The Shaman may only retain his power through the help of auxiliary spirits who are sympathetically united with him; they enable him to carry out his work according to the

62. Rasmussen: *Intellectual Culture of the Iglulik Eskimos,* pp. 111 ff.
63. Rasmussen: op. cit., p. 112
64. op. cit., pp. 112 ff.

directives given him by the old Shaman; he must also find
the ensured help of other similar spirits. He must engage
them personally, but it is not within his power to choose
them, because they will appear of their own accord. But
before reaching the stage where he gains this assistance, he
must go through a long period of hardship. He withdraws
from human contact and goes to some solitary place where
he may contemplate nature.

'But before a shaman attains the stage at which any
helping spirit would think it worth while to come to him,
he must, by struggle and toil and concentration of thought,
acquire for himself yet another great and inexplicable
power, he must be able to see himself as a skeleton.
Though no shaman can explain to himself how and why,
he can, by the power his brain derives from the supernatural, as it were by thought alone, divest his body of its
flesh and blood, so that nothing remains but his bones.
And he must then name all the parts of his body, mention
every single bone by name; and in so doing, he must not
use ordinary human speech, but only the special and
sacred shaman's language which he has learned from his
instructor. By thus seeing himself naked, altogether freed
from the perishable and transient flesh and blood, he
consecrates himself, in the sacred tongue of the shamans,
to his great task, through that part of his body which will
longest withstand the action of sun, wind and weather,
after he is dead.'[65]

But the Shaman's initiation is also subject to failure: its
metagnomic power may be replaced by the effects of a
sudden psychic trauma.

'Uvavnuk had gone outside the hut one winter evening
to make water. It was particularly dark that evening, as
the moon was not visible. Then suddenly there appeared
a glowing ball of fire in the sky, and it came rushing down
to earth straight towards her. She would have got up and

65. Rasmussen: op. cit., p. 114. This 'vision of one's own skeleton' is
closely connected to a phenomenon that is well-known to specialists in
the paranormal; it is called *autoscopism*. Internal autoscopism has been
observed in 'hysterical' subjects while under hypnosis and who were
being treated for the restoration of sensitivity. One of Sollier's patients
saw and described his blood-vessels, his heart, his blood, his lungs, his
intestines, his muscles, his tendons, his *skeleton* . . . and his brain.
(Osty: *La connaissance supernormale*, Paris, 1932, p. 22). One of Col-
mar's patients, although she was an ignorant country-woman, saw her
coxo-femoral joint and described it. (Osty; op. cit., pp. 22.)

fied, but before she could pull up her breeches, the ball of fire struck her and entered into her. At the same moment she perceived that all within her grew light, and she lost consciousness. But from that moment also she became a great shaman. She had never before concerned herself with the invocation of spirits, but now "inneru:jap inna", the spirit of the meteor, had entered into her and made her a shaman. She saw the spirit just before she fainted. It had two kinds of bodies, that rushed all glowing through space; one side was a bear, the other was like a human being; the head was that of a human being with the tusks of a bear.'[66]

Uvavnuk regained consciousness and returned home singing overcome with joy. The whole house was infected by this elation. And then Uvavnuk showed signs of her new condition:

'There was nothing that was hidden from her now, and she began to reveal all the offences that had been committed by those in the house. Thus she purified them all.'[67]

She had become a Shaman. She was now able to know everything, but only when she entered into a trance; before she could use her power, the spirit of the meteorite had to enter her.

Aua's calling, however, came about in quite different circumstances. The efforts of the other Shamans had been unsuccessful, so Aua sought out solitude.

'Then I sought solitude, and here I soon became very melancholy. I would sometimes fall to weeping, and feel unhappy without knowing why. Then, for no reason, all would suddenly be changed, and I felt a great inexplicable joy, a joy so powerful that I could not restrain it, but had to break into song, a mighty song, with only room for the one word: joy, joy! And I had to use the full strength of my voice. And then in the midst of such a fit of mysterious and overwhelming delight I became a shaman, not knowing myself how it came about. But I was a shaman. I could see and hear in a totally different way. I had gained my "gaumaneg", my enlightenment, the shaman-light of brain and body, and this in such a manner that it was not only I who could see through the darkness

66. Rasmussen: op. cit., p. 122
67. ibid. p. 123

of life, but the same light also shone out from me, imperceptible to human beings, but visible to all the spirits of earth and sky and sea, and these now came to me and became my helping spirits.

My first helping spirit was my namesake a little Aua. When it came to me, it was as if the passage and roof of the house were lifted up, and I felt such a power of vision, that I could see right through the house, in through the earth and up into the sky; it was the little Aua that brought me all this inward light, hovering over me as long as I was singing. Then it placed itself in a corner of the passage, invisible to others, but always ready if I should call it.'[68]

Beliefs in paragnostic powers are fundamental to the spiritual life of the Iglulik community. There is an intimate 'magic sympathy', a mysterious 'consensus' of souls which is believed to bind creatures to one another and to influence joys and suffering, hopes and fears. An Iglulik woman gives dramatic expression to the spiritual and human value of this belief, within its historical and cultural frame-work. The woman, Ourulo, tells:

'In the autumn, when the first snow had fallen, Qupanuaq decided to go up country with his wife Qiqertaunak and their son Torngraq ("the helping spirit"); my brother Qajakutjuk ("the little kayak") was to go with them. I remember my mother was very distressed about it, for she did not think the old man, armed as he was only with bow and arrows, would ever get any game. But she was not able herself to keep us, and had to agree to my brother's going with them.

Then a little while after, a strange thing happened. Mother had cooked some ribs of walrus, and was sitting eating, when the bone she held suddenly began to make a noise. She was so frightened, she stopped eating at once,

---

68. Rasmussen: op. cit., pp. 118 ff. Among the Coppermine Eskimos, the Shaman must become accustomed to his function from the moment of birth: 'Even as soon as the afterbirth has been extruded the infant is lifted up and allowed to look through it, a ceremony that gives the child second sight. Later on such children are called: those who have eyes in the dark.' (Rasmussen: *Intellectual Culture of the Copper Eskimos*, 'Report of the 5th Thule expedition 1921-24' IX, Copenhagen 1932, p. 27). The Shaman is also called 'elik', that is 'one who has eyes', whereas ordinary people are called 'inuin'ait' (op. cit., loc. cit.). The Shaman's body appears luminous to the air-spirits, which are thus attracted to him and wish to enter him, so giving him their powers, their sight and their knowledge (op. cit., p. 28)

and threw down the bone. I remember her face went quite white; and she burst out: "Something has happened to my son!" And so indeed it was; soon after, Qupanuaq returned late one night, and before entering the house, he went round outside to the window and called out "Dear Little Thing. It is my fault that you no longer have a son!" "Little Thing" was a pet name Qupanuaq used for mother. And then he came in and told us how it had come about. They had killed nothing, and had for several days been obliged to live on caribou dung; they were sadly worn out when at last they came to a place where he had stored away the carcase of a caribou he had killed some time before; but now they could not find the cache. They divided into two parties, his wife going one way and Qupanuaq with the two boys another. They searched and searched all about, but could not find the spot. The first snow had fallen, it was autumn, with a cold wind and driving snow, and they were poorly clad; so they lay down behind a shelter of stones to rest; all were much exhausted. The day was short, and the night very long, and they had to wait for daylight before they could begin searching again. Meantime, Qiqertaunak had found the cache, but she did not know where to look for the rest of the party, and being anxious about them, she ate but little herself, and gave the child she was carrying a small piece of meat to suck. She had made a stone shelter like the others, and lay half dozing when suddenly she awoke, having dreamed of my brother. She dreamed that he stood there quite plainly before her, pale and shivering with cold, and spoke to her and said: "You will never see me again. It is because the earth-lice are angry at our having eaten their sinews and their dung before a year had passed since my father's death."

I remember this quite distinctly, because it was the first time I realized that there were certain things one must not do after anyone had died. The caribou are called "earth-lice" in shaman language.

So lifelike was the dream that Qiqertaunak could not sleep any more that night. My brother Qajakutjuk was her favorite, and she used to say charms over him to make him strong.

Next morning, when it was light, and Qupanuaq was ready to start, my brother was so weak that he could not stand, and the others were too exhausted to carry him.

So they covered him with a thin, worn skin and left him. Later on they found the meat, but they did not go back to Qajakutjuk. He was frozen to death.'[69]

Awareness of the hidden meanings of signs, the symbolism contained in various phenomena and the examination of omens are all part of the Iglulik's spiritual life. The belief in metagnomic powers is an organic part of this ideological whole. The Shaman Takornak tells of how:

'Umaga and I were travelling from Iglulik to Tununeq when he dreamed one night that a friend of his had been eaten by his nearest kin. Umaga has the gift of second sight, and always knows when anything remarkable is going to happen. Next day we started off, and there was something remarkable about our journey from the start. Again and again the sledge stuck fast, but when we came to look, there was nothing to show what had stopped it. This went on all day, and in the evening we halted at Aunerit ("the melted place", in the interior of Cockburn Land). Next morning a ptarmigan flew over our tent. I threw a walrus tusk at it, but missed. Then I threw an axe, and again missed. And it seemed as if this also was to show that other strange things were to happen that day. We started off, and the snow was so deep that we had to help pull the sledge ourselves. Then we heard a noise. We could not make out what it was; sometimes it sounded like a dying animal in pain, and then again like human voices in the distance. As we came nearer, we could hear human words, but could not at first make out the meaning, for the voice seemed to come from a great way off. Words that did not sound like real words, and a voice that was powerless and cracked. We listened, and kept on listening, trying to make out one word from another, and at last we understood what it was that was being said. The voice broke down between the words, but what it was trying to say was this:

"I am now one who can live no longer among my fellows: for I have eaten my nearest of kin."

Now we knew that there should properly be no one else in this part of the country but ourselves, but all the same we could distinctly hear that this was a woman speaking, and we looked at each other, and it was as if we hardly dared speak out loud, and we whispered:

69. Rasmussen: op. cit., pp. 50 ff

"An eater of men! What is this we have come upon here!" '

The travellers finally find a woman behind a small shelter:

'We went. slowly up to the spot, and when we looked in, there lay a human skull with the flesh gnawed from the bones. Yes, we came to that shelter, and looking in, we saw a human being squatting down inside, a poor woman, her face turned piteously towards us. Her eyes were all bloodshot, from weeping, so greatly had she suffered.

"Kivkaq," she said (literally, "you my gnawed bone," which was her pet name for Padloq, whom she knew well), "Kivkaq, I have eaten my elder brother and my children." "My elder brother" was her pet name for her husband.'[70]

The aim of the whole religious system of the Eskimos is to 'maintain the balance between man and the rest of the world'.[71] This equilibrium is interrupted each time someone violates a 'rule of life' that has been decreed by tradition. If a taboo is ignored, the powers that regulate men and the world in general will transform themselves into supernatural forces that are malignant and hostile. The belief in the paragnostic powers of the Shaman is part of this ideological and affective ensemble. Once the taboo has been violated, the Shaman is called to identify the secret rupture that has thus been caused in the vital equilibrium, the balance of things that 'holds the world together' and assures the normal flow of both social and individual life. So, if someone falls sick, for example, then his sickness has been caused by the violation of some taboo. The Shaman must encourage the patient to confess what he has done; if the latter refuses, then the Shaman *tears the secrets from his soul*, by means of his mysterious powers. In Ollsen's report it is seen that the Shaman's procedures in this 'forced' confession a. e based mainly on the suggestive effectiveness of the interrogation. However, one cannot exclude the possibility of some elements of actual metagnomic power here and there in the seance, as occur in other seances of the same type. The seance follows these stages: the Shaman asks his helper-spirit the cause of the sickness; the patient (in this case a woman named

70 Rasmussen: op. cit., pp. 29 ff.
71. ibid. p. 62

Nanornaq who had fallen seriously ill and had extensive pains) replies that she has violated a taboo. Then the Shaman tries to discover which taboo she has transgressed, making general allusions, using vague images and suggestion, or very probably, actual paranormal knowledge. The other people present try to minimize the woman's faults and ask the Shaman to do away with the 'impurities' that have resulted from her action. Here are some passages from the Shaman's interrogation:

> ' "It is you, you are Aksharquarnilik, I ask you, my helping spirit, whence comes the sickness from which this person is suffering? Is it due to something I have eaten in defiance of taboo, lately or long since? Or is it due to the one who is wont to lie beside me, to my wife? Or is it brought about by the sick woman herself? Is she herself the cause of the disease?"
>
> The patient answers:
>
> "The sickness is due to my own fault. I have but ill fulfilled my duties. My thoughts have been bad and my actions evil."
>
> "I see a woman over in your direction, towards my audience, a woman who seems to be asking for something. A light shines out in front of her. It is as if she was asking for something with her eyes, and in front of her is something that looks like a hollow. What is it? What is it? Is it that, I wonder, which causes her to fall over on her face, stumble right into sickness, into peril of death? Can it indeed be something which will not be taken from her? Will she not be released from it? I still see before me a woman with entreating eyes, with sorrowful eyes, and she has with her a walrus tusk in which grooves have been cut."
>
> Listeners:
>
> "Oh, is that all? It is a harpoon head that she has worked at, cutting grooves in it at a time when she ought not to touch anything made from parts of an animal."
>
> "A seal comes forth, plain to be seen. It is wet. One can see how the skin has been scraped on the blubber side; it is all plain as could be."
>
> The patient:
>
> "I did scrape the skin of a seal which my son Qasagaq had killed at a time when I ought not to have touched seal skins."

"What is that I begin to see now? It must be blood unless it is human filth. But it is outside the house, on the ground. It looks like blood. It is frozen, and covered with loose snow. Someone has tried to hide it."

Patient:

"Yes, that was in the autumn. I had a miscarriage, and tried to conceal it, I tried to keep it secret to avoid the taboo."

"There is still something more I seem to see; something that as it were comes and disappears just as I am about to grasp it. What is it? Can it be the man Amarualik, I wonder? It looks like him. I think it must be he. His face is bright, but he is blushing also. He is as bright as a living being. It looks as if he wanted to show me something. And yet another person. Who is that? The patient must have no secrets. Let her tell us herself. Let her speak to us herself. Or can it be my cousin Qumangapik? Yes, it is he. It is Qumangapik. The size is right, and he has a big nose."

Patient:

"Alas, yes, it is true. Those men have I lain with at a time when I ought not to have lain with any man, at a time when I was unclean." '72

Martin Gusinde's very extensive documentation of the Fuegians shows how paragnostic beliefs have inserted themselves organically into a defined cultural group. It must be noted that the Selk'nam and the Yamana have a particular rapport between individuals, as well as between persons and objects, which is encouraged by a certain psychological climate, one that is derived from a very strong empathy. The Selk'nam take part 'very often and very actively' in a dream-world.[73] If a Selk'nam sees a sick relative in a dream, the next day he will send a messenger to enquire about his health.[74] The Teesesk magic-man had the habit of entering a half-conscious psychic state in the middle of the night so that he could contact his helper-spirit: in these psychic states he was able to predict future events, for the good of his

---

72. Rasmussen: op. cit., pp. 133-141. Naturally, the confession may not require any active exploration by the Shaman if the 'guilty' person is sincere and already willing to confess. Such is the case when there is a general purification of the community with the aim of clearing the obstacles that retain marine animals in the region of Tanakapsaluk; cf. op. cit., pp. 128 ff.
73. Gusinde: Die Feuerland-Indianer, I, p. 714. Cf. p. 716, 'A bad dream is often followed by a whole day of anxiety, agitation and anguish.'
74. ibid. p. 716.

people.[75] The Yamana also have an intense dream life and have great faith in the truth of dreams. This is confirmed by the fact that from time to time some dream-prediction comes true:[76]

'On the 26th July, 1923, Nelly (a Yamana woman) was upset when she told me that, the night before, she had dreamed of some very unpleasant things: "Several families came here from Mejillones (the island of Navarin) and told me that there is general mourning going on down there. Someone will certainly come from there to-day and we shall know who has died. After this dream I awoke and could not sleep any more." She was convinced of the truth of what she said and did not cease being worried when I tried to convince her that dreams were of no importance. In fact, for several days nobody from Mejillones had come to see us (at Punta Remolino) and we were afraid that some epidemic had broken out. To our considerable surprise, Alejandro arrived and told us: "Last night two of our women died. Anita, Willer's wife, and Sara, the wife of Masemikens. Masemikens himself and old Emilia are seriously ill and will soon die." '[77]

The dream of one famous Yekamus helped the community to find food:

'To give me an example of the skill sometimes encountered in former times, Nelly Lawrence told me the following story, which had been told to her by her aunt Flora. Among Flora's relatives there were two Yekamus who were considered to be the most powerful ones there had ever been. It happened that those living in the western region were going through a period of great hardship because the bad weather was preventing the capture of sea-lions, and even the gathering of shell-fish was impossible. The Yekamus became aware of this situation; then one of them went to sleep, with the intention of working through his dreams. The next day he said to the people of his village: "Go towards the West and stop at the southern coast." Without wasting time, all the families set off for this particular place. The next night the Yekamus dreamed again, and the following day, said: "I have seen two whales approaching. They are sisters. They are both pregnant and

75. ibid. p. 728
76. op. cit. II, p. 1296-1297
77. ibid. p. 1298

each has an almost completely-formed baby whale inside her belly. An enraged 'asoula' (Pseudorca crassidens) came up to the two whales in the middle of the sea and threatened them. The two sisters begged: 'Do not kill us; if you kill us, our babies will also die, and you will kill four creatures at once!' But the asoula was not moved by these words and he killed them ferociously. You will soon see the two whales when they are beached near here." Sure enough, the same evening, the tide deposited two young whales on the bank. They were females. Their bellies were opened, and each was carrying young.'[78]

Among the Selk'nam, the acquisition of paragnostic powers is particularly important to the witch-doctor. One must distinguish between an extra-ordinary (or spontaneous) calling and an ordinary (or artificially produced) calling. The first one becomes evident even in childhood. Its presence is indicated when the child often sings in its sleep, or even in day-time. The child often appears to be in a psychic half-sleeping state, when the singing-habit usually appears. In the other type—the ordinary calling or vocation—the aspirant tries to induce (through willing it), contact with the spirit of a dead witch-doctor who was related to him. In the case where the father is a witch-doctor, the suggestion provided through his practices will have only an initial effect. This exterior imitation will be interiorized until the sleep and hypnosis appear unconsciously. In his dream, the young man will see a related witch-doctor who appears to be favorable towards him. The novice becomes more and more pre-occupied. He goes more and more frequently and intensely into a state of great concentration on himself. He meditates for long periods in his hut or in the forest. During this self-introspection, the image of the dead witch-doctor appears with increasing regularity. One day, the novice announces that he has seen his relative in a dream and that he has received the power (Waiyuwen) from him. He now sings

78. Gusinde: op. cit., II, p. 1388 ff. Gusinde speaks of the 'claims' that dreams have proved true (op. cit., II, p. 1297) and denies implicitly that oniric consciousness may have access to paranormal consciousness. This is an *a priori* judgment which is inadmissible because the author made no systematic analysis of the facts. In fact, the *belief* in the truth of dreams has a firm foundation and consequently, it is possible that certain dreams may come true because they are either clairvoyant or telepathic.

very often: the soul of the dead witch-doctor causes him to sing, or rather, the soul itself sings through him. But he must still master his power completely; that is, he must be able to pass at will from waking into the hypnotic state, and also be able to contact at will his helper-spirit's soul and the power that comes from it. He must practise a great deal before attaining this perfection. He carries out difficult tasks, is violent towards his own body so that his mind may become more submissive to the image of the dead witch-doctor and so that the two personalities may become united. Then a new interior experience intervenes to show that this intimate union has taken place. Sometimes this does not happen, even though the efforts to attain it may last for years.

This contact with the dead witch-doctor is not an end in itself. Its purpose is to acquire certain *specific powers*. The novice must make still more preparations if he is to gain these powers. The efforts of concentration, the dreams, the hypnotic states and the singing must all continue. Then the *paragnostic aptitude* makes a gradual appearance: the natives call this 'ategn' or 'yauategn':

'People say: "He must work very hard, dream a lot and, above all, sing without interruption, so that his waiyuwen (i.e. the soul of the dead witch-doctor, together with his powers) will appear more often and remain with him longer." This means that the novice will concentrate even more, avoiding all distractions offered by his surroundings, or else he will enter the mysterious silence of his own ego in order to meditate upon one thought, his waiyuwen. (The people say): "He begins to work on his waiyuwen until he sees things that are far away." The novice's "strength of psychic vision" must be intensified until he is able to see the waiyuwen of other witch-doctors. He tries to contact these at a very early stage. When this has been achieved, he tries, through his "yauategn", to use his power at a great distance. During this particular period of preparation, the young man is instructed by an old expert. The latter says to him: "Go on working until you see my waiyuwen!" The novice's efforts may take from four to six weeks. Then he tells his instructor that he has been successful and the latter usually replies: "I saw your waiyuwen when it approached mine. Continue your efforts now so that you may approach others." '[79]

The belief in paragnostic powers does more than simply play an organic role in the ideology and institutions of the Selk'nam culture: it has its very own ideological organization. It is interesting to analyse how the Selk'nam imagine this 'psychical power of vision'. As we have seen, the novice tries to create a rapport with the waiyuwen of a dead witch-doctor. The waiyuwen is either the soul ('kaspi') of the witch-doctor —a guiding soul or a helper-spirit—or else it may be the gathering of exceptional powers that the novice is gradually taking into his possession. If the first sense is interpreted according to psychological conceptions, it would be called the 'second personality' which replaces the normal person when he enters into a trance; the second sense means that it is 'the combination of the witch-doctor's power and energy, together with all the capacities and activities that develop in his body, that he is sometimes able to exteriorize with the aim of applying this force in an area that is outside his body.'[80] The waiyuwen, seen as a collection of powers coming from the guiding spirit, works in the same way as what we know as metagnomic powers. The 'hamen' is a particular form of the waiyuwen, it is the power of lucidity that is used by the witch-doctor in matters concerning war, or else it may be described as the particular waiyuwen used exclusively in these matters:

> 'While the witch-doctor is singing and dreaming, the hamen communicates all its observations to him: how many men are assembled, where they are situated at the time, what route they have followed so far, what direction they will take, how far away they are, what they are discussing and what they intend . . . then it comments on the eventual outcome of the war: how many losses will be suffered on each side and other smaller details.[81]

The hamen is not simply a 'psychic seeing'; it is a vision that materializes in the form of 'an animal as big as a guanaco'; this animal is the 'messenger' or the 'informant'

79. Gusinde: op. cit., I, p. 783
80. Gusinde: op. cit., I, pp. 746-748
81. ibid. pp. 749 ff.

that the witch-doctor sends into the enemy camp.[82] Neither
is the 'yauategn', another form of the waiyuwen, just a simple
psychic vision; it is active and capable of changing, sometimes completely, the object that is seen:

> '(By this term) the Indians mean the psychic vision of
> the witch-doctor. The yauategn does not consist of just the
> ability to reproduce an object photographically; it is also
> able to exercise an actual influence on material objects and
> on the souls of other individuals. This power is depicted
> as an eye that leaves the witch-doctor's body and travels
> in a straight line to the object in his view, while still
> remaining connected to the witch-doctor. The eye distends,
> like a sort of "thread made from gum" (this is how the
> Indians expressed it): it is able to function from any side
> of the head like the eyes of a lobster, and may be with-
> drawn, like a snail's antennae.'[83]

The Selk'nams' formulation of the yauategn as a kind of
'active vision' may be seen in a peculiar competition that
takes place between the novice and the old witch-doctor.
They both go to a certain place, without this having been
predetermined in any specific way, because the witch-doctors
'with their spiritual eye, have no difficulty in following the
movements of a colleague'.[84] It is a purely visionary type of
test, taking the following form: to demonstrate his power,
the novice takes a small object into his hand, which he keeps
closed. He stares at his hand, then opens it slowly and, in
his imagination, sees the object shoot into the distance—as
far as his yauategn is able to send it. Then the old man's
soul—using his own yauategn and imagination—tries to out-
distance the object . . . Sometimes the old man will use
another method to show the power of his psychic vision: he
goes slowly towards the place where the novice's object has
fallen, seizes it with his yauategn and takes it back to its

82. ibid. p. 749
83. Gusinde: op. cit., I, p. 751. The clearest demonstration of the witch-
doctor's power is the 'canem'. Here, the idea of visual power is replaced
by the materialization of a human force: ('The form of the canem
resembles either a wreath of smoke or a patch of mist; sometimes it is
like an enormous packet and, more rarely, like a large, fat guanaco.'
Op. cit., pp. 750 ff.). The canem, in this materialized form, represents
the bad intentions of the witch-doctor, and it is particularly dangerous:
even more dangerous than the material cause of all physical or moral
ills, the 'kwake'.
84. Gusinde: op. cit., I, p. 784

original position. Then the novice must admit the superiority of the old man's power. Sometimes it is the old instructor who provokes the novice by throwing the object a great distance away: then the novice must try to use his yauategn to go beyond this point. He may fail and he may succeed; or he may have only partial success in which his yauategn reaches the place where the object lies and is confronted by the yauategn of the old man. If the success is complete, the novice is able to seize the object and carry it back to its owner. In any case, the old witch-doctor will usually contest any success by saying, for example, that the object was not the one that he had thrown, that the place had not been reached or that the necessary distance had not been covered.[85]

In all procedures that are directly connected to a belief in metagnomic powers, we come across a sort of *active vision*. It is not only the paranormal perception of objects or of mental states, but a *force* that is in itself dynamic. It is one that can change an object almost completely, or can itself take on some material form. This concept is found among many 'primitive' peoples: for example, when Unaleq, the Iglulik shaman, discusses some voyage that Rasmussen intends to take, he is not limited just to 'seeing'; he takes on the form of a bear and claims to influence what he 'sees', so that his vision actually determines what is really going to happen. Rasmussen tells how Unaleq goes out (according to his wife, Tuglik) in the form of a bear, so as to explore the route that the voyage will take. He sweeps away all obstacles such as accidents, sickness and death and predicts that they will return the following summer, safe and sound.[86]

Here we have entered another dimension of magic reality: an area where the witch-doctor claims to have wonderful powers over people and things. These are usually called 'physical' powers, because they control matter, and they appear frequently in beliefs that concern paragnostic powers. If, for the purpose of study, we isolate these beliefs in paragnostic powers, it must be remembered that they are not isolated in the cultural frame-work of magical actions in general. Physical powers become an organic part of a par-

85. Gusinde: op. cit., pp. 784 ff.
86. Rasmussen: *Intellectual Culture of the Iglulik Eskimos*, p. 122.

ticular cultural order and they express certain human attitudes and desires. In the fire-walking at Mbenga, for example, the smoke that rises from the furnace is not just ordinary smoke; it is considered as something living, as a protective 'spirit'. Nor is the fire just ordinary fire; it is also a spirit that lives in the flames that shoot up between the stones in the pit. These spirits, led by Tui Namoliwai, precede the participants: a dried fern-tree log is placed on the burning pit, pointing towards the direction that will be taken by the participants, and this log indicates the way that the spirits will come. If it is placed incorrectly, the fire-walk will fail, because Tui Namoliwai and his spirits will be unable to use their protective powers. Besides, it is taboo to cross the same way as the spirits as it would prevent their participation. The pit, also, is not just any ordinary burning ditch, because the roots of the 'draecena' have special ties with it: only these roots shall be cooked in the fire, all other vegetables shall remain raw. The test also requires an adequate psychic preparation, including no sexual relations, legitimate or otherwise, during a prescribed period.[87]

In the fire-walk at Mbenga, the nullification of the burning property of fire expresses a communication with 'spirits', made possible through the particular privilege accorded the descendants of Na Galita. The pit is consecrated in gratitude for the communication, as is the food. This food is also part of the ceremony and participates in the 'mana' that is created. But the suspension of the burning may be explained by other ideologies: for example, a man who is being persecuted by the spirits will pass over the fire in the belief that, in doing this, he is placing the fire between himself and the harmful

87. Kingsley Roth: *The Fire-Walk in Fiji*, in 'Man' XXXIII, 1933, No. 49

contact that is causing his suffering. J. G. Gmelin observed the Tartar custom of crossing the fire after a funeral, so that 'the dead person may not follow them through fear of the fire.'[88] The fire-walk may also have the value of a purification, one that destroys any evil influence from which a victim may be suffering.[89]

87. Kingsley Roth: *The Fire Walk in Fiji*, in 'Man' XXXIII, 1933, no. 49.
88. Frazer: *Balder the Beautiful* II, p. 18
89. ibid. p. 17. Concerning this purificatory element, see R. U. Sayce: *Fire-Walking Ceremony in Natal*, in 'Man' XXXIII, 1933, No. 2.

We have now seen the paradox of a *culturally-conditioned* nature, and all its embarrassing implications. But, at the same time, a new way has opened up before us: this cultural conditioning of nature has been examined in its own cultural frame-work, in its historical setting. Whether magic powers, even to some extent, are real or not, is a question that depends upon *what is meant by 'real'*. The meaning of 'real', in this context, may be obtained only by admitting that magic does play a role in history. We now turn towards the 'historical drama' in the hope of resolving the awkward paradox with which we are faced.

PART II

The Historical Drama of the Magic World

Research into one peculiar psychic state has been carried out in an area that covers arctic and sub-arctic Siberia, North America and Melanesia. It appears that the natives of these areas enter this state frequently, as if they have a natural disposition towards it. It is called 'latah' by the Malays, 'olon', by the Tungus, 'irkunii' by the Yukagires. 'amurak' by the Yakuts, 'menkeiti' by the Koriaks and 'imu' by the Ainus. It has been observed and described by several authors.[1] Sir Hugh Clifford describes the native who is in the state of latah; how, for longer or shorter periods and to varying degrees, he loses his own unity and is no longer able to control either himself or his actions. When this happens—usually after some emotional experience or after some surprise—the subject is receptive to any suggestion.[2] For instance, if his attention is caught by branches moving in the wind, he will imitate this movement. If two latah are surprised by a sudden noise, they will fall into an automatic miming of each other's actions; this mutual imitation may last for half an hour; if one undresses, so will the other; if one puts his hand over a flame, the other will follow suit.[3] According to Clifford, any adult Malay may become latah.[4] The Tungus call the state 'olon' from which Shirokogoroff derived the term 'olonism'. They sometimes set out to exploit the individuals who are susceptible to becoming olon and will carry out actions that the olon, having been surprised, proceeds to imitate in a completely passive manner. This is considered an entertainment, a sort of social game. Shirokogoroff witnessed the following incident: one individual was eating his millet in a circle of other people; his attention was drawn by one of the others, who pretended to fill his mouth with millet to the point of choking. The first immediately entered a state of echopraxia, one of the main characteristics of the olon situation: he immediately imitates the action and fills his mouth with millet until breathing is impossible. To extract himself from the suggestion, the olon runs away, and the audience laughs

---

1. Czaplicka: *Aboriginal Siberia, A Study in Social Anthropology*, Oxford 1914, p. 315
2. Clifford: *Studies in Brown Humanity*, 1898, p. 189
3. ibid. pp. 191, 193 ff. 195, 200
4. ibid. pp. 195 ff.

heartily.[5] A further incident is described: during a meeting, someone catches a Manchurian unawares and taps his hand lightly; the latter imitates the action automatically, and taps his neighbor's hand. The fun of the game is in the various reactions of people who are not familiar with the 'trick' and who are disconcerted or indignant when touched by the olon. This causes general hilarity, particularly when the person is a woman or an old man.[6] V. L. Priklonski reports an interesting case of collective olonism: during a parade of the third Transbaikalia battalion of Cossacks, one unit, composed entirely of natives, suddenly entered a state of olon. Instead of carrying out their colonel's orders—he was a Russian—the men repeated them in chorus. The colonel naturally became angry and began to abuse the men; they repeated his abuse.[7] Shirokogoroff remarks that the phenomenon 'because of its simplicity and its potential universality, may appear in ethnographic situations that are quite independent from one another', that is, it is not due to any simple diffusing process, but is a basic component of 'the normal psycho-mental make-up'.[8]

If we analyse this state of olon, we find that it is characterized by a complete abandonment of control, as if there is some element present that surrenders itself completely to an outside force. It is as if this insecure, unstable presence is unable to withstand the' shock of some emotive force; it cannot accept and master this force within the framework of relationships with which it is familiar. The subject does not seem to be aware of what he is faced with; his fragile 'control' reaches an 'impasse' that it is incapable of surmounting, and so it abandons all effort. When this barrier is down, there is no longer any distinction between his control and the action that he sees: instead of hearing or seeing the rustling of leaves in the wind, he *becomes* the tree that has rustling leaves; instead of hearing a word, he *becomes* the word

5. Shirokogoroff: *The Psychomental Complex of the Tungus*, p. 248
6. ibid. loc. cit.
7. Priklonski, quoted by Shirokogoroff: op. cit., p. 251
8. Shirokogoroff: op. cit., loc. cit. In regard to olonism, compare with Muhlmann: *Rassen und Volkerkunde*, Brunswick, 1936, pp. 403 ff. (I was unable to have access to the work by Lohnberg.) *Die Typen der Nachahmung bei den primitiven Volkern*, published in the *Archiv für gesam. Psychol.*, LXXXVIII, 1933, pp. 77-130, quoted by Mühlmann in *Methode der Volkerkunde*, Stuttgart, 1938

itself, etc. There is no longer any discrimination—the image cannot prevent itself from becoming the act . . . In this psychic situation, the peculiar 'presence' within the subject acts as an echo of the world; the object or action that stimulates his reaction may change at any time and become the center of his attention: Scheler calls this 'affective heteropathic fusion'.[9] In general terms, the state of olon is similar to the state of 'amok' that is encountered in almost all Malays. In the state of amok the loss of the 'control' may take another form: in the event of unexpected emotions such as fear, anguish after a death etc., the victim falls prey to a storm of gestures that are released completely and impulsively. He will leap about, arm himself, run like a madman and will hit out at or kill anyone he meets, even if it is his own father.[10] The psychic states of olon, latah and amok may not be considered as part of a culturally-formed magic because they represent the dissolution of the 'control' and the taking-up of an indiscriminate 'koinonia' (communion) where there is a complete unleashing of uncontrolled impulse. The negative fragility and imbalance of the control distinguish it from any cultural creation—the latter always implies a positive manner of facing the world; an experience may lead to a problem, but there is a development leading to a solution. Olonism does show one aspect which could lead to cultural developments. In certain cases the olonized individual makes a visible effort to resist the influences. He does not accept his susceptibility and will not give himself up passively when faced with these influences; he reacts. He becomes anguished, and this anguish expresses *his will to retain his identity when confronted with the threat of losing it*. Its fragility is the problem—he must defend and redeem it as best he can; he tries to reintegrate it. Jochelson reports a case where an old woman was olonized by a Cossack who made her run behind him. She was unable to escape the suggestion

9. Scheler's expression (Einfühlung) Einsetzen is found in his *Wesen und Formen der Sympathie* (Fr. Trans. *Nature et forme de la sympathie*. Paris 1928, p. 34). According to Scheler, in the heteropathic form of the affective fusion, the ego is attracted, captivated and hypnotized by an outside entity, to the point that the latter takes the place of the ego, substituting all its own basic attitudes for those of the ego.
10. Jochelson: *The Yukaghir and Yukaghirized Tungus*, p. 37, quoted by Czaplicka: *Aboriginal Siberia*, p. 252

and cried out for him to stop, after trying in vain to stop herself. In the previous case, with the eating of the millet, the victim saved himself only by running away. Sometimes the defence may be more violent: Jochelson reports that, on another occasion, a woman, trying to escape an irresistible suggestion, took hold of a knife and went in search of her persecutor.[11]

We have seen a rough outline of one part of the drama that helped create the world of magic, as well as evidence of its cultural diversity. The cases we have just examined, with their destruction of the 'controlling presence', their indiscriminate koinonia and their unleashing of uncontrolled impulses, represent only one pole of the magic drama: The other pole consists of the redeeming of the 'controlling presence'. When the presence resists because it wants to be free to function, a typical and easily-recognizable type of anguish is produced. The presence may then become aware of the need to redeem itself, and it does this by creating certain cultural forms. If the presence fades, without any effort or reaction taking place, then the magic world has not yet appeared. If the presence is redeemed and consolidated and is no longer aware of its own fragile nature, then the magic world has already disappeared. It is between these two stages that the magic world makes its appearance—in the struggle and opposition that arise between them—here, the magic world becomes manifest as movement and development: it displays its many cultural forms and is born into the history of mankind.[12] In an attempt to prove this, we will analyse some basic themes of magic.

11. ibid.
12. This examination of the problem reveals the many limitations of any research that aims to determine the actual structure of the primitive mentality; important things are glossed over and the real historical drama of magic is often ignored. When Levy-Bruhl talks of a primitive mentality governed by the law of participation, or speaks of a mytho-magical reality in which the individual has sympathetic ties with the world and with other people; when Cassirer theorizes about the primitive sentiment of 'Gemeinschaft alles Lebendigen' (communion between all living things) which makes impossible either the slightest contradiction between man and nature or the least expression of nature itself; when modern irrationalists, from Klages to Dacqué, talk about an affective mystical fusion during the first ages of history; when Heinz Werner and the 'Entwicklungspsychologie' underline the complex, unreliable structure of the 'primitive person'; when ethnological specialists, from Preuss to Graebner and Thurnwald, etc., give illustrations of this same structural character—although the interpretations may differ—and imagine

A. C. Haddon reports that a Turik (Borneo) refused to be separated from certain irregular-shaped stones because they 'held back' his soul and prevented it from leaving his body. This small psychological anecdote introduces us to one of the most important cultural themes of the magic world— *the danger of losing one's soul and the overcoming of this danger.* If we are to understand as fully as possible, we must consider the subject of our analysis without the interference of any personal views. Our interpretation must be colored as little as possible by our awareness of the Christian meaning of losing one's soul. A Christian conscience considers this fall into a finite and limited state (part of this individualization) as sin: the soul is lost when we become conscious of our individuality as a given fact, or when we consider this given fact as something finite, and yield passively to 'the pleasures of the flesh'. This whole complex historical world made up of experiences and moral judgments, *presupposes* the singularization of the individual and expresses the establishment, within the conscience, of questions that ask the meaning and value of one's individual being. But this presupposition turns into a *problem* in the world of magic. In the magic world, the soul may be lost; its existence is not founded on the same principles—it is rather a fragile presence that the world may swallow up or make disappear. In the magic world, the identification of one's soul is not a fact, but a task to be carried out, and one's being within the world is a reality that must be established. It is from this that there arises a whole series of experiences and images, protective measures and practices which express either the magical

that these explain the magical fact itself: all of these form only one moment in the existential magic drama. The danger that the subject feels—that he will not be able to exercise his 'control' is disconnected from its concrete relationship with the other moment—when he overcomes this danger—and is made part of a 'type' of mentality, part of a 'psychic structure' etc. The redeeming of the controlling presence is not taken into consideration, and the actual threat loses all its dramatic force, so that it becomes a limited, indiscriminate koinonia. This distortion is easily explained: the self-consciousnous of historiography leads it to deal with particular problems and to use categories that are particular to historic judgment. As a result of this, in the eyes of historical reason, the primitive individual is always qualifiable within the framework of a special problem and a special category. It is precisely this type of historical interest that has always been lacking in the area of magic; instead of an historical tableau being made of the primitive individual, the interest is limited to making just a general outline of a 'type'.

moment of danger when the soul may be lost, or else the cultural redemption—it is the dramatic opposition of these elements that forms the historical world of magic. The personal presence of oneself, one's 'being present', the soul, may escape from wherever it resides, may be ravished, stolen, eaten etc.; it may be a bird, a butterfly, or a breath; it must be protected, recuperated or else held back, fixed or localized.[13] The Turik who believes that his stones will hold back his soul is by no means a superstitious person who is the prey of his own ridiculous fears: in a universe where the 'being here' is exposed to the risk of not being here, one may, in actual fact, *not* be here, as in the case of latah when the subject was induced to imitate the rustling of leaves. And it is also possible that your soul, or your existence as a present being, may be tricked into subjection by someone else, as happened to the old woman who was forced to run behind the Cossack. The Turik rids himself of his anguish by means of his stones (or by means of the images and associations that they stimulate—his stones were hook-shaped) or at least overpowers and reduces it, thus recovering something that, to him, was no less real than the danger he was in. If the Turik's beliefs and actions appear superstitious to us, it is because we measure them anti-historically—that is, in the light of our own 'being here', something, in *our* culture, that is fixed and guaranteed. We regard our own historical mode of existence as valid for all cultural forms. And because the Turik's beliefs and practices have no real basis, according to our existence, we designate them as 'superstitions'. Our cultural assumptions limit our understanding of the existential drama of magic and its characteristic cultural themes.[14]

13. To prove the validity of this interpretation of magic, we recall that, in psychopathological cases where the psychological synthesis is weakened or where there is a more or less serious dissociation of the personality, the subject reacts by tending to reconstruct, even in a fragmentary way, this magic cultural theme of a presence that is in danger of being lost then overcomes the danger. We will return to this very important point.

14. To show to what point the magic risk of 'losing the soul' is *real*, we repeat the following incident, as told to Sir J. Frazer in a letter of the 26th August, 1898, from the Rev. Lorimer Fison: a Fuegian from Mukutu who was suddenly wakened by somebody treading on his feet, began to implore his soul to come back into him. He had been dreaming that he was far away in Tonga, and when awake, was greatly perturbed to find himself in Mukuto. Death hung above his head as long as he was unable to convince his soul that it should cross

The theme of the possible loss and eventual regaining of the personal presence is illustrated very clearly if we analyse the 'atai' that is found among the natives of Mota. Codrington writes that 'the word atai seems to have had the sense . . . of something that is connected to a person in a particular and intimate way and which, because of this, is sacred: *something that struck the imagination from the moment it was seen,* something that the individual considered marvellous, unless it was other people who had made it appear to him as such. Whatever this thing was, the person believed that it was a reflection of his own person; he and his atai would prosper, suffer, live or die together. However, there is no reason to suppose that this original meaning of the word was later extended to mean the soul. The word has a sense that applies both to the second self that is the visible object connected so mysteriously to the individual, as well as to the other second self which we whites call the soul.'[15] But Codrington's interpretation of the experience of the Mata natives is unreliable in so far as it is colored by his own Christian cultural bias (particularly by his concept of the soul). However, his account is interesting as a vivid illustration of what happens when the inhabitant of one cultural world comments on the realities of another.[16]

According to Codrington, the atai, as an experience and an occurrence, consists of the perception of something that strikes the imagination and astonishes or excites a lively affective reaction in the subject. But this presumption that the atai has psychological origins is no real explanation and cannot serve as a distinctive trait. We come across things that 'strike the imagination' or astound us several times a day—we do not create our atai out of such experiences. There is a gap between the feeling of astonishment and the atai which will persist as long as we presuppose dogmatically as Codrington does, the existence of a decided and guaranteed 'being here' which may be astonished or frightened,

the sea as quickly as possible and come back to its rightful place. (Frazer: *Taboo and the Perils of the Soul,* pp. 39 ff.).
15. R. H. Codrington: *The Melanesians,* 1871, p. 250. The italics are ours. For a related treatment, see Levy-Bruhl: *L'âme primitive, passim.*
16. For ethnological research on Dilthey's 'wechselseitige Erhellung', see W. Muhlmann: *Methodik der Volkerkunde,* Stuttgart, 1938, pp. 96-100.

but does not run the risk of *becoming* the actual thing that causes these reactions.

To understand the atai as a cultural institution, we must return to the existential magic anguish or distress and to the drama of redemption that is rooted in it. The possibility of becoming some emotive object (surprising, terrifying, etc.) causes the subject to adjust and redeem (provided he foresees the possibility as dangerous). His 'presence' is fascinated, it risks being led astray and remaining fixed upon the object, without being able to go beyond it, and so, no longer sustains itself as a presence. The redemption consists in experiencing and considering the object as an 'alter ego', with which a regulated and lasting relationship is established. The presence does not yet have the strength to crush the object by mastering the emotional charge that it causes. The process of objectification is half accomplished in the form of a compromise—the presence that is in danger of losing control masters itself by attaching its own problematic unity to that of the object. By means of this paradoxical compromise, and the rapport that follows it, insight is gained into the being as a unitary presence. Thus the dangerous process of annihilation and complete surrender is avoided, through a developing and meaningful cultural creation that liberates the presence. The product of this creation (the rapport between the ego and the alter ego) carries all the signs of the existential drama of which it is the complex solution: the atai is linked to the individual by an intimate shared destiny (both 'prosper, suffer and die together') and, at the same time (as Codrington remarks) the atai *is* the individual; we are again in the presence of a problematic 'being' that is still within the sphere of human decision. Because of this, it is impossible to relate the image and experience of the atai with our concept of soul, which carries with it the presupposition of a guaranteed identity. On the other hand, the atai is understood only within an historical world where identification is a task that must be accomplished; the atai is the drama of a presence in danger of dissolution that eventually succeeds in regaining control and re-establishing itself through the alter ego.[17]

In the case of atai (and similar phenomena) the threatened presence is held back and conquered by localizing it within the alter ego; but it may also be redeemed through practices that express the need to remove and thrust away the threatening object. This method of magical recovery is closely related to death and the treatment of the corpse. Death 'sucks away or steals' the soul (i.e. the presence or the 'being-in-the-world-of-the-living') of the living person: the corpse gives off something contagious that may lead to death. The natives give different reasons for the corpse's activity: the dead person's affection for somebody still living, jealousy or fear of going alone on the voyage, etc. The real reason is that the presence cannot accept death, and expresses its awareness of the danger that threatens it through its attitude towards the corpse; it is seen as something that steals, attracts, sucks away, infects or comes back to haunt.[18] From this there arises the need to detain the body (for example, by tying it up) or to thrust it away and put it at a distance etc., so that it may not return among the living or exert its evil influences. Among the Arunta, once the dying person is 'untied', i.e. has become a corpse that is capable of exerting its contagious and evil influences, they begin the process of overcoming these dangers: they destroy the dead person's abode to prevent him from returning to it; his name may not be mentioned because the word may induce him to return; the earth that covers the body is stamped down to make the grave more secure. The night after the funeral (night-time is particularly dangerous) the men gather together and shout so that the dead man is

17. The problems and misunderstandings that result from missionaries' use of the presupposed 'soul' are wide-spread. A European missionary once said to some Australian aborigines: 'I am not one, as you believe, but two'. When the aborigines laughed at this statement, he insisted: 'laugh as much as you like, but I tell you that I am two in one: the body that you see is one, but inside, there is another smaller, invisible me. The body dies and is buried, but the small one flies away when the other dies.' The aborigines replied: 'Yes, yes. We are also two. We have a small body in our chest.' (*Journal of the Anthropological Institute* VII, 1878, p. 282). It is unnecessary to point out that this was a purely verbal agreement; the ambiguity arose because the missionary was unable to cross the historical and cultural chasm that separated him from the natives.
18. On the magical attitudes surrounding the corpse, see Preuss in *Globus* 1905, p. 361 and Levy-Bruhl: *L'âme primitive*, pp. 275 ff.

frightened off. They gather again at dawn when the dead man's sister and cousin go to fetch water in a conch and return to the camp, raising and lowering the conch and crying out 'wa, wa, wa!' actions that express separation and distance. Then the conch is carried to the grave with cries of 'ba, ba, ba!' the hands are raised and lowered, still with the idea of frightening and chasing off the dead man. During the mourning, which is an expression of anguish at the threat to the presence, the water is poured over the grave so that the earth will be more compact. The same day, the men assemble nearby and begin the process of 'separation': at one point the men stand and stretch upwards, as if they wish to raise themselves off the ground; at the same time they chant: 'The dead man is rising, rise up further! Go on your way towards the land of the dead!' Then the youngest brother carries out the following rite with a cord made from the dead man's hair: he places one end against his stomach, in the place that he feels the distress or anguish. Then he bites the cord to indicate the end of his distress. All the men go through the same action, then the widow and all the women. The youngest brother then throws away the spindle that was used to twist the hair cord in the direction of the land of the dead, again crying out 'ba!' Another procession begins, with more hand movements and more cries of 'wa, wa, wa!' Bones are spread over the grave, so that when the dead man discovers them he will realize that his skeleton is now like these and will leave his grave and go to the land of the dead. The women leave the grave, protesting that they no longer wish to be near it. The men circle the grave, still making the up and down gestures; their legs tremble and they cry out 'trr, trr, trr!" They prostrate themselves on the groud and the rite ends with a prolonged 'baa!'[19] The dead man is now driven away and separated. The danger to the presence is over; it has been redeemed by a system of liberating 'guarantees' and the necessary balancing compensations.

In general, the magic drama—that is, the struggle of the 'being here' that is threatened and the consequent redemption —takes place at certain critical moments of existence when

19. Strehlow: *Die Aranda- und Loritja-Stämme in Zentral-Australien,* in *Veröffentlichungen aus dem städtischen Museum,* Frankfurt s.M. IV, 2, pp. 15 ff.

the presence is called upon to make an extra-ordinary effort. A rupture in the usual order of things is sometimes enough to excite the need to compensate, through magic, for any violation of tradition. A goat that eats its excrement, an ox beating the ground with its tail, the first sight of a white man or of a missionary's habit, the sound of a missionary church's bell, a plant that bears fruit out of season, a fruit found at the middle of the stalk instead of at the end, more than one fruit on the same stalk or a change in landscape—all these are dangerous events which call for a re-establishment of balance.[20] There are still other situations that give rise to the relationship between the magic world and the presence's critical moments. Such a struggle may be seen in Uvavnuk's experience. As we have seen, Uvavnuk was afraid of losing her 'being here' when faced by the terrifying and unexpected appearance of the meteor; but as soon as she interprets this apparition as a spirit that has entered her, then it is possible for her to redeem her presence. Instead of an uncontrolled take-over of the presence, we have a spirit that is seen as having changed through its relationship to the presence, so that it becomes something with a cultural and functional significance, something that will come when called upon and will carry out whatever the Shaman demands. In this case, as with the atai, the process of disintegration is arrested through compromise: and it is precisely this that is necessary if the soul (in the magical sense) is not to be lost.

To illustrate this, we will examine an example of spontaneous vocation among the Yamana and the Selk'nam. A young man goes off into the forest to look for some wood to make a harpoon. He becomes so tired in searching that he enters a psychic state that is very close to the actual loss of his presence. Finally, he finds a suitable branch which he begins to cut off with his axe—but with the first notch he releases a flood of water, something completely unexpected and, for him, an extraordinary 'sign'. He is greatly perturbed and returns to his hut. Something has happened to him that

20. For the relationship between the unusual and magic, see Levy-Bruhl: *Les fonctions mentales dans les sociétés inférieures*, pp. 35 ff., 70, 73; *Le surnaturel et la nature dans la mentalité primitive*, pp. 13 ff., 33 ff., 102, 182, 218 ff; *La mentalité primitive*, pp. 27 ff., 41, 125, 295 ff; *La mythologie primitive*, pp. 28, 36, 45.

compromises his fragile presence; he becomes obsessed with the incident in the forest. Although the Yamana is no longer in the forest, and the branch is no longer there, his presence is now fixated on the experience. In his dreams, he sees his soul or 'kespix' before the branch, the water pouring out of it. But now the scene is crowded with other spirits; some of them are familiar, but for the most part, they are strangers. Among them he sees some of his friends who are magic-men. They are benevolent and come up to meet him; they talk about his 'soul'. Gradually, all the spirits come and sit near him; they offer precious gifts to the dreamer's kespix; they invite him to eat and drink with them and he begins to feel at ease in their company; everything is pleasant and agreeable. Thus, the cultural redemption of the presence that was threatened has already begun in the dream situation. The original experience in the forest is transformed through traditional magic themes, so that it is no longer menacing or strange; he is being prepared to see a meaning in these things and to enter into a relationship with them. But the danger is still there: his dream-vision fades and disappears, beyond his control. The Yamana awakes and finds himself all alone in his hut. Still greatly moved by his vision, he is distressed and calls out to his neighbors. The magic-men arrive and, from the state of the man, they presume that he has been in contact with the spirits. Using suggestion, they sing a song that causes the man to see the scene once more, even though he is awake. He is again sitting at the banquet, along with the spirits, and is happy; but when the song is finished, his vision disappears. He tries to grasp it again, at night-time, when he is resting. Little by little, he masters his vision: he becomes skilled in finding it again, at will. In this new relationship, the meaning of the scene becomes clear to him: during the banquet, the spirits are inviting him to become a magic-man and to choose his helper-spirit. Finally, one morning, the Yamana gets up, gathers his possessions together, leaves his family and goes to see a famous magic-man whose image appeared to him in the previous night's vision. He remains with him and receives instruction: he will soon be a magic-man himself.[21]

21. Gusinde: *Die Feuerland-Indianer* II, pp. 1936 ff.

Here is another similar case. A Yamana crosses the forest, unaware of himself. Suddenly, a large group of spirits appear. They have a human form, but are smaller than men. He falls asleep and his vision becomes clearer. The dwarf-spirits now sit around a fire, talking to each other and warming themselves. They speak in a friendly manner of the dreamer's soul, and one of them appears particularly benevolent. They all invite him to sit with them near the fire; he complies, and feels at ease in their company. After some time, the Yamana awakes; the image persists and takes some minutes before it fades. The magic-man who had appeared particularly benevolent during the vision will become the helper-spirit.[22] Gusinde also reports another form of vocation among the Yamana: a man is walking slowly along the coast, lost in private dreams and thinking of nothing in particular. Suddenly, he is plunged into a complex vision; there is an enormous crowd of animals: herrings, whales, sword-fish, vultures, cormorants and petrels. All of them appear kindly towards him. The dreamer's soul enters into a rapport with the spirits and derives extreme happiness from this. The scene fades and the man regains consciousness and returns home. He then falls asleep and sees the scene again, in his dream. Once more, one of the spirits is particularly benevolent towards him, and will later become his helper-spirit, whilst the others will be at his disposition, as friends and protectors.[23]

Through these various stages of the magic drama, the initial situation (danger and fear that the presence shall disintegrate) is finally redeemed. The magical establishment of a vocation, the feeling of being 'called'; the identification of the spirits and the successful effort to master them; the presence of a whole series of traditional themes and images, of rites and practices that help in the interpretation of the call so that one may read a universe of culturally-meaningful

22. Gusinde: Op. cit., II, p. 1397
23. ibid. pp. 1397 ff. Among the Arunta, the Arumburinga spirits seem to have the same origins and functions. These spirits may be good or bad: the bad spirits may try to cause a man's life to be lost when he is walking in the bush: if this is the case, they hide their heads in a sort of large bag, made by scorpions and often seen hanging from Seringa and Acacia trees. The Arumburinga follow their victim and make him 'erita wideriga', that is, silly. If, however, the friendly Arumburinga find his tracks, they will bring him back to the camp. (Spencer and Gillen: *The Arunta* II, pp. 422 ff.).

forms into the chaos—all of these play a part in preventing the disintegration and have an actual saving effect. The being comes out of the conflict as 'one within several' or as 'several within one', but no longer susceptible to the one being completely lost in the several; and the several are now obedient to the one.

It may seem paradoxical that the 'threat' can be seen sometimes to endanger the presence, but also at others to have some superior and sought-after purpose. It may appear that things such as loneliness, darkness, fasting, difficult tests, frenzied dancing, monotonous chanting, extreme concentration, drum-beating, dreams and drugs, are techniques used to provoke a state of trance, in that they encourage a deliberate breaking-off from reality. It is up to us to show that the existence of such techniques is not a contradiction but a confirmation of the theme of the 'being-here' that is first threatened and then redeemed. First of all, we must examine more closely the significance of those practices that aim to establish a 'contact with the spirits'. Martin Gusinde, in his very extensive work on the Fuegians, describes the medicine-man's practices in detail, particularly those that lead to a state of trance and the consequent appearance of the second personality, or spirit. The author reports: 'The magic-man makes his helper-spirit appear by singing. It is the natural effect of this interminable and monotonous chanting, accompanied by the complete concentration of all his psychic forces. It produces a state of torpor that is much the same as a loss of consciousness. Then a series of most varied images is unleashed in his over-excited imagination; through intense concentration, he is able to make them appear over and over again. He creates a sort of autosuggestive situation for himself, a sort of autohypnosis through which he acquires his professional skills'. The 'second personality' is established quickly: veterans may enter into the control of this 'mediating personality' within thirty or forty minutes, whereas novices must concentrate for a longer period. If the attempt fails, the magic-man interrupts his chanting for a period of rest, then he begins again. If he has a second spirit, or more than one second personality at his disposal, he calls on this if the first still refuses to come.[24] Gusinde comments that 'The monotonous uniformity of the chanting was always painfully boring to me after the first ten minutes. Even someone who is just listening becomes so nervously excited that he feels he is about to go insane. The song they chant has the minimum modulations and is based on one basic series of tones, and because it was always "mezza-voce", there were hardly any variations in intensity. The basic theme remains the same, the only difference is that the voice is sometimes sharper, sometimes more mellow. The rhythm is rather jolting, and the chant begins suddenly with each new inspiration. There are no precise words, but sounds like "lolololo . . . hoiyoiyioi. . . ." The chant of each man differs only in minor detail and they all induce a trance-like state. This is when his actual activity as a magic-man begins; that is, when it is no longer he who is chanting, but his second personality; the latter takes up the chant and continues it, whilst the magic-man's only participation is to lend it his voice.'[25]

The Selk'nam magic-man's technique seems to be deliberately designed to weaken the integrity of the presence, which is why the monotonous chanting provoked the characteristic distress experienced by Gusinde. The slow, monotonous drum-beat used by the Tungus Shamans has a similar effect; so does the fixing of concentration upon a particular point, polarizing consciousness and preventing it going beyond this point. Concentration may not require the assistance of an outside object; it may be an entirely interior concentration, achieved by the methodical rejection of all thought-content that comes into the mind. In this instance the beyond is destroyed by depriving the consciousness of all outside objects.

In general, the weakening and reducing of the 'being-in-the-world-of-the-living' is closely connected to the diminishing of the world itself, in which the being is necessarily situated. Consequently, there are special magical techniques aimed at reducing this world, that is, aimed at reducing the matter that the world presents to the consciousness. The use of shadows and darkness is designed to help make this world

24. Gusinde: Op. cit., p. 754
25. ibid. p. 774

disappear by reducing the objects that may be seen. Shirokogoroff mentions that the Shaman's operations are usually carried out in darkness or dim light. The Tungus believe that the spirits go to the Shaman's house during the latter part of the day and that they cannot be contacted during day-light. This is true, not only of the Shamans, but of others as well.[26] The Manchous also operate at night and they, like the Tungus, consider that the spirits come more easily at night.[27]

K. Rasmussen once invited an Iglulik shaman named Unaleq to give a demonstration of his skill. He consented to hold a seance to find out information about the explorer's intended voyage in order to assure him of a favorable outcome. Rasmussen continues:

'In the evening, after dark, he came in, followed by his whole family, ready to fulfil his promise. The spirits, however, were not called upon until after he, assisted by his wife and children, had devoured a mass of walrus meat sufficient, in his judgment, to act as ballast in his inner man. Not until then did he declare himself ready to begin. There were several Eskimo visitors present, and all were eager to see what the evening would bring forth. We had hoped that Unaleq could have his trance in the mess room, where all could be present and witness his transformation to Tulorialik, but the old man declared very firmly that the apartment in question, being used by all, was too unclean for his spirits to visit. The invocation must take place in my little study, for he took it for granted that I, when I shut myself up there alone, would be occupied with lofty thoughts, like himself. He then required all the lamps to be put out, and crawled in under my writing table. His wife carefully hung skins all round the table, so that her husband was now hidden from all profane glances'.[28]

These techniques aimed at weakening or diminishing the unity of the presence may take a quite different direction: they may take the form of an artificial provocation of a psychic trauma, similar to an unexpected and unsolicited incident (such as the appearance of the meteor to Uvavnuk).

26. Shirokogoroff: op. cit., p. 325
27. ibid. p. 363 and note
28. Rasmussen: *Intellectual Culture of the Iglulik Eskimos*, 'Report of the 5th Thule Expedition 1921-24' VII, no. 1, Copenhagen 1929, p. 35

The orgiastic element of certain techniques (music, dancing) and the fasts and various tests of endurance are all part of this frame-work. The technique of sound or visual monotony tends to make the 'being-here' languid and weak; in a purely interiorized concentration (aided by darkness) there tends to be a rejection of all thought-matter. In an artificially-provoked emotional experience, magical technique tends to intensify and isolate a particular content so that it is absolute and autonomous, distinct and apart from any relationship through which it could turn into the content of a presence. All these techniques may alternate or combine in different ways[29] and are carried out with consummate psychological skill. It is a skill that has taken shape through several generations, made up of the formulation of individual inventions, ones within a traditional frame-work that have matured through numerous existential dramas.

A word must be said about the techniques that are based on dream-consciousness or the use of drugs and toxic substances. The exploitation of the uncertain sleeping-state and of dream consciousness to bring about a state of trance or direct communication with the 'spirits' has a psychological motivation that is quite clear when one remembers that the barrier between waking consciousness and dream consciousness is much less distinct in the magic-orientated person than in the rationalized individual of our own culture. It must also be remembered that the magic consciousness, under certain conditions, considers that dream-content is as valid, and sometimes more valid than events that have been actually experienced by the waking consciousness. Lastly, in the magical person, the dream consciousness may be guided and directed by the waking consciousness (through intentionally-provoked dreams and reveries).[30]

To return to the paradox noted earlier: we observed that

29. This weakening process of the 'being-here' through the repetition of one content may be preceded or followed by the emotional intensification of either this content or of one achieved through the use of music, chanting, solitude, fasting, dance, etc.
30. On the subject of dreams in the magic world, apart from the few mentions in Levy-Bruhl's work, see Rivers: *Dreams and Primitive Culture*, London 1935. For the use of toxics, see G. Wagner: *Entwicklung und Verbreitung des Peyote Kultes*, 'Baessler Archiv' XV, 1932, pp. 59-144; and V. A. Reko: *Magische Gifte. Rauchund Betaubungsmittel der neuen Welt*, Stuttgart 1938 (2nd edition).

the techniques which are apparently aimed at deliberately weakening and diminishing the presence are also in some way part of the process of its redemption and ratification. It is accomplished in the following way: by breaking down the various elements of the 'beyond' which normally sustain the presence, the magical person, often suffering considerable anguish, ventures into a void in which he exposes himself to that which threatens its dissolution. It is at this point in the magical drama that instead of finding a void he discovers himself in rapport with his helper-spirits. This is his victory and his redemption. The magical techniques that have been used to weaken the unified presence do not aim to suppress it completely; it must remain sufficiently intact to hold the trance in check so that it does not turn into an uncontrolled possession and so that the spirits' activity may be adapted to the actualities that arise during the seance. Although the 'being here' has itself recognized 'another consciousness' during the trance, and although this 'other consciousness' is accepted as a 'host', it is nevertheless not an absolute in itself, but a new, active member of the historical magic world, an element that has penetrated into the network of rapports and rites that form cultural tradition. The hard-earned equilibrium remains unstable; there is always the risk that it will return to disorder and chaos. But the tension, anguish, and the deliberate struggle to combat the threat, help the 'being here' to redeem itself and attain a psyche that creates its own possibilities and limitations. Czaplicka reports that, despite attacks from every side, the Shaman manages to maintain considerable self-control. He must know exactly when and how to give way to the attacks and crises of inspiration that sometimes approach madness. He is able to function only so long as he does not cross the thin line that separates him from madness. Cases have been known of Shamans who lose control of their spirits and become dangerous, sometimes for long periods. The Shaman's vocation comes to him in the exterior form of a psychic disequilibrium which is cured by the acceptance of his vocation.[31]

Sierozewski tells of a Yakut woman who fell seriously ill when she was twenty and began to see and hear things that

31. Czaplicka: *Aboriginal Siberia*, pp. 169 ff., 172

others did not. For nine years she suffered great conflict and said nothing about it, being afraid that people would not believe her and would make fun of her. When she was sick to the point of death, she began to practise as a Shaman, which resulted in her recovery. If she did not practise her skills for a period she risked the breakdown of her health.[32] Most documents dealing with shamanic magic agree that there is considerable stress and danger in the period between the first 'calling' and the eventual complete mastery of the spirits.[33] Shirokogoroff writes that, during the trance there is a varying degree of success in the attempts to induce the dual personality and eliminate conscious elements; there are, in any case, definite boundaries placed on these attempts; the Shaman must not induce an attack of uncontrolled hysteria, while maintaining the ecstatic state. Neither uncontrolled hysteria nor a complete suppression of ecstasy would allow the second personality to function as it should, and would prevent the subsequent independence of intuitive thought.[34] One example of the dangerous period between the first 'calling' and the mastery of the spirits is the example of Aua's vocation. It is likely that Aua, in the same way as the Yakut woman, was persuaded to become a Shaman through a serious psychic instability or through the distressing diminution of the united presence. Aua interprets his sickness as an invitation to become a Shaman, a vocation,

---

32. Czaplicka: Op. cit., p. 172
33. ibid. pp. 178, 179, 182 ff.
34. Shirokogoroff: *The Psychomental Complex of the Tungus*, p. 363. The need to remain in a trance and not to make the spirit disappear once it has been invoked, may help to explain the Selk'nam magic-man's particular technique. This consists of speaking detached and usually nonsensical phrases during the second personality's activity. Here is one document that refers to this technique: 'During the chanting, which is continued automatically by the spirit (when it is present) the magic-man speaks some brief phrases and mentions thoughts as they pass through his head. They are usually concerned with mythological matters, his own life, or just facts of general interest. These phrases are only allusive and do not communicate any ordered learning. They follow one another in a disjointed fashion' (Gusinde: Die Feuerland-Indianer I, p. 774). Here is the list of phrases that Gusinde heard from the magic-man Tenenesk when he, or rather, his spirit was chanting: 'Kausel was a powerful magic-man and a good man: he has been dead a long time. My father had the reputation of being the best hunter of all my ancestors: he never returned without a catch. When I was small, oh, how many Selk'nam there were then! Today there are only a few. All my sisters and brothers are dead, and I am old. My helper-spirit is very powerful, he is bringing me news from far away. Now he is worn-out and tired . . .'

and this is the beginning of his salvation. His attempts to be initiated through other Shamans are unsuccessful. Then he looks for solitude, for a condition that will help to intensify and unleash his instability so that he may read within it and finally master it. In his solitude, the danger to his 'being here' increases; joy and sorrow alternate inexplicably. The joy bursts into uncontrolled singing, almost as if a host—an anguished psychic alien—was singing within him. Finally there is the redemption, the conquest that leads to a new psychic equilibrium, the identification of the host and the formation of an alliance with it. It was in such an 'access of mysterious and irrepressible joy' that Aua became a Shaman. All these mysterious, unqualifiable, unrelated and chaotic elements became Aua's second self—a defined form with a justified existence, a spirit that would come when called with paragnostic power. Instead of the disintegration of the united presence, a double existence has formed, shared between Aua and his alter ego. Although it is a double existence, it is under the control of one united presence that has risen victorious from this extraordinary psychic adventure. Then a second spirit, the shark, appears and prevents another lapse into instability. So, the Shaman Aua comes back into the world and into actuality. From now on he will make this existence participate in the world and in history by his recognition and mastery of the danger that was threatening it.[35]

The regulating function of the 'being-here' is seen when the so-called normal consciousness seems to have disappeared completely, as in the case of the Shaman's psychic voyage to heaven or hell. The psychic voyage of reconciliation that is undertaken by the Iglulik Shaman for the purpose of visiting the Mother of marine animals, Takanakapsaluk, is a manifestation of this function, not only because the vision is intentionally provoked, but because its actually-experienced content (during the trance) is adapted to the ends of the seance and formulated through traditional mythical themes.[36]

The subject should now be considered from another quite

---

35. Rasmussen's documents should now be re-examined in the light of this new interpretation.
36. This voyage is examined later.

different angle. The magic-man's risk and redemption is not a strictly personal drama. It is the community as a whole, or one of several of its members, who, through the figurehead of the magic-man and through the drama in which he plays, become aware of the adventure of the loss and recovery of the 'being-here'. This relationship is particularly evident in shamanic magic. Whilst the ordinary members of the community may lose their united presence, so that their own 'being-here' becomes a fragile, hesitant psychic universe that threatens to slip into chaos—the Shaman takes on the dimensions of a hero who has ventured to the very threshold of chaos and has concluded a pact with it. Precisely because the Shaman has become absolute master of his own instability, he is also able to pass beyond the limits of his own 'being-here' and become the clairvoyant means, and the regulator, of other people's psychic instability. His own redemption makes a similar redemption possible for all the members of the community; without a Shaman, the community is in danger. Shirokogoroff says that the Shaman is able to master the spirits and free the members of the community from their influence. If the Shaman defaults, the spirits become free. As no one is controlling them any longer, they begin to enter the various members of the community, producing evil effects. A hunter, for example, may not be able to kill animals. If the others are made aware of this, they may suffer from the same ill effects. An idea establishes itself in their minds that the spirits, in preventing the hunt, wish to call attention to themselves. Some of the young people will lose their normal sleep; they will sit about talking, only half-awake, and will not have their necessary rest: they become absorbed in the spirits that are persecuting them and behave in a distracted, absent-minded way, becoming gradually incapable of doing socially-useful work. Some members of the tribe will flee into the forest whereas others, inclined towards day-dreaming, may turn dangerous in moments of absent-mindedness. Others will have 'crises' while doing daily jobs that require care and skill. The incidents mount up and some of the people will die. The community is almost paralyzed, its whole existence is in danger. The chaos may be overcome—and is overcome—when a man or woman successfully uses shamanic skills to regain control of the spirits.[37]

This community participation in the Shaman's drama is particularly evident in a large public seance. Several Shamans told Shirokogoroff that they could not function without an audience. One of them said that a number of participants helped him to reach the nether regions of the spirit-world. The public is also under the continuous influence of the Shaman. He emits an uninterrupted current of influences that are received in an intensified form by the public and then deflected to the Shaman as stimuli to his state of excitation. The shamans do not approve of non-participating spectators because they feel that their presence may weaken the trance. However, they have no objection to the presence of non-tribal members or even people from different ethnic groups, provided they do not disturb the harmony. . . . A hostile or sceptical attitude may spoil the seance.[38]

The magician endows magic with the character of a great collective and redemptive drama (but one in which salvation has a radically different meaning from our religious sense). So long as the instability of the presence remains uncompensated, and the 'being here' dissolves into an echoing of the surrounding world (as in the case of 'latah', with the imitation of the rustling leaves), then magic has not yet made its appearance. It appears only when the instability

37. Shirokogoroff: *The Psychomental Complex of the Tungus*, p. 246. The author asserts elsewhere that the shaman is 'the safety-valve', that shamanism is a working-method of ethnic units and that the shaman is a vital part (pp. 267, 273)
38. Shirokogoroff: Op. cit., p. 325. In the account of the seance held on the 5th May, 1928, at the Schrenck-Notzing laboratory in Munich, with the medium Rudi Schneider, G. H. Heier made the following observations: 'During this seance I once more observed the considerable influence of the 'togetherness' of the group and the placing of the participants. At the beginning, Hans Driesch (the famous Leipzig biologist and philosopher, who attended the seance) did not say a word but was intently observant and in an unrelaxed and critical frame-of-mind. Schneider, or rather, his second personality, Olga, tried to correct this attitude several times, asking Driesch to take up a conversation with Dr. Probst. Driesch gradually adapted himself to the instructions, but without forgetting the controls. When he had attained the state of psychic passivity that is necessary before phenomena may be produced, there was no longer any obstruction to their taking place.' (Schrenck-Notzing: *Die Phanomene des Mediums Rudi Schneider*, p. 120). This confirms our interpretation of the Selk'nam sorcerer's practise of saying certain phrases while he is chanting. He does this to distract himself and so maintain the presence of the spirit. Schneider encourages Driesch to do the same thing by conversing with his neighbor.

and fragility become a problem, when the subject is aware of the danger that threatens and feels the necessity for redemption—redemption within a well-defined cultural order which acts as a system of guarantees for the threatened 'being-here'. Culture means an inspired initiative that has been consolidated by a tradition, while tradition itself conditions and sustains this initiative. In the center of the cultural world of magic there is the magician, the living synthesis of initiative and tradition; it is he who opens himself to the magical drama and overcomes the danger in a victory that is applicable to others, besides himself. The anguish and distress that, for others, may mean the threat of an insurmountable danger, acts as a stimulus for the magician. The 'not being here' that causes others to lose their presence is recreated by him into an order of identified and mastered spirits. For the others, to 'lose oneself' may be a permanent state, whereas, for the magician, it is transformed into just one stage of the process towards salvation. He recognizes that to prevent this disintegration one must go deliberately to the limit of one's own presence through a clearly-defined practice; one must go to the very essence of the outer limits and completely master it; the spirits must be identified and evoked and one must develop the power to call upon them at will and profit professionally from their activity. These are the steps taken by the sorcerer; he transforms the 'being-here's' critical moments into a courageous and dramatic decision—one that shall establish it in the world. If the 'being-here' is considered as an accepted fact, it runs the risk of being dissolved: it is not yet a given fact. The magician, through the establishment of his vocation and successful initiation, *undoes* this presumed granted fact and *reforms* it through a second birth; he goes to the limits of his presence in order to reform himself into a new and clearly-defined entity. The techniques he uses to increase the instability of the presence, the trance itself and other related states, are the expression of this 'being-here' that disintegrates so that it may be reformed, the being that goes to the very end of its confines in order to discover itself as a sustained and guaranteed presence. The mastery that the magician has acquired allows him to penetrate not only his own instability, but also that in other people. The magician knows how to *go beyond himself,* not in the ideal sense, but in the actual, real sense. The man whose being-here is a problem and who has the power to establish his own presence, is not just an ordinary presence, but a 'being-here' that can penetrate others, understand their problem (for example, identify other people's spirits) and influence their course (for example, by freeing the victim from the 'spirits'). This means that the whole community, through the sorcerer's redemption, may also be redeemed and attain salvation. In this sense, the sorcerer becomes a kind of *magical Christ,* the mediator for the whole community, through whom the 'being-here' may be redeemed from the danger of not being here. It is a cultural redemption in the sense that the individual experiences connected to the magic existential drama do not remain isolated and without inter-relation, but are moulded into a tradition and, as such, form the ideological and institutional expressions which will be the starting-point of new individual experiences; through these, the dangers, audacities, failures, and victories which characterize the magic world shall arrange themselves and unfold in their own unique way.[39]

The many gaps in ethnological documentation make it very difficult, and sometimes impossible, to demonstrate the link between the magic world and certain critical moments of

---

39. The institution of the helper-spirit consists basically of dividing the threatening instability between two or more simultaneous psychological existences of which one, the historical one, controls the others. (On the subject of simultaneous psychological existences, see Janet: *L'Automatisme psychologique,* pp. 314 ff.). But the magical redemption of the being-here is probably also accomplished among successive psychological existences (cf. op. cit., pp. 67 ff.). Heinz Werner writes: 'In primitive societies, there is usually a regulating way of life, to which the individual must gradually adapt himself: birth, puberty, marriage, entry into the warrior-society or into the secret magic society. These life patterns do not mean a simple exterior transformation of the individual, they also express changes that occur in personal magical forces. For example, when a young Australian aboriginal reaches the age of puberty, the initiation ceremonies transform him into a member of society: he changes his magical forces to some extent because he passes from a phase where he was assimilated with the women, to a phase the essence of which is virility and manhood . . . The transformation of the child into a young man, and the young man into an adult is, in one way, a magical metamorphosis which shows the instability of the primitive subject: They pass from one age to another and are recreated each time, which means that the magical individual has not yet reached unification. And yet, within this very magical instability, one finds a tendency towards unity and stability, because, with each age of life, the continuity and constancy of the ego are reinforced: this time-regulated stabilization makes them lucid and sentient.' (Heinz Werner: *Einführung in die Entwicklungspsychologie,* pp. 383 ff.).

the 'being-here'; nor does it clarify the theme of salvation that has been discussed. Ethnologists have been in the habit of starting their documentation with the presupposition that magic is nothing more than a collection of superstitions that the primitive or naive mind either creates when faced with something it does not understand, or uses to stimulate emotions or the imagination. This results in the documentary evidence being only partially valid. We have some examples in the treatment of magic among the Aruntas. The document makes quite clear allusions to the link between the demons or bad spirits and certain critical moments of the 'being-here'. Spencer and Gillen tell us that the 'erintja' or 'eruncha' appear only when the victim is *alone in the dark*.[40] Strehlow reports that the 'kokolura' attack men who wander *alone near the camps at night*. They drag the victim's soul down into their vast underground abode, where it is destroyed. The 'tjimbarkna' are female demons that are probably linked to critical moments of the 'being-here' at night-time. They imprison the victim's soul in a net, then disappear. The victim becomes sick and loses weight rapidly. The following night the tjimbarkna return and pull lightly at the net and the sick man is able to get up and walk a little. On the third night they give it a more violent pull and the victim dies. Other Arunta demons seem to be connected to critical experiences in winds and tempests—'Rubaruba' is the cyclone demon and is depicted with a large head hanging down, its long hair lifting up the dust and its thin legs trailing behind. The tempest demon has a thin body, long teeth, bony fingers with long nails, and long toes.[41]

These demons warn of extreme danger to the 'being-here' at critical moments, such as those caused by solitude, darkness and tempest. But to be warned is not to redeem; the spirits may free themselves completely if some member of the community does not contact them and succeed in mastering them. 'The sorcerers use their strength and their art to influence the evil spirit ("erintja kunna") that "makes" the sorcerer. The evil spirit *takes away the reason and the hearing*

40. Spencer and Gillen: *The Arunta*, London 1927 I, pp. 110 ff.
41. Strehlow: *Die Aranda- und Loritja-Stamme in Zentral-Australien* I, 1, p. 11.

of a man who is on walk-about so that he wanders about the whole night like a madman ("ruburubulema"), unable to rest, even for a minute. During this wandering, the bad spirit throws "ngankara" stones at the victim, and these penetrate his body, particularly his thigh, thorax, tongue, head and fingertips. These magic stones are about the size of peas and are black, red, yellow or white. Then the evil spirit leads the man to the entrance of his underground abode, and here, he *throws him to the ground several times,* until the victim is unconscious or "eregna". Using a thrower, the spirit then pierces the victim's head with a kangaroo's splint-bone and throws more smaller ngankara stones into the humerus and the hips. At dawn, two more spirits come and take the victim's hand and lead him to the camping area where they burst into raucous laughter that is heard by the other members of the tribe. Then the two oldest witch-doctors go to meet their new colleague; they embrace him and *expel the two bad spirits that are still in him,* which then return to their abode. The two witch-doctors take him back to the camp where he *no longer recognizes anybody,* not even his closest relatives. They place some of the ngankara stones, taken from his body, into his ear, so that he may regain his sense of hearing. The novice still feels very sick and is so tired that he sleeps the whole day; he visibly loses weight and becomes very thin. Then the old witch-doctors prepare a shelter for him, and give him food and drink. They then carry him to the hut and paint some black stripes on his body and a black and red circle on his forehead. Then some food-taboos are prescribed, followed by two practices which will allow the novice to extract the cause of sickness from his patients' bodies: a pointed magic stick is used to perforate the index of the right hand and also the tongue. There is a final ceremony, and the new witch-doctor is ready.'[42]

Whatever deficiencies this document may have from a psychological point of view, it nevertheless seems to confirm the theme of risk and redemption of the presence. The witch-doctor's vocation begins with a crisis of incertitude and instability, with an uncontrolled possession and an invasion

42. Strehlow: op. cit., IV, 2, pp. 38 ff.

of psychic realities that submerge the presence. The fact that this happens when the man is wandering away from the camping area is related to the critical moments of the 'being-here', such as the loneliness and fatigue that have been seen in other cases. The crisis is not just a spontaneous, disconnected happening; *it follows a scheme* and, with an effort, attains a cultural and traditional significance. This means that the presence reappears, even if only in an incomplete and vague manner, and recognizes the evil spirit; it then makes itself receptive to the drama of the new birth and the second existence. The disintegrating 'being-here' tends to form itself into a new equilibrium: even an organic change is felt and takes place as the stones penetrate the body. Yet the crisis has by no means been overcome; the major danger of uncontrolled possession reappears at the threshold of the spirits' lair. The victim is thrown to the ground twice and becomes unconscious. The adventure continues: the 'being-here' slowly begins to look for itself: its presence is that of a dream and through this it experiences the new elements that lead to its transformation. At dawn, the novice gets up and goes to the camp, his presence subjugated and divided, interiorily, between himself and the spirits that have not yet been mastered. The victim is a sick man, a 'being-here' that is in peril, one that has not yet attained its equilibrium and has not yet been reborn. It needs help. The restoration of the presence proceeds in various stages: the two old witch-doctors exorcise the spirits, they use certain suggestion-practices, aimed at restoring the lost or diminished sensibility and they prepare an isolated place for the novice, one where he will be able to spend this delicate period of convalescence. Finally, when the novice has sufficiently recovered to be able to practise his profession, there is a conclusive ceremony and the new witch-doctor is ready: he is now a presence who is able to master the spirits, who has acquired certain powers and who, through his own redemption, has become the center of redemption for all the possible existential dramas that may be experienced by the community.

Spencer and Gillen make a distinction between three forms of initiation for the Arunta witch-doctor: the first is by means of the 'iruntarinia', spirits that wander about at night, and usually appear when a man or woman is alone; the second is through the 'eruncha' (Strehlow's 'erintja'), and the last is brought about by other witch-doctors.[43] In the first, the man who thinks that he may be able to become a witch-doctor leaves the camp and goes alone to the abode of the iruntarinia. He sleeps there, in a state of excitement and anxiety. He does not venture inside the cave, for fear of being permanently 'spirited' instead of just obtaining magical powers. At day-break, one of the iruntarinia appears at the cave-entrance and exerts its influence over the novice, after which he falls into a stupor. This does not last very long, and when he is 'cured' to a certain extent, the iruntarinia allow him to return to his people. The spirit returns to the cave and the man continues to act strangely for several days. One morning, the others discover that he has painted himself with charcoal-dust and grease—usually a wide stripe over the nose. His strange behavior has disappeared and the community has a new witch-doctor. However, his professional activity will not begin for another year because he must undergo another period of instruction with an older witch-doctor.[44] During the initiation through the iruntarinia, the process of risk and redemption unfolds in the following manner: there is a call, i.e. the distressing threat that the presence shall disappear; there is a period of incubation at the cave entrance until the spirit appears at dawn and the presence is engaged in a difficult and dangerous struggle, during which the novice undergoes a profound existential renewal which is also a second organic birth; the subjugated presence gradually frees itself of its possessor until it is again its own master through a second effective existence that has a rapport with the spirits. This is only a general outline, but the document does not give further information.

Thanks to its witch-doctors, the community has at its disposal the powerful and really efficacious means to combat the threat of instability to individuals and the group alike. Strehlow is surprised that the witch-doctor is able to fight

43. Spencer and Gillen: *The Arunta* II, pp. 391 ff.
44. ibid. pp. 392 ff.

and repel the spirits that gave him his powers.[45] But this is exactly what the magic drama consists of: to obtain a rapport with the evil elements (i.e. with his own distressing instability) and to acquire the power to vanquish and repel it (which means that he acquires the power to master his own instability, as well as that of other people). Here is how a witch-doctor actually operates in a particular case: 'When a bad wind rises up from the west, the witch-doctors gather in a circle and watch the wind approaching. If they see evil elements in it, ones that have the form of large cats and are called 'erintja ngaia', they begin throwing ngankara stones at them, afterward battering them to pieces with their sticks. Then they show the dead erintja only to their colleagues'.[46] In this case, the magic drama begins with the moaning of the wind. It is not a matter of simple pre-occupation or terror before a merely frightening object, but one that may not lend itself to being mastered and which therefore distresses the presence which, in its anguish, senses the wind's malignancy. The object does not have clearly-defined outlines, it can not be seized hold of as an object; it has infinite and unknown possibilities that suggest a 'beyond' that is fraught with mystery. Who shall be able to read into this 'beyond' of the wind, who shall identify the form of its reality and who shall re-establish the limit that renders the being present in the world? Only those who, through their own existential drama, have mastered the limit, the explorers of the beyond, the heroes of the presence. The witch-doctors gather together to read the forms that make up the wind's reality: these are the demon-cats or 'erintja ngaia'. Only the witch-doctors see them, only they can fight and kill them. Once the task has been accomplished, the wind's magical horizon has been duly exorcised and all have been liberated from the malignancy that was endangering their presence.

We now turn towards another great cultural theme of magic: *sortilege* or *evil spells*. The existential magic drama is once more enriched with new elements. Strehlow reports

45. Strehlow: *Die Aranda- und Loritja-Stamme* IV, 2, p. 40. 'Although the witch-doctor receives his powers from the evil elements, he strangely enough also claims the power to repel them.'
46. ibid. pp. 4 ff.

that: 'The witch-doctor's or sorcerer's art consists mainly of nullifying the malignant influences of hostile *men* or evil creatures. He is consulted in serious cases when sickness has been caused by either hostile men or evil spirits. . . . The natives consider that all sickness is due to outside influences, that is, hostile men who say they are able, with the help of magic, to bring about the death of another individual, or it may be due to evil spirits (erintja) who approach their victim in animal form or disguised as natural phenomena—for example, bad winds—and who do them harm. So the witch-doctor is called, not only to combat the instabilities that may arise in every-day life, but also the instability caused intentionally by other witch-doctors through magic spells'.

Once again, we are dealing with a cultural magic theme that seems to contradict the fundamental idea of risk and redemption: in witchcraft and in black magic practices generally, the endangering of the victim seems to have become the aim of the magical operation. We shall examine the problem closely and begin by showing the *reality* of the danger created by this type of magic.

Spencer and Gillen report that an Arunta will die from even a superficial wound if he believes that he has been struck by a weapon that has been 'sung' and supplied with an 'arungquilta'. He will gradually weaken, refusing food until he wastes away. The case of a man from Borrow Creek is mentioned. He was wounded in the groin, not very seriously, but insisted that the spear had been charmed and that he was about to die; he died several days later. Another man caught a light cold while travelling from Tennant Creek to Alice Springs. He was then told by the local witch-doctor that a group of people, about twenty miles to the east, had taken his heart away from him; the man lay down and began to pine away. At Charlotte Waters another man appeared with a light shoulder-wound. He was assured that there was no serious damage and received the appropriate medical treatment. He persisted in saying that the spear had been charmed and that he would die; his prediction was verified soon after. Many such examples could be quoted and, although it is not possible to say that death would not have intervened in any case, one needs only to be aware of the many serious injuries from which the Aborigines recover when they do not suspect any magical intervention. Death, in such cases, can only be explained by its relationship to the victim's belief that the arungquilta has entered his body and that he must therefore die.[47]

We must conclude from this that the person who believes he is the victim of witch-craft is exposed to real and actual danger. Let us now consider the spells from the point-of-view of the sorcerer. According to Spencer and Gillen:

> 'To punish a man who has stolen a wife and who belongs to a distant group, or to one which is too powerful to make it advisable to allow matters to come to an open fight, two men, perhaps the former husband and another man to whom the stolen woman is Anua—but they need not of necessity be either of them Anua—prepare a special implement of magic. A thin flake of flint or quartzite, in fact a miniature knife blade, is made, to the blunt end of which a lump of resin is attached, and to this a miniature spear is fixed. Then a very small spear-thrower is made, and into this a hole is bored so that the end of the spear fits tightly into it. To this implement the name of Arung-quilta is applied. It is painted all over with red ochre, and when this is dry, cross bars of white, yellow and black are added along the whole length.

> 'It is now sung over and left in the sun for some days at a secluded spot, the men going to it every day and singing to it a request to go and kill the man who stole the woman, the words of the request being "Go straight; go straight and kill him." Finally the two men come to the spot, and after singing for some time, one man kneels down, huddling himself together with his forehead touching

---

47. Spencer and Gillen: op. cit., II. pp. 403 ff. The actual danger to a victim of witch-craft is closely related to the result of a violation of taboo. In *Old New Zealand by a Pakeha Maori*, London 1884, pp. 96 ff. mention is made of a slave who one day ate the left-overs from a chieftain's meal and consequently suffered violent convulsions and stomach-cramps which continued until he died, early the next day. W. Brown, in *New Zealand and its Aborigines*, London, 1884, p. 76, reports that a Maori died after eating a fruit that was taboo. E. Tregear, in *The Maori of New Zealand* ('Journal of the Anthropological Institute' XIX, 1890, p. 100) writes: 'The taboo is a fearful weapon. I have seen a strong young man die on the same day that he has violated a taboo: the victims of a violated taboo die as if their strength pours out of them like water'. For other such examples, see Frazer: *Taboo and the Perils of the Soul*, pp. 314 ff. We will examine, at a later stage, the place of taboo within the framework of the magic existential drama.

the ground in front of his knees, while the other man takes up the magic implement, and, standing between the feet of the first man, throws the thing with all his force in the direction in which his enemy lives. When he has done this he kneels, huddled up in the same position as the other man, and with his head between the latter's feet. In this position they remain in perfect silence until they hear the Arungquilta, which is regarded in this instance as an evil spirit resident in the magic implement, saying, "Where is he?" Upon hearing the voice—and sometimes they have to remain in this most uncomfortable position for several hours—they get up and return to camp, where they abstain from talking and are always listening. By and by if the Arungquilta be successful—and it is generally supposed to be so—they hear a noise like a crash of thunder, and then they know that, in the form of a great spear, it has gone straight to the man, mutilating and thus killing him.'[48]

The document does not tell us whether such a procedure is successful, but we quote another where the magical operation is similar to the psychologist's 'post-hypnotic suggestion' and is completely successful:

'In Murray Island the writer obtained a description of a species of sorcery, called 'maid', which was formerly inflicted by any of the older men, in cases of hatred (maid urkerlam) or adultery (maid koskerlam). Finding his victim alone, the avenger takes up a chance stone, and, pronouncing over it some magic words (zogo mer) in a half-whisper, spits once or twice on it, and hurls it with great force to strike the back of his enemy. The latter falls to the ground, breathing heavily, and loses consciousness. The assailant and certain relatives who have accompanied him now close in on the prostrate body of the victim, and belabor it with their clubs. They then rub the body with a mixture of herbs and coco-nut oil, and give the victim coco-nut milk to drink. The assailant, while rubbing him, tells him to go up a coco-nut tree and to fall down from it, breaking his leg; or he orders him to be bitten by a centipede (esi), which will produce fatal blood-poisoning; or he may tell him to go to a certain point in the island, and then to return home and die. The avenging party now withdraw to a short distance, leaving the man's knife and some bananas and coco-nuts beside him. When he awakes

48. Spencer and Gillen: *The Arunta* II, pp. 414 ff.

and begins to wonder what has happened to him, one of the hiding party takes up a stone and hits a tree near the terrified man. This makes him start, forget his bruises, and rush home, where he lies thirsty and comatose for some days. Then (according to the order of his assailant) he will say to his wife: "I think I shall go up that coco-nut tree". He goes up, falls down, breaks his leg, and perhaps dies. As the informant said, "He no go up himself. Medicine [i.e. the magic ceremony] make him go up".'[49]

One must also take into account the cases of spells that have been cast from a distance, when the victim does not know, through normal channels, that he is the object of witch-craft. Shirokogoroff mentions that the Tungus make a kind of receptacle and call their victim's soul to it, then hit or partially-destroy the receptacle. They do this because they believe that as the exteriorized soul is inside the container, if it is destroyed, the soul shall also be destroyed. Shirokogoroff mentions the possibilities of telepathy and thought transmission, but recalls other similar cases and writes: '. . . perhaps in the case of similar actions there is more than a simply groundless hypothesis of the possibility of influencing people from a distance'.[50]

One solution to witch-craft is exorcism: it is possible to un-do the spells. The elimination of the danger to the victim is as real as the danger itself. Here is such an instance among the Arunta:

'An Arunta native was hit by a boomerang, which inflicted a wound by no means dangerous as such, but the difficulty was that the wounded man declared that the weapon, which had come down from the Ilpirra tribe which lives away to the north of the Arunta, had been "sung" by an Ilpirra man. An Arunta medicine man was of no use under such circumstances, but fortunately there was an Ilpirra man in the camp, and he was brought and "sang"—that is, went through the usual pantomime of making passes, sucking and muttering over the wound. As he belonged to the same locality as the man who had originally "sung" the boomerang, it was supposed that he

49.   C. S. Myers, in the *Encyclopaedia of Religion and Ethics*, IV, p. 725.
50.   Shirikogoroff: *The Psychomental Complex of the Tungus*, pp. 181 ff.

could counteract the influence of Ilpirra Arungquilta, which he successfully did'.[51]

The very strong prejudice which holds that witch-craft is no more than a *superstitious* idea arises from our habit of endowing the magical person with the same identity that our civilization guarantees us[52], and we can only understand the phenomenon if we can penetrate into its *historical function*, within the framework of the existential magic drama. What is this function? Through sortilege and exorcism, the risk and redemption of the 'being-here' receive a new humanization and intensification. This time, it is man who controls each stage of the magic drama, not only at the culminating point, but also the actual production of the risk or danger. The risk no longer arises from demoniacal attacks that are beyond human control, attacks that occur during solitary walks, at night, with the appearance of a corpse or a meteor, when there is a break in normality that causes astonishment or stupor . . .; in sortilege, the magical initiative goes back to the beginning of the drama and is, itself, the center of the evil spells. The fact that the sorcerer is able to *create* the spell, intentionally, and that another person can *un-do* it, makes the existential magic drama a kind of struggle—one that will be won by the stronger presence. Spell-binding and exorcism, taken as historic institutions, as a collection of forms, experiences, practices and counter-practices that have been consolidated by tradition, drag the entire community into the struggle—an enforced participation.

Another important institutional theme of magic is *imitation*. The English anthropological school considers that imitative magic arises from false association caused by resemblances, in the same way that contagious magic arises from false association through contiguity.[53] On the other hand, Alfred Vierkandt says that 'expressive movements' ('Ausdrucksbewegungen') are at the base of imitative magic. These are

51. Spencer and Gillen: *The Arunta* II, p. 405.
52. Here we are speaking of a characteristic of our own civilization, where instances of black-magic are certainly infrequent, although not entirely non-existent.
53. Frazer: *The Golden Bough*, I³, pp. 53, 221 ff., 233, 420.

impulses that are used to free oneself of certain feelings.[54] For example, if I throw a stone and it veers to the left against my will, I will bend towards the left; anger may cause me to punish and mutilate an image of my enemy, etc. In opposition to the anthropological school, it has generally been observed that imitative acts are not symbolic of the desired result; through the 'complexity' of magic thought, the resemblance between the imitative action and the actual action is dissolved into one, simple identity, so that, by imitating what one wishes, one obtains the desired object.[55] In the bison-dance, among the Dakota, we consider the bison, as represented by the dancer, and the actual presence of the bison, as two quite independent facts; but, in the dancer's mind there is a double presence, seen as one, and this influences his desire and his impulses so strongly that there is no longer any difference between the two.[56] Ernst Cassirer has examined the magic imitation of basic characters in the area of myth, which is a form of thought that has its own particular laws: 'Wherever we find a pure analogy, that is, a pure rapport, the myth is dealing with real and concrete reality, with the immediate presence'.[57] Imitative magic is not a symbolic representation of what will actually happen; the cosmic eventuation and the man's action 'are immediately united with each other' ('sich unmittelbar ineinanderschlingen').[58]

These interpretations considered separately are all quite inadequate. The theory of association takes the initial attitude that magic imitation has an *aim* (for example, to make rain fall); the theory considers that this characteristic is essential to the imitation and does not understand the actual communion that it establishes. Vierkandt's theory *reduces* imitation to its *first motive*, expressive movement; it does not understand any progress *beyond* this motive: from this point, the imita-

54. A. Vierkandt: *Der Ursprung der Religion und Zauberei*, in 'Globus' 92, 1907, p. 22.
55. Th. H. Preuss: *Die geistige Kultur der Naturvolker*. Leipzig (Teubner), 1923 (2nd Edit.), pp. 29 ff.
56. A. Vierkandt: *Die entwicklungspsychologische Theorie der Zauberei* in 'Archiv fur die gesamte Psychologie' 98, 1937, p. 478. Cf. Heinz Werner: *Einfuhrung in die Entwicklungspsychologie*, p. 336.
57. E. Cassirer: *Philosophie der symbolischen Formen* II (*Das mythische Denken*), Berlin 1925, p. 87.
58. Cassirer: op. cit., p. 234; cf. pp. 193 ff.

tion that has a certain aim takes on the appearance of a
posterior ideological 'superimposition'. Finally, if one reduces
imitative magic to a form of mythical thought, and not to
an original psychological motive, the imitation becomes a
sort of prisoner of what is considered to be the characteristic
form of this thought. Therefore, it becomes just a communion between the subject and the object, of an immediate
presence, etc., without having the justification of an action
that has a particular aim.

What must be understood is that the institution of magic
is *both* an immediate presence *and* an action with an aim,
and it is only as such that its positive function is revealed
to historical examination.

The case of 'latah' in which the subject repeated the
rustling of the leaves and the movement of branches in the
wind is a form of passive imitation where subject and object
are fused. It is, however, completely unrelated to any magical
imitation. This appears only when there is an awareness of
the danger that threatens the 'being-here', which then becomes
the pivot of the imitation and directs it towards a particular
end, that is of retrieving the presence from the danger of
possession, or of becoming a mirror of the world that
surrounds it.

We shall try to make this *historical* interpretation of
magic imitation a little clearer. The myths and legends of
the Arunta and the Loritja tell that the totemic ancestors,
in mythical times, established certain ceremonies with the
dual purpose of initiating the novices into the sacred rites
and making the totemic animal or plant stronger, or causing
it to multiply.[59] The Arunta obey the wishes of their ancestors by celebrating the sacred rites, but whereas, in mythical
times, there was but one ceremony (with a dual purpose),
there are now two ceremonies with quite distinctive aims.
One is the initiation during which the novices are taught how
to carry out the sacred rites that will multiply or develop
the totemic animal or plant; the other is the 'corroboree' of
the actual totemic species.[60] Imitative magic has a very
important role in the corroboree, which the Aborigines call

59. Strehlow: *Die Aranda—und Loritja-Stamme in Zentral-Australien* I, 1
    (1907) and I, 2 (1908).
60. ibid. I, 3 (1910), pp. 1 ff.

'mbatjalkatiuma' (to 'make grow', 'make fertile' or 'place in the best possible conditions').[61] The ceremony proceeds in the following stages: the participant (or participants) in the corroboree dresses himself as his totemic ancestors, wearing objects that represent the latters' bodies or body-parts; he then takes his position in a hollow that is used as a 'stage'. The elders give a signal and the young men run to the central figure, make a circle around him, crying out 'wa-wa-wa-jai-jaijaijai': they exhort him to carry out the necessary movements to the best of his ability. The cry means, literally, 'go on, get up, start moving'. It is believed that the cry has the effect of multiplying the totemic species. Meanwhile, the performer enters an 'ecstatic' state (Strehlow's term) and his body begins to tremble or imitate the movements of the appropriate totemic animal. In the Choritja tribe, at Alice Springs, the totem is a sort of edible grub (witchetty-grub) and the participants come out of a structure made of branches, in imitation of the insect that leaves its chrysalis.[62] In the 'tonanga' ceremony (tonanga = flying red ant), the two participants hold branches and imitate the flying movements of the ant;[63] in the 'ultamba' (= a kind of wingless bee) ceremony, the participants (an elder with several young men) imitate the animal in the following way: the elder crouches on all fours, his body vibrating like a bee's, while the young men lift up the right foot and then the left and buzz in imitation of the insect.[64] In the 'mulku-mura' (= a large fly) ceremony, the oldest participant and the young men imitate the buzzing of the fly.[65] The 'mbat-jalkatiuma' rites usually end by one of the elders leaving his group, which is usually some distance away from the ceremony, and going towards the performer. He embraces him, takes him by the shoulders and sometimes shakes him to bring him out of his 'ecstasy' and arrest his movements.

The young men help the old one by crying out 'wa-wa-wa-jaijaiiaijaijai-trr-trr-trr', which indicates that he should stop.

What do all these ceremonies mean? Are they aimed at

61. Strehlow: op. cit., 1, 3, loc. cit.
62. Spencer and Gillen: *The Arunta*, I, p. 152.
63. Strehlow, op. cit., I, 3, p. 84.
64. ibid. pp. 89 ff.
65. ibid. p. 94.

the magical increase of food, as Spencer and Gillen suggest? But the same authors note that certain totems, like those of the evening star, stones, shadows, flies and mosquitoes are not of the edible kind. Flies and mosquitoes, particularly, are such a curse in this region that it would be astonishing if the ceremonies were directed towards their increase. Strehlow also observes that, as the totemic species are usually taboo to the tribe, it must be concluded that their ceremonies are performed for the benefit of groups other than themselves. According to Strehlow, the ceremonies are performed because 'the ancestors want us to' (this is the aborigines' usual reply), and the increase of the totemic species is only of secondary consideration.[66]

Strehlow's interpretation, however, is far from enlightening. In his list of totems, 411 out of 442 are animals or vegetables and 20 others belong to nature (sun, moon, star, milky way, fire, water and rain, mythical elements, etc.). Among the edible animals some are of a demoniacal nature and others of a disagreeable taste or too small; among the plants, some are poisonous and others lack any nutritive value. One can appreciate the ceremonies for the increase of fire in winter, of rain in drought, or moon-light to help in the hunt for opossums, but it is difficult to understand the purpose of the fly and mosquito ceremonies, or other ceremonies involving either dangerous or useless animals.[67] One also wonders why the ancestors wished such rites to take place?

These ceremonies should therefore be considered within the framework of the existential magic drama. The main point is the danger that threatens the presence: an emotive reality appears and makes it difficult for the presence to maintain control; it is in danger of becoming the emotive object itself, through the passivity of the echopsychosis. The totems of the Pleiades, shadows, 'Musco vomitoria', the mosquito or other harmful and frightening animals originate in some critical moments of existence when the presence was almost subjugated or restrained. This subjection or restraint is noticeable in the performer of the rite; he acts

66. Strehlow: op. cit., p. 59.
67. ibid., I, 2, pp. 72 ff.

like some sort of machine that is being started and stopped by its driver.[68]

This passivity and imitation form part of a group of ceremonies tha⁺ are referred to by the general term 'mbatjal-katiuma', meaning 'to make grow', 'make fertile', etc., i.e. to invigorate and strengthen ('corroborare') the totemic species. With this in mind, the imitation is transformed into something active and creative: the fire is imitated in order to revive it, as is the rain, and the edible animal is imitated to forestall a shortage of food. The actual content of this activity is of secondary importance: the significance lies in the fact that these actions, through their imitation of some aspect of reality, adjust an initial malignancy and redeem a presence that was in danger of being completely subjugated.

One theme that is closely related to the other basic themes of the existential magic drama is that of *force or strength*. The *magic force*, in much the same way as the exteriorized soul, the mastery of spirits, the casting of spells and imitation, is an institution that expresses the existential drama of the 'being-here' that is exposed to the danger of *not* being here but is recovered from this risk. The fact that the disintegration of the 'being-here' is seen as a malignant force already indicates a certain resistance: the disintegration becomes a force according to how much the being-here resists. Here, it may be seen that the magic strength has acquired a second significance and proves its necessity: at the moment of redemption, when the presence is on the point of being saved, the magic strength resists the threat of disintegration; it makes an effort to overcome the evil, and functions as a protective measure. As in the case of the Turik who attached his soul to the hook-shaped stones, the force that undermines the soul is beaten down by the strength of the stones that keep the soul 'hooked'.

The magical elements that have to do with the body are related to this fundamental experience of a presence under tension which must be held in check, mastered and directed. The individual's strength may escape through the natural orifices of the body, and these may also allow malignant

68. Cf. the case of catalepsy; if a patient's arm is moved, the motion will continue until arrested. Cf. Janet: *L'automatisme psychologique*, p. 17.

influence to enter (through the nostrils, mouth, ears, etc.). This limits the risk to a certain degree and allows the presence to be redeemed through compensatory or liberating beliefs and practices. Let us take an example: defaecation is sometimes seen as a loss of personal strength that must be re-established and re-integrated.[69] Elsewhere, delivery from the existential magic torment may be obtained through other more mediatory forms that bring about the mastery, increase and regulated use of the force, so that the malignant and threatening element is transformed into a benign power that will be at man's disposal. The so-called 'ornaments' that are worn in the nose, ears, lips, etc. are actually methods used to 'control' the flow of strength in and out of the natural orifices, and so they compensate for the existential anguish or torment. The breath that is expelled through the nostrils is considered as 'strong', as a force that is being discharged: the forms of embrace, such as a kiss or the rubbing of noses, derive from the need to combine the respective forces that are emitted with the breath. This mastery of the breath's force, to consolidate, use and direct it, is a common trait of the magic world: breath may be used to kill, to protect oneself from evil, to regenerate and create. The use of breath in incantation and, generally, as a controlled and directed force, has led to the practice of extracting and deforming the teeth so that the breath may be exhaled and inhaled more easily.[70]

The magic quality of certain organic functions is related to the emotional experiences that they cause. The intense emotional experiences that derive from the genitals—the sexual function that leads to orgasm and the communion through coitus—are seen by the magic world in their relationship to its own fundamental problem, the threat of the presence. Modesty is more often the desire to protect the sexual organs from the evil eye; coitus is seen as a "strong" act, absolutely necessary to rid oneself of potentially dangerous energies; sexuality is seen as a magic force that must

69. Cf. Preuss: *Der Ursprung der Religion und Kunst in* 'Globus' 1904, pp. 356, 324 ff., and 'Globus' 1905, p. 416.
70. On the subject of the relationship between magic and the natural orifices see Preuss: op. cit., 'Globus' 1905, pp. 416 ff. Regarding breath, see ibid. pp. 375, 384 and cf. 'Globus' 1904, pp. 375 ff. On the extraction of teeth, see Preuss: op. cit., 'Globus' 1904, p. 362 and 'Globus' 1905, pp. 375, 394, 414 ff.

be mastered, consolidated and liberated through certain practices (such as circumcision and subincision); finally, coitus
is a magic fertility rite: all of these are mediate forms that
lead to delivery from, and redemption of, the risk of disintegration that threatens the presence; because of this the emotional side of sexuality is of particular importance.[71] Furthermore, the localization of the personal strength within a particular part of the body is part of the pedagogy surrounding
the presence, one which places the 'being-here' above any state
of dispersal and leads to a unified subordination and centralization.[72] The magical experience of a presence under tension,
that is in danger of discharging and must be restrained
(remember the Turik's hooked stones), is expressed in the
representation and experience of a 'beyond' that is outside
of the presence, a reflection, an echo, a shadow, a similarity,
a double, etc.: the man and the stone, the man and the
animal or the man and his shadow are as 'two in one' or
'one in two', and the presence that cannot hold its ground
when confronted by the world rids itself of the risk by
making a compromise.[73] But the historical content of the
magical force is by no means exhausted yet. The magic risk
of the chaotic irruption of the world within the ego, or of
the uncontrolled discharge of the ego into the world, also
implies a risk to the objectivity of the world: the crisis
involved in the limit that separates the presence from what
confronts it is, in fact, a crisis of two quite distinct spheres
that should result from it. The guaranteed presence and the
world of objects (and of clearly-defined events) condition
each other, with the result that the crisis of the presence is
also that of the objectivity of the world. Consequently, the
way in which the 'being-here's' resistance to disintegration
engenders (i) the representation and experience of the 'malignant influence' (to which the presence is exposed), and (ii)

71. On the relationship between magic and coitus, see Preuss: op. cit.,
    'Globus' 1904, pp. 324 ff., 356 and ibid. 1905, p. 416.
72. 'Whilst each part of the body contains in itself the essence of the
    person, we see, in the more elevated phrases of the development of
    thought, the formation of an articulation between parts that are
    magically important and those that are magically unimportant—there is
    a centralization and subordination, as if they are the kernel and husk
    of the person'. (Heinz Werner: Einfuhrung in die Entwicklungspsycho-
    logie, p. 380).
73. For such examples (atai, tamaniu, etc.) see Levy-Bruhl: L'âme primitive.
    passim.

the 'personal magical force' (which allows this influence to be overcome), is echoed by the resistance of the 'being-here' to the disintegration of the world which engenders (i) the representation and experience of a dangerous 'beyond' of things and events (a tension or force belonging to these things and events and of so many obscure possibilities that their limits and outlines become hazy) and (ii) the representation and experience of a pragmatic, ritual order which allows this 'beyond' to be explored, expressed and mastered so that the process of disintegration is arrested, the objectivity re-established, and so the order of the world within a defined framework is maintained. Nowadays people usually begin with the presupposition that magic, as in our own civilization, has a *given* world to which a *guaranteed* 'being-here' presents itself: with such a point-of-view, magic may appear to us as a false science or an abortive technique. In fact, magic is not basically concerned with 'knowing' the world, nor with changing it, but aspires to guarantee the world to which the being may make itself present. In magic, the world is not yet 'decided', and the presence is still engaged in the task of making a decision about itself and about the world. We may analyse this particular statement through the examination of a concrete case. Rasmussen, who was an actual witness, shows us the Eskimo (Coppermine) Shaman who tries to subjugate the force of the Arctic gale.

The Shaman was Horqarnaq, a young man, who took some time to enter into a trance. He explained to Rasmussen that he had several helper-spirits at his disposal, the spirit of his late father, the latter's helper-spirit, an imaginary human figure, made of snow, and a red stone that he had found one day when out hunting. He is dubious about his skills, and is encouraged gently by the village women. . . . He slowly enters into an almost frenzied trance and the audience increases, trying to stimulate his frenzy. . . . Finally he no longer recognizes the people around him and asks who they are. He keeps repeating that he cannot do it. Then one of the helper-spirits enters his body; he no longer has control over his actions; he jumps and dances around, and invokes his father's spirit, an evil spirit. His recently-widowed mother is also present, and she tries to calm her son, but the others encourage him to greater frenzy. He then names several other spirits

of dead people, whom he sees in the hut, among the living.
He describes them, even those he has never known. The
old women try to guess who it may be, becoming more
and more excited as they attempt to solve the mystery.
Then one old woman comes forward and calls out the
names of the people whom her sisters had not dared to
mention: a couple from Nagiugtoq who had died quite
recently. The Shaman cries out that it is they. They have
been turned into bad spirits and are the cause of the
tempest. The seance goes on for another hour, amid howls
and cries and the noise of the storm outside. . . . Then
a fearful thing happens. Horqarnaq leaps at old Kigiuna
and seizes hold of him, he shakes him brutally and pushes
him into the center of the hut. They struggle and grunt
and eventually he, also, is in a trance and follows the
shaman docilely until they fall to the floor where they
roll around, possessed. The old man seems to be dead and
is dragged over the floor by the Shaman, like a sack of
old rags, and finally allowed to fall heavily. . . . The
tempest has been killed symbolically. The shaman bites
the old man on the neck and shakes him as a dog would
a rat. . . . The people are silent while Horqarnaq continues his dance. . . . Then he slowly becomes calmer,
kneels down by the body and begins to massage life into
it. The old man revives and eventually gets to his feet.
But he has only just managed to do this, when the whole
scene is repeated, and he is again seized by the throat.
This happens three times: three times he is "killed", in
order to show that man is superior to the tempest. Finally,
it is the young Shaman who faints, and the old man rises
up and describes the images that are racing before his
eyes—naked men and women flying in the air, causing the
tempest to swirl behind them . . . they are afraid and are
fleeing. . . . Among them there is one whom the wind
has filled with holes; the wind blows through these, causing a whistling noise . . . he is the strongest of the people
in the winds, but will be mastered by the old man's helper-
spirit. . . . Then the younger Shaman recovers and they
both begin to chant and sing plaintively, addressing the
Mother of marine animals and begging her to send away
the evil spirits, to bite them to death. . . . So, the two
Shamans struggle until the tempest is finished, and the
people return, reassured, to their huts, prepared to sleep'.[74]

74. Rasmussen: *Intellectual Culture of the Copper Eskimos*, pp. 33 ff.

The initial situation to which this document refers is as follows: an upsetting incident, the Arctic gale lasts for three days; in the face of such an event, the presence becomes distraught and bewildered; the gale begins to take on a 'beyond', some evil force that threatens to quell the gale's limits. The presence is threatened and ready to give in, so, in order to restore it and, at the same time, prevent the gale's 'beyond' from making chaos in the world, the gale must be 'decided' or 'resolved' and its beyond must be explored and expressed. This leads to the eventual mastery of the gale by using the 'charge' of the spirits that are evoked. The Eskimo Shaman explores the gale's beyond in the same manner as the Arunta witch-doctor tries to read into the bad wind that comes from the west, and discovers the 'demoniacal cats' that are in it, or rather, that *are* the wind itself. Only the presence's hero, the Shaman, is able to 'make the hidden forces appear', because he alone knows how to place himself deliberately on the same plane as this 'beyond' and then act accordingly. All this implies dramatic tension, force, in two senses: (i) knowing how to attain rapport with the helper-spirits, through the trance, with the purpose of operating with them (Horqarnaq says that it is a difficult task to make the forces appear and does not believe himself capable of doing it) and (ii) being able to avoid the danger of uncontrolled possession (we are told how some force has possessed him and that he is no longer in control of what he does and says). The control is gradually re-established and the exploration of the beyond begins: the gale appears as a couple, man and wife, who have recently died. But there is no immediate identification; the magic torment is a reality that develops, disengaged from its physical tie, and roams about in search of figurations and incarnations. Within this dramatic fluidity, the magical torment is first of all within old Kigiuna, killed three times, and then it passes into Horqarnaq, who is killed in turn; it is finally concentrated in the ultimate, liberating vision of the victorious Kigiuna, that is, in the troop of spirits that appeared, led by their most powerful member, the whistling sieve-like body. The final liberating action is accomplished with this ultimate evocation of the beyond: Kigiuna's helper-spirit advanced against the unleashed spirits and stops them. The magical horizon of the gale has been explored, evoked and then cleansed of the tormenting malignancy that was disturbing it. Then the beating of the big birds' wings, the weeping of Narsuk that burst the lungs of the air and the sinister noise of the sieve-body all disappear from this horizon; when this has been reduced, there remains only the demarcated, precise event, confronted by a presence that has been re-established; in other words, the tempest returns to much the same form as it would have for us. In this new situation, arrived at through great effort, a different attitude, almost resembling prayer, becomes possible: the invocation to the Mother of marine animals, living at the bottom of the sea.

Therefore, corresponding to the magical risk of *losing the soul,* there exists the danger of *losing the world.* Together with the experience of the soul that leaves its abode and is attacked, compromised, violated, etc., we have the experience of objects that go beyond their tangible horizons, escape from their limits and fall into chaos. When a particular tangible horizon enters a critical stage, the danger lies in the possibility that every limit will disappear; everything may become anything, or a state of nothingness looms ahead. But the magic elements that warn of the danger, also intervene to arrest imminent danger and re-establish order. When considered in this light, magic becomes a restorative power that brings back threatened horizons, and returns the world to mankind.

The beyond of a particular tangible horizon may first appear as a simple invisible presence. The beyond of the bad wind from the west was present before the Arunta tribesmen read into it and saw the 'demoniacal cats'; there is a beyond of the arctic gale before the Eskimo shamans see the 'nude spirits'. But the beyond may also be manifested as a persistence of the object, even though its tangible reality has gone. This is particularly so in the cases of 'nunuai' among the Mota natives. It expresses a persistent or recurrent sense-impression. For example, a man who has been frightened during the day by a horrible cry of pain will continue to hear the noise in his ears: the cry has stopped and the sound is no longer there, but the nunuai persists.

Or a man goes out to catch flying-fish; he rows, alone, all day long, with the long line tied around his neck. At night, he settles down to rest, having first unknotted the line from his neck; but he feels the line pull at him as if the fish had taken the bait: this is the line's nunuai at work. For the natives, these are not imaginary happenings: the nunuai is a reality, albeit without tangible form. Pigs, ornaments, food, all have their nunuai. The word is related to 'niniai', which means a shadow or reflection. If we hear a cry of pain we may say 'I still hear it in my ears', but this is nothing more than an image that is completely unsupported by actual physical sensation. In the magic world, however, things may be prolonged beyond their actual limits, in the sense that the perceived reality may persist beyond the actual perception.[75] In other words, the sensed actuality has not yet been

75. Codrington: *The Melanesians*, p. 251. At this point it is appropriate to remember Jaensch's research in the area of so-called eidetic experiences. Jaensch shows that, at certain stages of psychic development, there is no differentiation between the sensation and the representation which gives rise to various forms of lived experience that retain traits of both. In visual eidetics, the subject is capable of visualizing in a material form, of projecting a certain image onto a screen after having received that sensation and after the stimulus has been removed. The eidetic image is as vivid as the sensation; the subject is able to describe it, down to the smallest detail, even those that had not been noticed in the original image; but it may also be influenced by the will and modified by the imagination. The colors of the eidetic image are mixed with experienced colors, exactly as if they were sensations. For example, the eidetic image of a blue square, projected onto a white screen, is transformed, according to the laws of color composition, into a gray square if one replaces the white screen with a yellow one while the image is still there. The eidetic phenomenon is normal in children under fourteen. But there is considerable evidence to show that it is also wide-spread among so-called primitive man and that, in this context, it is closely related to magical experiences and events. On the subject of eidetic phenomena, see E. R. Jaensch: *Der Aufbau der Wahrnehmungswelt und ihre Struktur im Jugendalter*, 1923; also his *Die Eidetik und die typologische Forschungsmethode*, 1927, and *Eidetische Anlage und kindliches Seelenleben*, 1934. cf. Heinz Werner: *Einfuhrung in die Entwicklungspsychologie*, pp. 112 ff. In the magic world, the representation is stamped with tangible reality and it may take an objective form at any moment by imposing itself upon the senses. Rasmussen one day asked the Eskimo Shaman, Anarqaq, to draw his helper-spirits. He applied himself to the task and, after a long period of concentration, his eyes closed, during which he tried to fix the image in his mind, he drew the figures on the paper with a sure hand and no hesitation whatever. Sometimes the image he drew had such an effect upon him that he shivered and had to give up the task. (Rasmussen: *Intellectual Culture of the Copper Eskimos*, p. 44.) This powerful interior image could convert, at any moment, into an actual sense perception: Anarqaq. at certain critical moments of his existence. saw the spirits in material form, particularly when he was preparing for bed or when he was out alone hunting for caribou (op. cit., p. 45). It is possible that topographical memory and the sense of orientation may be related to the magical proximity of the representation and the sensation: cf. Heinz Werner: op. cit., p. 116.

'fixed', but is still within the area of human decision. The object that cannot be mastered, at certain critical moments of the presence, and cannot remain as a given fact, is restored or redeemed through a culturally significant institution, such as the nunuai, reflection, shadow or echo of the thing. This cultural transformation recuperates and saves the object, giving it entry into a network of clearly-defined rapports.

But the restoration or redemption of the beyond may be achieved through other means. For example, a tangible horizon that is 'suffering' a crisis may redeem itself through the representation and experience of the *force* that emanates from it and that can be used by man. Or else the beyond may be interpreted as a dangerous tension that threatens to discharge and that may be held in check through the observance of certain taboos. In some cases, the taboo takes the form of a law that forbids certain 'strong' objects to be changed or modified.[76] Chaos is overcome through remodelling: a universe is born which, although it is not ours, is nevertheless a universe, governed by creative human action. The following procedure is used on Pentecost Island (New Hebrides) to encourage rain-fall: a 'mana' stone is chosen and its energy is increased through a spell, then a hand-full of leaves are placed in a hollow stone, and some Piper methisticum twigs are slowly crushed and pounded, the mana stone is added to it and magic formulae are chanted, so that the spirit Tagoro will intervene; the whole lot is then covered and allowed to ferment. It is believed that the fumes from the fermentation, full of mana, will produce both the clouds and the rain. According to Preuss, the Huichol Mexicans identify deer with a certain variety of cactus called 'peyotl'. They believe that during the day the stars are hunted and captured, so they are identical to the deer, which is the principal game of their area. All prosperous growth on earth depends upon the hunt for the stars (= deer). Therefore the deer is the principal sacrificial ani-

---

76. To change the form of objects, according to the Zuni, is to profane them; any change in their visible outline releases dangerous forces (Cushing: *Zuni Creation Myths* in the *Report of Ethnology of the Smithsonian Institute* XIII, pp. 361 ff.) The Loango people consider any modification in the landscape as a destruction of its magic balance (Pecuel-Losche: *Die Loango Expedition* III, 2, p. 209, quoted by Levy-Bruhl: *Fonctions mentales*, pp. 35 ff).

mal at all the fetes. The peyotl, because of its stimulatory
and hallucinatory effects, has become a kind of magic object.
But the peyotl grows far away from the Huichol mountains,
in the eastern plains, and each October the Indians organize
the picking of the plant in order to ensure a good harvest
in the following season. They arrive at dawn and the first
peyotl is seen as a deer and is shot with bow and arrow.[77]
So, a new order of magic appears against this background
of problematic objectivity. Here is an account of the psychic
voyage of the Iglulik Shaman to the abode of Takanakapsaluk,
Mother of marine animals:

> 'The journey may be undertaken at the instance of a
> single individual, who pays the shaman for his trouble,
> either because there is sickness in his household which
> appears incurable, or because he has been particularly
> unsuccessful in his hunting. But it may also be made on
> behalf of a whole village threatened by famine and death
> owing to the scarcity of game. As soon as such occasion
> arises, all the adult members of the community assemble
> in the house from which the shaman is to start, and when
> he has taken up his position—if it is winter, and in a
> snow hut, on the bare snow, if in summer, on the bare
> ground—then men and women present must loosen all
> tight fastenings in their clothes, the lacings of their foot-
> gear, the waistbands of their breeches, and then sit down
> and remain still with closed eyes, all lamps being put out,
> or allowed to burn only with so faint a flame that it is
> practically dark inside the house.
> The shaman sits for a while in silence, breathing deeply,
> and then, after some time has elapsed, he begins to call
> upon his helping spirits, repeating over and over again:
> "The way is made ready for me; the way opens before me!"
> Whereat all present must answer in chorus: "let it be so!"
> And when the helping spirits have arrived, the earth
> opens under the shaman, but often only to close up again;
> he has to struggle for a long time with hidden forces, ere
> he can cry at last:
> "Now the way is open".
> And then all present must answer: "Let the way be open
> before him; let there be way for him".
> And now one hears, at first under the sleeping place:
> "Halala—he—he—he, halala—he—he—he!" and afterwards

77. Preuss in 'Globus' 1905.

under the passage, below the ground, the same cry: "Halele
—he!" And the sound can be distinctly heard to recede
farther and farther until it is lost altogether. Then all
know that he is on his way to the ruler of the sea beasts.

Meanwhile, the members of the household pass the time
by singing spirit songs in chorus, and here it may happen
that the clothes which the shaman has discarded come alive
and fly about round the house, above the heads of the
singers, who are sitting with closed eyes. And one may
hear deep sighs and the breathing of persons long since
dead; these are the souls of the shaman's namesakes, who
have come to help. But as soon as one calls them by
name, the sighs cease, and all is silent in the house until
another dead person begins to sigh.

In the darkened house one hears only sighing and groan-
ing from the dead who lived many generations earlier.
This sighing and puffing sounds as if the spirits were down
under water, in the sea, as marine animals, and in between
all the noises one hears the blowing and splashing of
creatures coming up to breathe.

An ordinary shaman will, even though skilful, encounter
many dangers in his flight down to the bottom of the sea;
the most dreaded are three large rolling stones which he
meets as soon as he has reached the sea floor. There is
no way round; he has to pass between them, and take great
care not to be crushed by these stones, which churn about,
hardly leaving room for a human being to pass. Once he
has passed beyond them, he comes to a broad, trodden
path, the shamans' path; he follows a coastline resembling
that which he knows from on earth, and entering a bay,
finds himself on a great plain, and here lies the house of
Takanakapsaluk, built of stone, with a short passage way,
just like the houses of the tunit. Outside the house one
can hear the animals puffing and blowing, but he does not
see them; in the passage leading to the house lies Takanakapsaluk's dog stretched across the passage taking up all
the room; it lies there gnawing at a bone and snarling. It
is dangerous to all who fear it, and only the courageous
shaman can pass by it, stepping straight over it as it lies;
the dog then knows that the bold visitor is a great shaman,
and does him no harm.

These difficulties and dangers attend the journey of an
ordinary shaman. But for the very greatest, a way opens
right from the house whence they invoke their helping

spirits; a road down through the earth, if they are in a tent on shore, or down through the sea, if it is in a snow hut on the sea ice, and by this route the shaman is led down without encountering any obstacle. He almost glides as if falling through a tube so fitted to his body that he can check his progress by pressing against the sides, and need not actually fall down with a rush. This tube is kept open for him by all the souls of his namesakes, until he returns on his way back to earth.

Should a great shelter wall be built outside the house of Takanakapsaluk, it means that she is very angry and implacable in her feelings towards mankind, but the shaman must fling himself upon the wall, kick it down and level it to the ground. There are some who declare that her house has no roof, and is open at the top, so that she can better watch, from her place by the lamp, the doings of mankind. All the different kinds of game: seal, bearded seal, walrus and whale, are collected in a great pool on the right of her lamp, and there they lie puffing and blowing. When the shaman enters the house, he at once sees Takanakapsaluk, who, as a sign of anger, is sitting with her back to the lamp and with her back to all the animals in the pool. Her hair hangs down loose all over one side of her face, a tangled, untidy mass hiding her eyes, so that she cannot see. It is the misdeeds and offences committed by men which gather in dirt and impurity over her body. All the foul emanations from the sins of mankind nearly suffocate her. As the shaman moves towards her, Isarrataitsoq, her father, tries to grasp hold of him. He thinks it is a dead person come to expiate offences before passing on to the Land of the Dead, but the shaman must then at once cry out: "I am flesh and blood" and then he will not be hurt. And he must now grasp Takanakapsaluk by one shoulder and turn her face towards the lamp and towards the animals, and stroke her hair, the hair she has been unable to comb out herself, because she has no fingers; and he must smooth it and comb it, and as soon as she is calmer, he must say:

"Those up above can no longer help the seals up by grasping their foreflippers".

Then Takanakapsaluk answers in the spirit language: "The secret miscarriages of the women and breaches of taboo in eating boiled meat bar the way for the animals".

The shaman must now use all his efforts to appease her

anger, and at last, when she is in a kindlier mood, she takes the animals one by one and drops them on the floor, and then it is as if a whirlpool arose in the passage, the water pours out from the pool and the animals disappear in the sea. This means rich hunting and abundance for mankind.

It is then time for the shaman to return to his fellows up above who are waiting for him.'[78]

For us, this voyage takes place in an unreal world; but if we rid ourselves of the limitations of our historical concepts and take into consideration not only the Eskimo culture, but also our own cultural system (Einstellung), then the dogmatic character of this attitude becomes obvious.

In a civilization such as ours, where the decision of the self and of the world is no longer a characteristic problem of major importance, we are, ourselves, 'given facts', and the objects and events of the world are therefore considered by our empirical minds as given facts. Even transcendental research is conditioned by actual lived experience, in which the 'presence within the world' and the 'world that makes itself present' are both decided and guaranteed. In the magic world, however, everything revolves around this lived experience of which the duality between presence and world creates a major and characteristic problem. In the realms of magic, the presence is still searching for its identity as a unified factor; it is still trying to control itself and mark out its boundaries; nor is the world yet separated from the presence, it is not yet controlled and independent. In such a historic situation the presence within the world and the world that makes itself present are continually at odds as they try to define their respective boundaries. It is a struggle that involves certain hostilities, defeats and victories as well as truces and compromises, and the outcome is very important. Reality, when conceived as the independence of the given fact, as the installation of an observable world, as a decided and guaranteed 'otherness' is a historic configuration belonging to our civilization, and so is correlated to the decided and guaranteed presence that is characteristic of it. This reality, which we could also call 'naturalness', is expres-

78. Rasmussen: *Intellectual Culture of the Iglulik Eskimos,* pp. 124-127.

sed in the following manner: I see myself as a given fact within the world, and I see the world as it presents itself to me, without this double 'invention' giving rise, within me, to any cultural problem. But the magic world, which is in the throes of decision-making, contains forms of reality that, in our civilization, have no cultural value and are, in fact, polemically rejected and denied.[79] These magical forms of reality are: a simple beyond of the world, a 'present becoming' that is diffused and vague in its development, but full of dangerous possibilities and of definite force; there is a beyond that is redeemed through the institution of the echo, the prolongation, shadow or double of objects; there is a beyond that is redeemed through spiritualistic activities; and there is a beyond that has boundaries imposed upon it through a system of participation (the part that has characteristics of the whole, or 'wholes' that have an inter-participation). These may be related to a tangible form, through the intervention of a privileged being, for example, the shaman or magic-man. In the area of the being-in-the-world, there is a magic reality of the presence which may escape, be violated or stolen, etc.; there is also the magic reality of the beyond of the presence that is organized by the echo, prolongation, shadow or the double of the presence itself; there is the reality of the beyond of the presence that is redeemed through the helper-spirit, or localized in some part of the body, etc.

All of this evidences a reality that is occupied with making a decision, one that is trying to give itself a form. In some cases, magic reality takes a form that is very close to the

79. Obviously there are marginal situations in our own civilization where such forms may have subsisted or may have reappeared, even taking on, in some cases, cultural importance . . . it is enough to think of certain magical traditions within peasant populations, the activities of spiritualistic circles and even the magical elements that are related to certain psychopathical states, such as psychasthenia, schizophrenia, and paranoia. In all of these cases there are more or less authentic forms of aspects of magic reality and of the existential drama of the magic world. . . . Even the educated and normal man may sometimes be touched in his everyday life, however slightly, by these archaic realities. The fact that magical elements may be found to occur even in the educated man of the Western world indicates that the decided and guaranteed presence is an historical acquisition that may be revocable in certain circumstances. . . . Suffering or severe privation during a war or famine, etc. may cause the being-here to lose its resistance when confronted with great tension, and it may well open itself up once more to the existential drama of magic.

'objectivity of facts', as if it has been released, during its wanderings, into a world that is quite different from ours. Once more we are confronted with the problem of para-normal magic reality and real magic powers. When the imperiled beyond of the presence redeems itself, as in the establishment of the exterior soul, then the rapport resulting allows certain real bonds to appear, ones that we are tempted to call objective, in the historical sense of this term: if the 'nagual' dies, its master dies, and vice versa; the master may guide his 'nagual' from a distance, etc. When a real struggle between presences takes place, through evil spells and curses, the perpetuator is able to gain control of an individual or even kill him; the victim may also be saved through the intervention of a more powerful magician who has the power to undo the witch-craft: here again we have something that is actually effective, but which, to us (because of our attitudes), does not exist. Furthermore, the presence that is trying to establish itself is able to read, telepathically, the thought of other individuals and is able to communicate its own content to other presences; or make itself present to events which, considered from our cultural view-point, are far away in either time or space. That is, within the magic world, they are included within the realm of human decision through the rapport desired, and may also be suppressed through the same channels. In the same way, the beyond of the world may be redeemed through certain paranormal physical powers—to what extent, however, may only be known through research into each case.

It is nevertheless true that paranormal reality is not the same as the positive reality of the scientist; strictly speaking, one cannot speak of real magic powers in the same way as a positivist would refer to any particular object. Even if such powers were proved real to the satisfaction of everyone, through the recordings of instruments (e.g., photography), and if the paranormal act causes the introduction of some definitive element, there still remain elements that are unacceptable to *our* positivist way of thinking. Paranormal events are, by definition, still part of the realm of human decision; they are dependent upon this decision and are influenced by psychic effort. Because of these factors, they are not yet sufficiently independent, mastered, objective or given. We are concerned with another order of reality here that is linked to the historical and cultural order of magic and which is foreign to our civilization.

So we come up against the problem of magic powers expressed in explicit terms. Research dealing with the reality of such powers is becoming more conclusive and, with this new perspective, we are able to examine documentation, experimentation, observations and controls, from a position that differs radically from the narrowness of our former perspective. Previously, it was rather a case of the blind leading the blind, with much over-simplification, and too much involvement in polemics. The emphasis was upon negation rather than affirmation. We are now aware of what was limiting our outlook. We are ready for critical analysis not only of the magic world, but also of our own reactions to this world. A kind of catharsis has taken place within us, a radical change, a profound metanoia. We can now look at the object of our research—and ourselves as researchers—in a new light. The documentation quoted in the previous chapter now, and only now, permits us to say with complete and utter certainty that there are paragnomic aptitudes, that the burning power of fire may be suspended, and that there are real instances of telekinesis. It is no longer these phenomena that appear absurd to us, but rather the hypotheses and explanations put forward by men of science for the purpose of denying them. It is a fact that Wundt was scandalized at the violation of the 'grandiose universe of Galileo and Newton' that now scandalizes us, while also providing the impetus that directs us towards a new understanding. A scientist once said to William James that if the existence of telepathy was ever proved, a whole league of scientists would be obliged to arise to defend themselves against such a dangerous phenomenon and against its equally-dangerous supporters. The great scientist Helmholtz once declared that, in the case of telepathy, he would utterly reject even the evidence of all the members of the Academy. The most important discovery, for the ethnologist, is not the reality of telepathy or other paranormal phenomena, but the fact that he has uncovered, among the men of his own civilization, very revealing attitudes towards the problem of the reality of magical powers: attitudes that uncover all the limitations of their cultural Einstellung.

A new era gives rise to new questions and therefore new problems. The naturalist has been tempted many times to bring paranormal phenomena into the physical order: it is indicative that Richet defined metapsychics as 'the science of unknown vibrations'. Bernhard Bavink writes, 'Telepathy could be interpreted in the following manner: certain people who are able to enter more readily than the average man into the depths of the unconscious (or rather, are able to seize something from these depths) could, through this, have access to spheres that are normally quite inaccessible to the consciousness (the ego); that is, they would be able to gain knowledge of structures belonging to other individuals (telepathy) or of a content that is considered as inanimate or dead (clairvoyance). Even spatial-voyance and prophecy would have their own place because, basically, according to Ninkowski's view of the universe, it does not matter if such exploration is carried out in the temporal or spatial order of the world'.[80] But, looked at from our newly-attained point-of-view, the limitations and even contradictions within this statement become obvious. In the first place, research that attempts to integrate paranormal phenomena within our physical order has nothing in common with the historical and cultural understanding of magic powers; this may be reached only through a reconstruction of the magic age and its characteristic existential drama. In the second place, one should not forget that paranormal facts, except in the abstract sense, are not natural facts. They are in contrast to the *physical world*, in the sense that they are not *given facts*, but are in the process of being formulated through intervention of a presence that endeavors—through an historical effort—to distinguish itself from and oppose the world. Natural facts *presuppose* the decided and guaranteed presence that is part of our civilization, whereas paranormal facts *presuppose*, if they are considered concretely, a threatened or endangered presence, a being-within-the-world that is try-

---

80. B. Bavink: *Ergebnisse der Naturwissenschaften*, Leipzig 1935, quoted by Muhlmann in *Rassen und Volkerkunde*, Brunswick 1936, p. 367.

ing to establish itself. Thirdly, one should be aware that paranormal phenomena, even if observed and recorded by instruments, do not lend themselves to the conditions of scientific experimentation, except to a very limited degree. Science is devised for the exploration of phenomena that belong to a *given* world, in which the presence is guaranteed; consequently, its methods are not completely applicable to phenomena of the magic world. Because of this, certain paranormal phenomena and certain subjects require the full or partial participation of the observer in the existential drama of the individual who is producing the phenomena. For example, mediums sometimes ask the spectators to try to distract themselves through conversation, singing, etc., or they may complain that the observer's interior attitude, scepticism or over-intense concentration, is preventing the production of phenomena. This leads to a paradox—it is precisely the attitude that conforms to the rules of scientific observation which may have the unintended effect of making the phenomenon disappear. Also, the phenomenon will probably appear more easily if the spectator abandons his function as just an observer and makes at least some effort to collaborate with the medium. This has nothing to do with the fact, now accepted by modern physics, that the scientist, by means of his measuring apparatus, may sometimes influence the phenomena he is observing; rather, it implies a criticism of science—the observer is dealing here with a level of reality which, for him, is not sufficiently *given*: this seems to seriously compromise the whole aim of scientific knowledge, which is to rationally resolve a given fact. Paranormal phenomena seem to evade the imposition of laws; it appears that the plasticity of a world that has an immediate link with human intention prevents the phenomenon from finding its place in some regulated and clearly-defined mould, even though this is what it is endeavoring to do. The paragnostic aptitudes of the medium X seem to follow methods that are quite different from those of the medium Y, while the medium Z, using various methods, produces physical paranormal phenomena. All these contradictory elements create a tormenting confusion in the scientist's mind; he feels that he has entered an unknown region, one that is completely foreign to him, and his distrust prevents him from venturing very far. He may withdraw from it, completely disorientated, or he may abandon his life's work (and this happens more frequently than is suspected) and turn spiritualist (as, for example, the physician Lodge). This uneasiness that the scientist experiences when confronted by paranormal phenomena has been analysed in depth by V. Germicca: 'How can one refer to the metaphysicians' ecto-plasms and teleplasms as matter in the scientific sense of the term? This matter that, in certain cases, cannot even be photographed, may detach itself from the medium and, instead of being dispersed within the encompassing milieu, it may go towards some other place: for example, it may take a table and lift it from the floor or it may condense itself into a particular form, such as a specter or a human face, or else it may become tangible and leave certain traces before disappearing. No gas or radiation could produce analogous phenomena. And even if it were possible to analyse this ectoplasm and find some new composition or radiation within it, this would still not provide an explanation, because scientific method is unable to explain this joining-together into an expressive form, this habit of moving in one direction instead of another . . . The ectoplasm could be photographed, the weight of the table that it lifted could be recorded, as could the period the table was suspended etc., but no calculation or measure would give any real insight into the actual mechanism . . .'[81]

To attempt to reduce paranormal incidents to natural facts and to consider them as if they *must be proved* and under-stood on the same level as *given facts* are quite valid methods in the effort to uncover their nature. In fact, they help to establish that paranormal incidents are *real*, even if the final conclusion indicates that the reality concerned is not that of the given fact. The failures that occur during scientific research, the contradictions and doubts, the researcher's fears that his work lacks authenticity and the choice he must sometimes make between incomplete acceptance and an impossible rejection—all of this is, in its own way, instructive, because it contains the seeds of a deeper crisis that is related

81. Extract from a letter to the author, 10th February, 1942.

to cultural presumptions and to the fundamental anti-historical attitudes that these involve. Scientific or positive research is necessary and must continue to be carried out with the utmost care. At the same time, it has become possible to discipline it and place it within a new perspective that frees it from uncritical pretensions and makes it more decisive. On this last point, it must be admitted that there are certainly some legitimate and necessary exigencies if one is to gain guaranteed information, and these are often dictated by the type of research; but these never-ending and often-renewed requirements, as well as the final doubt that persists in spite of them, are frequently the expression of a research that is disorientated, one that has been following a false path. To a degree, the problem of magic powers is linked very closely to the question: 'quis custodiet custodem' or who shall supervise the supervisor? Obviously, the system of guarantees cannot conclude with some exterior guarantee that is utterly absolute and final; it must have the interior guarantee of a thought that can develop a clear, disciplined and comprehensive point of view, one that is able to defend itself and have the courage of its convictions.

We have a simple but instructive case: one day the missionary, Grubb, was accused by a Paraguayan Indian of having stolen gourds from his garden; the only basis of his accusation was that he had seen him do this in a dream. Although the missionary tried to convince the native of his innocence, the latter persisted, saying that Grubb must have taken the gourds, as the dream had showed him entering the garden and carrying them away.[82] This is what we would call an unreal incident: the native has had visions, and Grubb has stolen nothing at all; but can this view be valid if we take into account the relationship between the presence and the world that is part of the world of magic? In a situation where the presence is still undecided, and in a civilization where the presence and the world that makes itself present are intimately bound up with dream-

---

82. This case is reported by W. G. Grubb: *An Unknown People in an Unknown Land*, pp. 129 ff.

consciousness[83] (and where such consciousness is part of what this culture considers as real), it is quite possible that Grubb, in the native's dreams, is playing out a vital role in a life of which he is completely unaware. In order to find out something about this 'life', and to recognize the actions as his own, Grubb should have been deprived of his decided and guaranteed presence. Then, through this bridging of the cultural chasm between him and his accusor, he could have reached the historical region in which the latter moves and acts. If Grubb had been able to do this, he would not have considered the native's accusations absurd, because he would have penetrated a cultural order in which one may exist within the dreams of another individual, and where acts that one 'commits' in these dreams are accepted as real.

If one affirms, *in a completely absolute fashion,* that the missionary Grubb did not steal the gourds, then one is creating a sort of metaphysical transposition: Grubb, the historical form of his presence, his historically-determined sense of reality and the cultural order that has influenced him, are abstracted from historical movement and are crystallized into an absolute criterion that is supposedly valid for all historical epochs and all civilizations. There are, in fact, two Grubbs; there is the one that belongs to our culture and who, obviously, cannot carry out actions through the dreams of another individual; then there is the other Grubb who becomes part of the magical rapports within another civilization and who, unbeknown to himself, may even be stealing gourds in the 'real' dream of some native. A third, or 'essential' Grubb, who is an absolute truth, who is paradigmatic, exists only within the limits of a polemical attitude, within some metaphysical outgrowth, nourished by cultural presumption, and which historical reasoning must do-away with. The statement 'Grubb did not steal the gourds' is valid only within our civilization, or in some essentially-similar oriental civilization—it cannot be defended if our historic horizon is extended to include the magical epoch. So long as we allow our historical awareness to be con-

83. To understand this relationship between reality and dreams it must be remembered that certain links and bonds may be instituted through dream-consciousness: dreams are often used by the clairvoyant, or for contacting the 'spirits'.

ditioned by polemical attitudes and positions it will remain as limited as Grubb's. But if we include the presence and the world that makes itself present within the realm of historical movement, then we are reaching for a more elevated view-point: we go beyond the polemics that form part of our anti-magical civilization, and we are able to condone the statements of both Grubb *and* his accusor.

We suggested previously, that if Grubb had been able to transpose himself into the historical region of his accusor, he would have conceded the possibility of having stolen gourds in the dream of another person. Such a transposition may sometimes take place. It is then that the magical forms of reality begin to come into play and begin to be recognized for what they are. C. J. Jung reports that:

'In the Kitoshi region, south of Elgon, I went on an excursion into the virgin forest of Kabra. As I was walking among the long grass that grows there, I almost stepped on a viper. I only just managed to avoid it. In the afternoon my friend returned from the hunt, pale as death and trembling all over: He had just escaped, by a hair's breadth, from being bitten, fatally, by a seven foot "mamba" that had thrown itself onto his back . . . In the evening, at about nine o'clock, our camp was attacked by a pack of famished hyenas . . . Such an eventful day caused considerable talk among my blacks. What was for us a simple accumulation of incidences was, for them, the normal verification of a presage that had appeared in the forest on the day of our departure. We had fallen into a stream when crossing a bridge in our Ford. The boys had looked at one-another as if to say, "That's a good beginning!" Then we were caught in a tropical storm that soaked us all to the skin and caused out-breaks of fever that lasted for several days. That evening . . . I said to my hunter friend: "It seems to me that these things began a long time ago. Do you remember the dream you told me about before we left Zurich?" He had had a most revealing night-mare. He had dreamed that he was in Africa and had been attacked by an enormous "mamba".'[84]

As a commentary on the various forms of magic reality, and to illustrate the part they play in the existential drama,

84. C. G. Jung: *Seelenprobleme der Gegenwart* (Italian Trans. *Il problema dell'inconscio nella psicologia moderna,* Turin, Einaudi, 1942, pp. 179 ff.).

we shall quote a remarkable document furnished by a Fan, Mba Eyana, and told to Raoul Allier by the missionary, Charles Cadier. It concerns a sorcerer who is searching for a victim; one who will enable him to cure a sick man. After some vicissitudes, the sick man goes to see the sorcerer and asks him to choose between his son and his daughter-in-law.

'The sorcerer went to look at these two people in a dream and saw that it was the woman who should die. He called upon the other spirits of his clan to come to his aid and all these spirits left, prepared for war; they left their village and arrived at Akoghengol in the middle of the night. And all of the Fans knew that the spirits were there. The latter seized hold of the woman who then woke up and said to her husband: "I've just seen the spirits (beyem) who have thrown a hunting-net over my body." The husband gave the alarm and the whole village awoke. During the night, owls were heard hooting all the way along the road that the spirits had come by. Then the villagers became angry; their spirits also left, prepared for war, and chased away the spirits from the other clan, several of which were wounded by spears thrown during the night by the Fan spirits. Two of the other group died. A third one, wounded during the fight, asked a Fan, several days later, "Is the woman whom we seized dead?" "No, but she is very sick," was the reply. "She will certainly die," said the other, "and because of her, we will also die." The next day both the woman and the wounded man were dead.'[85]

This document will appear quite unintelligible if we look at it within the limitations of our historical consciousness, but if we consider it in the light of our conclusions about magical reality, we can arrive at a radically different interpretation. The sorcerer who goes to see the Fan couple in a dream, does, in actual fact, go to see them: in an historical world where the presence in still undecided, it may really visit another presence in dream. Once the victim has been sought out, the sorcerer calls all the members of his tribe to come and help him, and, in dream, the latter gather at the appropriate place; this is so real that both the victim and the Fans are aware of what has happened; the spirits, even though invisible, are felt to be present. This psychic state in

85. Raoul Allier: *Le non-civiliseé et nous*, Paris 1927, pp. 291 ff.

which the real presence of some invisible being is felt is called 'ngwel'. The presence of the spirits, as sensed by the Fans, is a reality that is felt during a state of ngwel, but it is nonetheless real. The victim senses that she is in danger and the spirits throw a hunting-net over her; it is a ngwel net, invisible, but present. Then we have the Fans' reaction to the invasion of the other spirits and there is a general unleashing of conflicts between presences. The conflict takes place at the ngwel level, with ngwel spears and wounds. One presumes at this point, that paranormal elements now come into play, and that the actual wounds do appear in much the same way that stigmata appear on the bodies of mystics.

This overlapping of the ngwel level of reality and the realm of the paranormal seems to give the most satisfying explanation of numerous concrete cases of magic that, otherwise, would remain completely incomprehensible. Thus, for example, sorcerers' sabbatical reunions would take place at the ngwel level of reality; in certain cases, a more or less complex paranormal reality sometimes also appears. One day, Father Trilles carved his initials on a rock on Mount Nsas, Gabon, a place considered by the natives to be the scene of the sabbatical congress of sorcerers. A sorcerer from a village forty miles away from Mount Nsas agreed to Trilles' request that when he went to this place for a gathering of sorcerers he would read what the priest had carved on the rock. He carried out his promise. Another time Father Trilles invited a native to accompany him on a fishing-trip, using dynamite, but the native refused. 'Why don't you want to come?' asked the priest.

'I won't be here tomorrow.'

'Where are you going?'

'To X.' (four days' walk away).

'But you couldn't be at X by tomorrow You wouldn't have time.'

'I have my means.'

'Very well, if you are going to X, will you carry out a message for me, as you will be passing through Aleva.'

'Certainly.'

'Go to Esab'Ava's place, the fourth house on the right,

along the river-bank, and tell him to bring me, as soon as possible, the packet of cartridges and the box of powder that I left at his place. But perhaps you could bring them yourself?'

'No, that would be impossible.'

When he was questioned closely, the native admitted that he was going to a special sort of reunion, and by special way and means that would not permit him to take or bring back luggage. Father Trilles was allowed to be present during the preparations for this strange trip. The sorcerer first smeared his body with a special mixture . . . then he lit a fire and walked around it, saying prayers to the spirits of the air and the guardian-spirits of the magic brotherhood. He then fell into a state of ecstasy, showed the whites of his eyes, his skin became insensitive and his limbs rigid. It was ten o'clock the next day when he came out of his trance, and during that time Father Trilles had not left his side. When he awoke, the man gave some details about the reunion at which he had been present and then, without being asked, said:

'Your message has been carried out. Esab'Ava has been warned. He will set out this-morning and will bring you the powder and cartridges.'

Three days later the catechist, Esab'Ava, arrived at the village with the goods. He did not know how he had received the message. Someone had called out, outside his house, towards nine o'clock in the evening, and had told him that Father Trilles wanted the packet that he had left at his place. Here is a possible interpretation of these happenings: the sabbatical trip, the details of the reunion, and the return, etc., usually all take place at the ngwel level. But this does not mean that they were *unreal* events—except from the point of view of our culture and civilization. Within the *historical* concept of reality, the ngwel level is something real, although in a form that differs from that of the given fact. The ngwel level may sometimes overlap with the paranormal level: in other words, another form of reality may appear during the ngwel journey—clairvoyance, telepathy etc., for example. And even if this form of reality cannot be integrated into the reality of a fixed and guaranteed world, it nevertheless has its own, historically-determined reality, exactly as does *our* 'given fact'.

Let us consider Trilles' remarks about the Fans:

> 'A vague rumor went around this peaceful village today . . . : "Ngil e shoa", the sorcerer is near-by; and in the long-house, where only the men have the right to stay, there were whispered, anxious conversations: "Why has the sorcerer arrived?" Then night fell, a black, starless night; each man hurried home and carefully barricaded his wooden door and the family talked in low voices: "Ngil e shoa va", the sorcerer is very close. Suddenly, a sharp cry rings out in the black silence, a cry that is never forgotten by those who hear it; the cry echoes around the village, then there is a deep, raucous noise, something inhuman . . . there are more cries, nearer . . . every one is silent, to speak aloud would be punishable by death . . . there are loud knocks at each door, violent and repeated knocks . . . all light and fire in the village must be extinguished. There is a frantic galloping, cries, calls, unknown voices with strange intonations . . . men or animals . . . ? perhaps both. Arrows fly in all directions, poisoned arrows that cause their victims to writhe and moan in hopeless agony . . . men, women and children maintain the terrified silence, then another door crashes down, more cries, a woman or child is carried off, never to be seen again . . . and then there is the mournful silence that nobody will dare break until morning . . . even weeping is stifled . . . "Ngil e lura . . .", the sorcerer has been and gone.'

It would be easy to interpret such a document as an account of a normal village raid, carried out by the sorcerer and his offsiders. But we are forced to reconsider our ideas in the light of our previous examination of the ngwel and the appearance of certain paranormal forms.

The common assertion that so-called magic activities are no more than the vulgar tricks of cunning men who can rely on the credulity of an ignorant public, might as easily be matched by a claim that religion is nothing more than a deception perpetuated by self-interested clerics. Certainly there are cases in which the magician or Shaman deliberately sets out to dupe his public. But as literary plagiarism is in no way related to artistic creation, so are the tricks of the false magician unrelated to authentic magic activities and to real, paranormal powers.

In a cultural milieu where forms of extrasensory perception may be verified and where the burning quality of fire can be mastered, one must have *positive proof* that personal powers *do not* come into play and that the magician's claims are not just clever tricks. Such proof is completely lacking in ethnological documentation. According to Bogoraz, the Chuckchee sorcerer is a ventriloquist, but there is no proof that this is so. On the contrary, even the phonographic documentation confirms the impression that the 'voices' were speaking directly into the gramophone horn.[86] Bogoraz also claims that the various actions of invisible hands, during shamanic seances, could not occur without the help of human assistants, but he gives no positive proof of such intervention. The woman Shaman who manipulated a stone in such an astonishing way is considered by Bogoraz as a prestidigitator, while he admits that he could not discover what techniques she employed. In these cases, proof is replaced with the dogmatic presupposition that magic powers are non-existent, and the whole question is avoided by thinking up some normal explanation, such as 'collaboration of assistants', or by indicating that there is certainly some reasonable explanation, but that 'it is just pointless to attempt to find it . . .' If we examine the documents of Gusinde and Trilles, not only do we find no positive proof of trickery, but the authors themselves appear to express a rather strange dilemma; Gusinde declares that there was no possibility of illusionism or trickery being used; Trilles describes the things he saw in such a way that the reader is intended to see the transfer of a fever from a sick man to a plant as an actual occurrence. In other words, in this whole question of magic activities and powers, the guarantee is rooted in the *dogmatic realism* of the Western observer, rather than in any close examination of the sorcerer's capacities: in many cases, it is precisely this realism that prevents the observer from understanding the magical experience and accepting the possibility of a magic reality—he

86. Bogoraz: op., cit.

is more inclined to see or look for the fraudulent products of some trickster.[87]

But the problem is more complicated than this. Even if no paranormal reality seems to accompany the claims to magic powers, and even if everything seems to indicate that the claims are fraudulent, it is still not necessarily a question of deliberate trickery and clever machinations. It must be remembered that, as well as paranormal reality, there is the ngwel level of reality, and one may discover, with *this* form of magic reality in mind, that the claims are not without foundation. Objects within the framework of the ngwel reality may take on a quite different meaning, undergo a complete transfiguration and enter into relationships that, for us (and only *for us*), are non-existent. We only see the co-ordinating factors that are part of the very real magical dream, and we judge these as if they are not part of the ngwel framework, as if they continue to be objects and relationships that belong to *our own* historically-determined reality. Rasmussen reports:

> 'One day a little boy came into the hut, crying, but unable to say what he was crying for. Such an occurrence is not unusual or remarkable with children, but Anarqaq at once perceived a chance of making an impression. As if driven by a sudden impulse, he dashed out of the hut without a word and raced off over the ice and was lost to sight. It was a dark evening, and very cold, Anarqaq was away for more than half an hour, and when he came back, the sleeves and lining of his fur were torn, and his arms and hands covered with blood. He breathed heavily, in great gasps, as if thoroughly exhausted, and without a word of explanation, sank down to the floor and lay there, apparently unconscious. All sat speechless, gazing at him with the greatest astonishment and respect, and no one present thought for a moment of doubting his word when he shortly after came to his senses and explained that the child had been attacked by an evil spirit, which he,

87. A typical example of this Western attitude towards magical processes is revealed in W. G. Hoffman's statement concerning the witch-doctors of the Amerindian tribes in the North-West: 'The exploits of some of the more famous of these prestidigitators even manage to convince the most intelligent and incredulous observer: it is not surprising that certain accounts . . . contain the most circumstantial and extraordinary stories concerning the powers that these characters supposedly possess.' (W. J. Hoffman in *University Medical Magazine*, Nov. 1890, p. 2).

Anarqaq, had now vanquished after a hard fight. It never occurred to anyone that he could have snatched up a lump of seal's blood out in the passage, where some had been set out to freeze after the day's hunting; nor did it enter anyone's head to suppose that he might have torn his clothes himself. It was taken for granted that he really had fought with an evil spirit and thus saved the child's life.'[88]

The difficulty that is experienced in admitting Anarqaq's 'good faith', and in justifying the powers of persuasion that he appears to hold over his public, obviously originates in our own lack of that dimension of reality which, for convenience's sake, we shall continue to call ngwel. It is the dimension of reality in which the seal's blood, put out to coagulate after the hunt, may become the blood of the Shaman who is struggling against the evil spirit, and in which the Shaman's clothes, that he has torn himself, may turn into the clothes that have been lacerated by the spirit during the course of the fight. The idea of trickery and fraud derivates from our insistence upon the absoluteness of our own historically-conditioned form of reality and from our measuring Anarqaq's claims according to this form. But his claims, in fact all magical claims, must be related to the forms of reality that belong to the historical and cultural world ·of which they are part.

On the other hand, authors have recognized the good faith of shamans and magicians without being aware of the complexity of the problem. Gusinde writes about the Selk'nam: 'I must reject firmly any opinion that claims that the sorcerers are impostors or charlatans who knowingly dupe their public through the use of tricks.'[89] And about the Yamana: 'It would certainly be unfounded and quite false to say that the sorcerer is an impostor and charlatan.'[90] Rasmussen admits that the Iglulik shaman, Anarqaq, was capable of using trickery in order to convince the public that he was communing with the spirits, but he thinks, despite this, that Anarqaq was 'always honest and sincere'.[91] Con-

88. Rasmussen: *Intellectual Culture of the Iglulik Eskimos*, p. 43.
89. Gusinde: *Die Feuerland-Indianer* I, p. 736.
90. ibid. II, p. 1393.
91. Rasmussen: Op. cit., p. 43.

cerning another Iglulik Shaman, Unalek, the same author
says, after a seance in which the spirit voices were heard:

> 'Despite the extreme naivete of the whole proceeding,
> this spirit seance was to me of great interest. For it was
> one of the first at which I was present, and I could not
> but feel astounded at the manner in which it impressed
> the Eskimos themselves. They were altogether fascinated,
> as if they really felt a breath of some supernatural power
> in the pitiful acting which any critical observer could see
> through at once. I saw here how great was the faith of
> these people in their wizardry, and how even the most
> mediocre practitioner can gain adherents, because all are
> ready to believe without question. And, as I was to learn
> in a moment, the old shaman himself believed in his
> helping spirit. He was a poor ventriloquist, but no humbug
> all the same.'[92]

There are other complex aspects of this question of
fraudulence. Ethnology is aware where magic is declining,
that what was in the past an actual, real power, may now
be functioning at the ngwel level of reality, or may have
turned into simply a spectacle during which the magician
deliberately tries to dupe the public with vulgar tricks.
Thomas, for example, writes about the fire-crossing ceremony
of the Fiji islands as a local custom which escaped the
general destruction wrought by the missionaries. Ocken
reports that the incantation that used to be chanted before
crossing the fire had fallen into disuse since the introduction
of Christianity. The old Maori chieftains, when told of
Gudgeon's report, claimed that their ancestors used to be
able to carry out this ceremony, but that it had not been
performed for a long time. Kingsley Roth, a more recent
witness at the Mbenga ceremony, observed that whereas
the dimensions of the pit were now fifteen feet in diameter
and three feet in depth, in former times it had been much
larger[93]: in actual fact, the pit that Ocken had seen in 1898
was twenty-five feet in diameter and eight feet deep. Roth
also remarks that 'in former times the walk was done three
or four times round the oven'[94] and not once only. According

92 ibid. p. 40.
93. Kingsley Roth: *The Fire-Walk in Fiji (Man)* XXXIII, 1933, No. 49.
94. ibid., loc. cit.

to Gudgeon, the pit was prepared and burning from dawn until two o'clock in the afternoon; according to Ocken, this took thirty-six to forty-eight hours. S. P. Langley, who was present at a ceremony in Tahiti, stated that the pit was not very deep at all, and had been lit only four hours previously. In the latter case, the fire-crossing had been reduced to just an exhibition, a spectacle, with no ritualistic value.[95] With these changes in mind, it is easy to understand that many European observers have seen nothing more than a semblance of the original ceremony, so their observations are of diminished significance. It is also likely that there has been a gradual introduction of changes that make for an easier or even quite harmless crossing (lack of depth, lessened width, moderated heat, rapid crossing, etc.), leading to a degenerate and decadent form of the ceremony. This would explain a judgment such as that of Mackenzie, who was present at a fire-crossing in India where the pit was only four feet long and two feet wide. He remarks that, having heard various descriptions of such a ceremony, he was expecting something quite extraordinary. He was shocked by the utter banality of the spectacle, during which there was not the slightest threat of danger to the participants . . . apart from the possibility of minor burns to their feet.[96]

The tradition of the greater powers of Shamans and magicians of former times is generally well-founded; in some cases tradition has an historical foundation, or one that reflects historical characteristics. A Chuckchee Shaman apologized to Bogoraz for not being able to carry out a particular traditional exploit and complained 'this is not a time for great shamanistic acts'.[97] Shirokogoroff remarks that, among the Tungus, there is the prevailing idea that shamanism is on the decline, and it is generally admitted that the Shamans of former times were much more powerful . . . The Birarcen also say that, although there were formerly very few Shamans, they were nevertheless powerful, whereas today there are many more, but of inferior quality.[98]

95. S. P. Langley: The Fire-Walk Ceremony in Tahiti (Folklore) XII, 1901, pp. 446-455.
96. Frazer: Balder the Beautiful II, p. 6, note 2.
97. Bogoraz: The Chuckchee, p. 448.
98. Shirokogoroff: The Psychomental Complex of the Tungus, pp. 391 ff.

The Selk'nam and Yamana also consider that the older Shamans were more powerful and were capable of exploits now considered impossible. Gusinde remarks that 'The present-day Indians are of the opinion that the former Shamans were both more evil, more powerful and more dangerous . . . One of their greater powers was the speed with which they could attain their destructive aims . . . The sorcerer's art shows definite signs of decadence, and hardly any aspect of the Selk'nam culture has escaped the influence of europeanization.'[99] Concerning the Yamana, he writes: 'My informers have told me in the clearest possible terms that the sorcerers of former times were more skilful and more capable in the practice of their art.'[100] The magicians' school in which Gusinde participated during his fourth voyage was the last reunion of this type, and the previous one had taken place twenty-five years before.[101] When Gusinde asked to be allowed to take part in the ceremonies, the three magicians that belonged to the group, as well as the older participants, were both puzzled and scornful; they made excuses, saying 'the times of the skilful and powerful magicians were long past, and that they, themselves, were only very amateurish magicians, incapable of carrying out those astounding practices and superhuman tasks with which the older members of their profession used to impress their public.'[102] So, the problem of the 'good faith' or 'trickery' of the magicians must be reconsidered according to a quite new set of criteria. It must be remembered that much of the so-called trickery is pure dogmatic supposition, and not positively proved by the European observer; we must remember that many of the processes that appear false to us undergo a vast change in significance if we accept the principle of an historical conditioning of various forms of reality, and that we are dealing with the drama of the magical epoch, involving a world that is still included in the realm of human decision. The deliberate, vulgar trickery is then reduced to almost negligible proportions, particularly when one is examining magical societies that do not show

99. Gusinde: *Die Feuerland-Indianer* I pp. 726 ff.
100. Gusinde: op. cit., II, p. 1388.
101. ibid., p. 1400.
102 ibid, p. 190.

any obvious signs of disintegration or decadence.

Storch's works on the relationship between schizophrenia and the mythico-magical (or archaic) mentality confirm the relationship between the magical drama of the danger of 'not being here' and the redemption of this danger, at an historical level. In schizophrenia, there is the manifestation of a more or less profound dissociation within the personality, a suppression of the distinction between subject and object, between the me and you, between the self and the world. The crisis suffered by the presence is sensed as a kind of occult power, an evil influence. The objectivity of the world turns into something almost wax-like, as if objects lose their resistance and contours and outlines are erased, or else run together. The world gives way, crumbles, loses its beauty and value and turns into something sordid. The schizophrenic subject sees his own catastrophe magnified into a cosmic upheaval; one of Storch's patients makes the following remark: 'Hundreds of stars have fallen and, like my body, a whole part of the planetary system has crumbled.'[103] For the schizoid, the great danger is that he may fall either into the utter passivity of a cataleptic state or else into the chaotic state of uncontrolled impulses. In the cataleptic state, there is a passive acceptance of any imposed positioning of the limbs, no matter how uncomfortable this may be (cf. the malleability of wax). There is an imitative automatism, expressed by various forms of echophrasia, echopraxia and echomimetism. The patient will react to this extreme danger of cataleptic passivity in an exasperated and spasmodic fashion; the presence is unsupported in every act, and, as every act or concrete relationship to the world constitutes a danger to the being-within-the-world, he will place barricades around his will and refuse to concede to the world. These are the origins of the peculiar psychic state that is referred to as 'catatonic stupor'. The presence attempts to redeem and save itself through a dramatic withdrawal from all stimuli, by placing a general veto on every action. Any attempt to encourage action is seen as a potential attack upon the presence: any action will cause the being-within-

---

103. Storch: *Die Welt der beginnenden Schizophrenie und die archaische Welt* in 'Zeitschrift Neurol. Psych.' 127, 1930.

the-world to escape, to be violated or to enter into a more critical state. The taking of food would cause the introduction of evil influences; natural bodily functions cause the loss of the presence's strength, etc. In the catatonic stupor, and in the negativism that accompanies it, there is a complete rigidity of the will: this leads to a kind of petrified immobility, the intentional retention of urine and bowel-contents, refusal to speak and to eat. Yet sometimes the force of uncontrolled impulses can cause a breach in this seemingly impenetrable wall.

Attempts to protect the endangered presence sometimes led to an effort towards the reconstruction of magic. Werner writes: 'The irruption of the encompassing environment within the ego and the discharge of the ego into the encompassing environment create a demoniacal vision of the world before which the only possibility of redemption is through the demonism of the ego and through the magical aspects of its operations.'[104] Further on, he writes: 'The pathological dissolution of the personality and of its activity would be avoided (the psychopath hopes) by his forcing himself to attain some internally coherent form of life. The ego that is continually disintegrating . . . reinforces itself in a certain way and saves itself through a kind of magical reconstruction, even though this effort may lead to a world that is completely different from the normal one.' In this way, the ego reaches out for a rational world through which there is 'a recomposition of the disintegrating concrete reality, leading to the re-forming of the personality.' If this new rational plane is far removed from normality, it nevertheless has one trait in common with the plane of normal activity: it tries to 'put some order into the surrounding environment and, through this newly-attained centralization, ensures that the personality has some kind of coherent effectiveness, even though this may be arbitrary and extravagant.'[105]

This comparison between the magic world and the schizophrenic mentality is of purely heuristic value; the shared traits should not cause one to forget or ignore the basic differences. In the magic world, we are concerned with an

104. Werner: *Einführung in die Entwicklungspsychologie*, p. 398.
105. ibid., p. 404.

historic epoch in which the being-within-the-world is *not yet* fixed and guaranteed, and where an attempt to defend oneself from the danger of not being here leads to a cultural creation that actually overcomes this danger. In the magic world, the individual drama is an organic part of the cultural ensemble, it has the support of tradition and of established institutions, it can profit from the slowly-accumulated experience of past generations: the whole structure of civilization is prepared for the resolution of this drama that is shared to varying degrees and in different forms by everyone. Considered as an historical epoch, magic belongs to the physiology of spiritual life and, in the variety of its forms and develop- ments, it has had one result that is most precious to the history of human civilization: a presence that is guaranteed in its relationships to a balanced, ordered world.

On the other hand, in schizophrenia the being-within-the- world is *no longer* fixed and guaranteed as it should be in its relationship to its historical situation. Here, the individual drama remains something entirely private; it is not an organic part of the cultural life, and it breaks out without the historic milieu being sufficiently prepared to accept and solve it through a system of accepted traditions and institutions. Basically, the pathological character of schizophrenia is determined by the direction that is taken by the dramatic movement; the schizoid's person disintegrates and any barriers that are raised in an attempt to prevent this are progressively broken down. The presence is detached from the historical plan to which, by rights, it belongs, and even if it resists and fights against this collapse, it does not have the force or strength to arrest it and redeem itself. In the magic world, salvation is the result, not only of effort within the indivi- dual, but part of a cultural drama that is not private, but public. In schizophrenia, the individual must struggle alone, or almost alone: the thread of tradition has been broken, and the efforts and experiences of others are either un-usable or non-existent because of the lack of defined magical in- stitutions; as for the prevailing cultural drama, far from being of any help, it is rather an obstacle in the way of recovery and may provoke new and more serious conflicts. The schizoid's efforts to overcome the danger, or to compensate for the threat through his stereotypy, mannerisms and amulets, are insufficient because they are isolated and autistic: if they persist, they will lead eventually to complete insanity.

In schizophrenia, the themes related to the threat of disintegration are far more decisive and radical than those that affect the man who is part of the magic world; those connected to redemption are different from the corresponding magical themes, in that they take on an unauthentic quality, and are therefore a wasted effort. In schizophrenia, the threat of falling into a state of cataleptic passivity or catatonic stupor, and the danger of uncontrolled impulses, are all very important elements, whereas, in the magic world, these would be rather the result of some rare accident—here, the dominating trait is not a vain effort, but the presence that succeeds in obtaining its own salvation. This salvation or redemption is never achieved through the barricading of the will or through the rejection of all rapports with the outside world. There are some actions that are taboo, but these are isolated and clearly-defined, as are taboo objects and people. Instead of rejecting food, certain nourishments are forbidden, either permanently, or under particular circumstances, or else there are ritual fasts; instead of the refusal to speak, there are words that should not be spoken, either permanently or in certain situations, and there is also the imposition of ritual silences; instead of the retention of body-matter, there are magic elements related to defaecation and the openings of the body. The soul that escapes, is violated, or must be restrained, is recovered through the institution of the alter ego; or through the intervention of the helper-spirit that is sought out and dominated through the spiritualistic trance or the shaman's spell, etc. The presence is freed and released into the world, although not without fear and confusion; its drama, which is a basis for wisdom, creates a civilization, one that may have things to teach modern man.

It was probably Karl Gustav Carus who first advanced the theory that psychoses are, in general, the repetition and returns of certain ancient phases of psychic development (*Vorlesungen uber Psychologie*, 1831). But it was an Italian psychiatrist, Eugenio Tanzi, who extended and developed these ideas in a series of monographs.[106] According to Tanzi, the disordered mentality of primitive man may be reproduced in modern, educated man as 'archaic survivance'. The disordered ideology of primitive man, supressed in normal man by ideas that have been created during subsequent human history, may reappear in all their former strength in the mentally-ill, producing an intellectual deformation containing traits that are simultaneously barbaric and cultured. It was also an Italian psychiatrist, Morselli, who warned against the hasty drawing of analogies between abnormalities in the psychosis and the cultural creations of a primitive society. In discussions with Freud and other German alienists (including Jung, although he was less concerned with this question), Morselli made the observation that the civilized individual who suffers from mental illness is not *the same* as prehistoric man because, between the two, there has flowed 'the whole historic course of human progress' which affects not only the individual, but the world as a whole. He added: 'The repetition cannot be an integral part because, on one hand, the civilized individual of today cannot free himself from elements that have been acquired "ab antiquo" and which have been firmly established within his psychic make-up by his ethnic, family and cultural heritage and because, on the other hand, the young, adult, or elderly subject cannot suddenly rid himself of all that life has taught him and placed in his subconscious.'[107] Morselli's observations are supported by the ethnologists who warn of the distortions that result from an uncritical comparison between magical elements and psychopathological states. Shirokogoroff writes that, if the observer takes the *standard* of normality or abnormality of his own ethnic milieu as his point of departure, he will probably find much more abnormality in an ethnically-different group, than in his own. Further on, he tells us that the Tungus, during their everyday activities, must come to grips with numerous psychic situations which a superficial observer would call pathological, or even madness. Many of these instances are no more than different

106. Tanzi's works will be found in *Rivista di Filosofia Scientifica* IX, 1890, and X 1891.
107. Morselli: *La psicanalisi* I, p. 318.

cultural phenomena, unknown to the ethnic group to which the observer belongs.[108] He goes on to say that when the observer is examining a strange ethnic group, his attitudes will reflect his own ethnic background, so that he might interpret perfectly normal phenomena as collective psychoses, while sometimes ignoring or failing to recognize what could legitimately be called psychoses; thus many cases which would appear to belong to hysteria are, in actual fact, 'possession by spirits' and, among the Tungus, these would not be considered as the products of individual abnormal dispositions.[109]

As awkward and naively naturalistic as these statements may be, they are nevertheless valid. If the magic existential drama is characterized by the threatened presence that saves itself from the danger of not being within the world, then the moment of danger and the moment of redemption, as well as the disturbance in the structure of the presence and the eventual control and mastery of the temporary loss of horizon, must be examined *within the specific framework of the concrete historical drama* that is characteristic of magic. The basic error of a psychopathology that is unaware of its limitations is that it tends to make abstractions of this *historicity* and to amalgamate everything into the concepts of symptoms, phobias, deliriums, etc. No consideration is given to the relationship between a certain psychological situation and the history and culture in which it arises; it is abstracted and compared artificially to a psychological situation that has a quite different historical background and which offers no real analogy. As an example, we could mention schizophrenic coprophilia and magical coprophilia. The first is the expression of a presence that has torn away from its rightful cultural framework, whilst the second expresses a still-undecided presence, one which is establishing its foundations and is participating in a cultural world and in a public, historical drama that has a permanent, progressive value within the history of civilization.

There is no doubt that the study of psychopathological material does have an important heuristic value for the person

108. Shirokogoroff: op. cit., p. 259.
109. ibid. pp. 263, 268, 269.

who is trying to reconstruct the magic existential drama. We shall recall some cases. There is, for example, the reproduction of magical traits in cases of psychasthenia. According to Janet, in this illness there is a break-down of 'mental tension', that is, a failing of the ability to synthesize and concentrate; this results in a loss of contact with reality and the ability to adapt to it. Consequently, there appears a state of anxiety, a sense of extraneousness and inadequacy and a feeling of alienation from the world outside. The subject feels stranger-like, dominated, depersonalized or divided and sometimes multiplied; he feels he does not have sufficient reality and the world about him loses its naturalness. Such an experience helps us to understand similar cases in the magic world, for example, the feeling that one is 'the victim of a spell'. When suffering from a general anxiety crisis, the psychasthenic patient worries about everything and nothing, and this psychasthenic pantophobia that lies at the basis of various phobias helps us to understand why Aua said to Rasmussen:

'We explain nothing, we believe nothing, but in what I have just shown you lies our answer to all you ask.

We fear the weather spirit of earth, that we must fight against to wrest our food from land and sea. We fear Sila.

We fear dearth and hunger in the cold snow huts.

We fear Takanagapsaluk, the great woman down at the bottom of the sea, that rules over all the beasts of the sea.

We fear the sickness that we meet with daily all around us; not death, but the suffering. We fear the evil spirits of life, those of the air, of the sea and the earth, that can help wicked shamans to harm their fellow men.

We fear the souls of dead human beings and of the animals we have killed'.[110]

But there is more than this. The whole system of compensations that are designed to liberate the psychasthenic from his existential anxiety reminds us of the system of guarantees through which the magic presence escapes the danger that threatens it, although it is necessary to be aware of the limitations of such a comparison.

On the subject of psychasthenic obsessions, Janet writes: 'The ideas that invade the mind during contemplation rep-

110. Rasmussen: *Intellectual Culture of the Iglulik Eskimos*, p. 56.

resent the ideas of another age, the ideas of childhood, the ideas of a former, inferior civilization or of a humbler social milieu, and ideas that are related to dreaming. In conclusion, I maintain that they are ideas that are *inferior* to the ideas that the subject should normally have, given his particular surroundings and circumstances'.[111] Later, he observes that psychasthenic anxieties may be considered as 'phenomena that are inferior to the emotions that should appear at that particular moment'.[112] Janet's comments correspond to what we have called the collapse of the cultural and historical plan to which the person rightfully belongs. The unauthentic character of psychasthenic magic, compared to its historical counter-part, is explained by this 'collapse', which does not occur in real magic. This historical unauthenticity places the *isolated* and *destitute* individual at the mercy of the threatening danger; the morbid trait derives from the evasion of the historical world. Generally, at the initial stages of lability of the presence, it is sufficient to make minor compensations, which we would call weaknesses, superstitions or peculiarities.[113] But in the more serious cases, when the existential threat is developed to its greatest extent, the individual does not have sufficient strength to redeem his presence. He is quite incapable of re-inventing the whole cultural world that would be necessary if the threat was to be made to disappear. This explains how the risk-phase becomes extended, in psychasthenia also, and why all the themes that are related to redemption are ineffectual.

Western civilization is impregnated with the principle of the autonomy of the self. From an *ethical* point-of-view, the first expressions of this great theme—the person as the center of everything—are to be found in the works of the ancient Greeks. In book X of Plato's *Republic,* Lachesis says to the souls: 'It is not the daemon that saves you, but it will be you who choose your daemon. Virtue has no master: each one of you will have either more or less virtue, according to how you honor or scorn it. The fault lies in him who chooses: God is not to blame'. But the real historical movement of the gradual discovery of the person began with

111. Janet: *Les obsessions et la psychasthenie,* Paris 1903, p. 252 ff.
112. ibid., p. 253.
113. cf. Raoul Allier: *Le non-civilise et nous,* pp. 193, 204 ff.

Christianity. It is a vast and complex movement that still forms our cultural destiny and assigns special tasks to the lives of historically-determined men. The basic problem may be found in Jesus' words to the Pharisees: 'The sabbath was instituted by man, not man by the sabbath: for the son of man is also master of the sabbath'. Today, we are still preoccupied with trying to break away from the influence of the 'sabbath', that is, to transform the being that is above us and weighs upon us, to the human liberty of doing and transforming. The task that our cultural destiny has assigned to us reappears constantly, not only in the *ethical* area, but in all the areas of spiritual life, in the theories of knowledge, art and language, in economic, juridical and political life, and in religious experience itself. It is a task that consists in combating the pharisee sabbath, in ridding ourselves of this ambiguity that is perpetually reappearing and which lifts the product of personal activity out of the drama of its production and then proceeds to consider it within the isolation of what is 'given' or 'laid down'.

In Western civilization, this awareness of the autonomy of the person has a sort of ideal high-point which is the discovery of the transcendental unity of self-awareness. So long as speculative thought understood the subject as a consciousness that is *granted* certain contents, then the way remained closed against the establishment of the 'possibility' of the person's autonomy. Whether the point of departure was the 'given fact' of sense-reception or the postulation of value as a given fact, in neither case did the consciousness arrive at an autonomy of form. The empirical analysis of consciousness started with the simple 'sense-impression' and tried to explain, through the rules of association, how the consciousness developed a variety of contents. But this theory of association ignored what constitutes the value and particularity of these contents and failed to explain how these qualifications could be reduced to specificity. On the other hand, the rationalist analysis of consciousness took, as its starting-point, the value that the consciousness would 'rediscover' within itself; but, once more, with this simple 'rediscovery', we come across a fundamental deficiency in the idea that is unable to arrive at autonomy of form. In

the critical treatment of the problem, the increasing consciousness of the self takes the decisive step. The elements
of the ego, the granted facts of reception, are not thought
of as isolated elements, but as presupposing totality of the
consciousness that conditions them.[114] All content of the
consciousness is determinable only as a certain logical,
aesthetic or practical value, etc. It is here that we become
aware of the 'supreme principle' of the transcendental unity
of the awareness of the self. To bring about the opposition
between a 'subject' and a 'world', or a distinction between
the subjective unity of the ego and the objective reality of
what is real, so that a qualitative 'many-valuedness' of
the content of consciousness is possible, it is necessary that
an act of synthetic transcendental fusion takes place, a
unification according to the forms. At this point a new
perspective opens up for research. The transcendental unity
of the awareness of self establishes not only the possibility
of the autonomy of the person, but also the possibility of the
risk to which this autonomy is continually exposed. For this
reason, the form is a constituting action, a 'self-creation';
it includes the opposition, so therefore the risk. In the form
of concept, the risk is error; in the form of art, it is ugliness;
in the form of moral life, it is evil, etc. Besides this, the
supreme principle of the transcendental unity of self-
awareness involves a *supreme risk* to the person—the risk
or threat of losing the supreme principle through which it
is constituted and established. This risk appears when the
person, instead of retaining his autonomy in his relationship
to the contents, abdicates, and allows the contents to act,
outside of the synthesis, as undominated elements, as 'given
facts' in the absolute sense. When confronted with this threat,
it is the person itself that is in danger of disintegrating, of
disappearing as a presence, *because it is incompatible with
the elements and the given facts.* Kant adopted the analytical
unity of apperception as a non-historical and uniform given

114. The relationship between the elements and the totality of the cons-
sciousness is explained in Cassirer: *Philosophie der symbolischen
Formen* I, p. 40. '. . . so, we must think of the general law of the
structure of the consciousness as already given with each of its elements or parts—not as distinct and autonomous contents . . . there is
a predominant quantity of relationships through which the form of
the totality expresses itself simultaneously in the consciousness of the
various parts'.

fact—that is, the thought that belongs to the self, and does not change with its contents, but considers them as an integral part; and he placed the transcendental condition of this given fact within the synthetic unity of the apperception. But elements and given facts of the consciousness do not exist (except through abstraction), nor does a presence exist— there is no empirical being-within-the-world that is a given fact, an original immediate that is sheltered from all danger and incapable, within its own sphere, of any drama or development, or any *history*.[115]

Here we find ourselves faced with a limitation that is characteristic of the historic consciousness of our own civilization. The choices and options authorized by this consciousness are concerned exclusively with what the mind accomplishes according to *particular forms;* in other words, only what one chooses and decides in the forms of art, language, religion and myth, scientific knowledge, economics, politics and law shall enter into history. But what one chooses and decides within the *fundamental form*—the 'supreme principle' of the transcendental unity of self-awareness—shall not enter into history. In fact, the elementary being-within-the-world of the person, which is conditioned and established by the transcendental unity, is our constant companion in cultural life. In other words, within the actual determination and limitation of our historical consciousness, the united being-within-the-world of the person—its presence—takes on the form of the *never-fixed* or similarly the *still-being-fixed* and, because of this, is the same as that which never enters the world of historical decisions. So *our* guaranteed and fixed presence is considered (still within the limitations of our historical consciousness) as the model for every possible historical presence: it is felt that the presence, in every

115. For discussion on our limitations within history, see Kant: *Critique of Pure Reason.* In support of our own ideas, it should be remembered that Pierre Janet was unable to study 'isolated psychological phenomena', except when the subject was in a cataleptic state, that is, when his 'presence' had disappeared and was replaced with that characteristic passivity that gives rise to such phenomena as echokinesis, echolalia, etc. (cf. P. Janet: *L'automatisme psychologique,* chap. I). In the state of 'olon', as previously analyzed, one finds a similar deficiency of the presence, in relation to the isolation of contents. In the techniques used by the sorcerers in order to attain a state of trance, or to reduce the intensity and extension of the presence, means are used to isolate a particular content from the consciousness, e.g. in visual or acoustic monotony, or in emotional intensification.

historical and cultural world, *must* follow this model, and that, in no civilization, can the reality of the absence of the presence become a problem or a self-established reality.[116]

The narrowness of our actual historical outlook is most obvious in the existentialist mind. There is a presupposition common to all existentialist writers—that man is a limited and finite being: 'man, enclosed within an inexplicably finite horizon, within the heart of a humiliated terrestrial existence'. This limitation of the presence is considered as a granted fact, but having an obscure and anxiety-ridden origin, as a 'here' and a 'now' that are independent of the ego, as something that takes on the form of a 'descensus', a collapse. But these experiences and ideas are reflections of our historical debt, as yet unpaid, to that magic age of history in which the being-within-the-world was still an 'in fieri' human option, when the presence was something to be aimed for, a task, a drama and a problem. We are prisoners of the cultural limitation that makes us think of a limited presence as something sinful; in the magic world, however, it is precisely this limited presence that provides salvation; the sinful thing, in the magic world, is the dangerous crossing-beyond of the limits. Greek-Christian anthropology, and the anti-magical polemics that are part of our civilization, have created a chasm and have provoked discontinuity; this is why the being-within-the-world is considered by us as a *perpetual granted fact,* as something given to man by nature, something that is inherent within him and quite apart from any creative activity on his part: consequently, it is considered by us as the acme of the unknown, the irrational, and the mysterious. How is man able to find the *reason* behind those elements

116. The ideas expressed here are an extension of the reaction of modern thought against *reality as such*. There are categorical modes of shaping reality, unifying elements that, by following certain rules, form the reality of the naturalist, the artist, the moral man, the believer, etc. Within each of these modes there is a history, a development of real products. Historical reason has penetrated very deeply into the historiographical reconstruction of reality, following different categorical modes, but it has failed to emphasize the transcendental unity of self-awareness. The presence and the world that makes itself present remain outside the historic process, and are crystallized into a reality which is considered as always having been so. More precisely, the historical form of the presence and of the world as given realities (i.e. fixed and guaranteed) is not considered in its correlation with western civilization, its historicity is not recognized, but is a distinct and separate unity, applicable to all possible civilizations, and hence, also to the magic civilization.

that seem to be quite distinct from any *formulation* that would result from human activity? One hardly crosses the limitations inherent in our present historical awareness than one discovers that the magic world is a form of civilization in which the individual being-within-the-world appears as a *mediate result*—we then develop a heightened awareness and recognition of our former limited outlook. The being-within-the-world is seen as it really is, as something that has been 'granted to me through my participation in human history'; it is seen as a cultural property that has come about through efforts and struggles, through dangers, failures, compromises and eventual victories; and finally, it is seen as a decision and a choice that continues to live today in each of our decisions and choices. Through the history of magic, the obscure 'I am', the dejection of our being-within-the-world, and the experiences related to feelings of sin and down-fall, are deprived of their position as supposed absolutes and are reassimilated into the historical process of which they are just one particular formation. A different epoch and an historical world that is different from ours—the magic world—have accomplished the task of establishing individuality, the being-within-the-world and the presence. Consequently, those things that for us are given facts were, at this stage of history, a task with slowly-developing results.[117]

117. Wahl writes: So, two 'Weltanschauungen' (world-views) come face-to-face; the Weltanschauung of the day, Hegel's, and the Weltanschauung of the night. . . . There are certain souls who reject the day-world, the world of manifest triumph and rational unity that is offered to us by Hegel's philosophy, because they feel themselves imprisoned within it. They choose the world of problems, ruptures and failures where, their eyes fixed upon that transcendance that they cannot see, they constitute a problem for themselves, they remain, for themselves, full of irreducible multiplicities and ruptures, but because of this they perhaps feel more intensely, both within themselves and in their rapports with the 'outside'. J. Wahl: *Etudes Kierkegaardiennes*, Paris, 1938, pp. 170 ff. Wahl bases his two Weltanschauungen on an opposition between two psychological types: there are personalities that prefer the day, and others that prefer the night, people who are at peace in a clarified atmosphere and others, more problematic, who make their interior, dramatically-divided experience into the law of the world. But at this psychological level, in this philosophized reduction of the hopeless fatality of a certain state of mind, all possibility of judgment is lost and there develops a real dilettantism of thought processes. In actual fact, things are quite different from this. Existentialism has put its finger on an obscure point, on an unsolved problem of modern rationalism: the individual as a given fact. But instead of widening the historical awareness of such rationalism until the concrete given fact is resolved in the historical drama of the magical development of the presence, it has pushed its polemics so far that it

If the narrowness of our historical outlook has so far prevented us from penetrating the magic world, the discovery of this world and its problems may serve as a mediating factor so that we arrive, through the widening of our humanism, at a betterment of historical methodology. The historiographical categories that are normally used to understand the various stages of our civilization (or of neighboring civilizations) are shown to be inadequate when dealing with the magic world. Notions that concern language, art, 'logos', 'ethos' etc., cannot be used to qualify and describe magical acts. If they are used, then magic takes on the form of a sort of impotence or penury, as something negative that gradually disappears with the progress of reason. From this point of view, it seems that one may only construct a history of magic art, magic language, logos or ethos, etc., without ever being able to construct a history of magic as such, because history is not made up of what is negative.[118] The characteristic impotence of traditional historiographical categories, in their application to the understanding of the magic world, was revealed, implicitly, by the statement that all the particular forms of the mind appear, in the magic world, as rudimentary, coarse and sketchy,[119] etc.; or when magic was considered as a sort of spiritual disintegration, as a malfunctioning of intelligence, and an obstacle in the way of moral progress, etc.[120] But we now know, as a result of our study, that the main interest of the magic world is not to bring about particular forms of spiritual life, but to master and consolidate the elementary being-within-the-world or presence of the individual. We are now aware that the ideology, praxis

has destroyed every form of rationalism and has elevated to the dignity of thought *not* the solution of the problem, but the experience of the crisis which may be passionately lived through. Through the history of magic, historical reason retrieves its proper rights and judges the claims of those who wish to unseat it from its rightful position.

118. In a letter, written to me on the 24th February, 1941, Adolfo Omodeo made the observation that 'in absolute logic, the history of magic does not exist, because one may make history of what is positive, but not of what is negative: magic is a power that one rids oneself of with the progress of reason, because it shows itself to be inadequate and uncreative'.

119. The thesis according to which all spiritual forms are found, in magic, is mentioned by Carlo Antoni in his commentary on my volume, *Naturalismo e Storicismo nell'etnologia* (in 'Leonardo' XII, 1941, p. 131). Allusions are also made to the absence of will of history, the anonymous and collective nature of life, etc.

120. cf. R. Allier: *Le non-civilisé et nous*.

and institutions of the magic world cannot be understood unless one considers them as the expression of one problem: the wish to defend, master and regulate the threatened being-within-the-world (and, at the same time, establish and maintain world order that is also threatened with disintegration). This anonymous and collective way of life that seems to characterize the magic world, this apparent incapacity to want history, the forbidding of audacious actions, of conflicts and developments—this is how the magic world appears when one persists in examining it according to criteria of development and struggle that are foreign to it, and are incompetent to explain and define it in a precise manner. It is therefore not surprising if we maintain that no drama is involved, that there is only a negative aspect to magic that cannot be the subject of any history. But if we see magic as a movement, as the expression of the dramatic wish to establish oneself and to maintain oneself as a guaranteed presence in a world of clearly-defined things and events then all its drama is revealed. Admittedly, there are also products in magic civilization that may be considered as belonging to art, philosophy, ethos, etc., but the collection and cataloguing of all these products would, in no way, refute our thesis.[121] The thing we want to underline here is that particular forms in the magic world cannot be a central point of interest, and that, consequently, any historical judgment that uses these categories exclusively is destined to fail. How, indeed, could the man of the magic world be freely aware of such interests, and devote himself to them, while his presence is still undecided and identity is still a problem, both for his existence and his life?

Any philosophical system that recognizes only the traditional forms is expressing the methodological moment of an historical experience that is limited to western civilization, and is therefore based on a limited humanism. Such historical reasoning does not acknowledge the essential characteristic of magic; it mentions magic only when referring to the shadows of spirituality that may be found within it and naturally enough prefers to study those manifestations of it

121. On this subject see Radin: *Primitive Man as Philosopher*, New York, 1927.

that occur during the great periods of the history of civilization such as the classical world, Christianity, the Middle Ages,
the Renaissance, etc. Such an interpretation reveals a lack
of true historical awareness, for instead of examining the
thought process that is unable to comprehend in its human
and historical context, it considers it as negative, and as
something deprived of authentic historical reality.

But it is now clear that the power of archaic traditions
that are still strongly active in our daily life, and which
secretly support the diversity of our cultural manifestations,
must be admitted and recognized within the perspective of
historical thought.

We now have before us the image, or at least the broad
outlines of the image, of the magic world. This historical
world plunges its roots into one fundamental experience:
the presence that is exposed to a risk and rises up in its
own defence. The presence does not resist the effort of
being here: it escapes, discharges, submits to evil influences;
it is stolen away, eaten, etc. It is discharged through body
orifices or steals away during solitary wanderings; it is
attracted by corpses, or subjected to some new or unexpected
event. . . . In some cases, the presence's loss of horizon
goes so far that the individual becomes merely an echo of
the outside world, or is possessed by uncontrollable impulses.
The presence is surrounded by a perilous beyond, one that
causes anguish and anxiety and disturbs the presence's horizons; the world also sees its own horizon enter a critical
state and is perpetually passing into this anxiety-ridden
beyond. At the outer limits, every rapport of the presence
with the world becomes a risk, a collapse of the horizon, an
inability to maintain itself, a complete abdication of control:
it is somewhat similar to the situation that causes the schizophrenic subject to enter into a catatonic state, when the
will is placed behind barricades which close spasmodically
against attacks from the outside world. Magic rises up to
fight against this and sets itself against the process of disintegration. It establishes a series of institutions that warn of,
and eventually overcome, the threat. The system of compensations, compromises and guarantees makes possible the
redemption of the presence. By virtue of this cultural formu-

lation, this institutional creation, the existential drama of each individual is no longer isolated; it establishes relationships, becomes part of the tradition and profits from the experiences that are conserved and passed on by tradition. The fleeing presence is apprehended and held in check; through the institution of the alter ego, it makes a dramatic recovery through a compromise with the object that is associated with personal destiny. The dead person sucking away the soul is separated, distanced, fixed and consolidated. The critical moments of existence, linked to long wanderings, solitude, night, etc., are now remodelled into clearly-defined horizons with which the presence develops a regulated and well-adjusted rapport. The world recovers from the threat of collapse, thanks to a new order of participation. The body-orifices are closely supervised and the strength that escapes from them is mastered, controlled, directed and converted into a powerful instrument. Yet all·these themes of magical redemption, and the myriad other themes that magic is composed of, would have been of little importance if it were not for the hero of the presence, the magical Christ— the sorcerer. Because of the sorcerer, the threatening collapse is deliberately averted through human creativity and becomes just a moment in the cultural drama. And, through the sorcerer, the whole community is open to the drama of risk and redemption, endowing it with a new intensity.

Finally, this struggle of the presence that wants to be within the world causes the emergence of forms of reality that are impossible in a civilization founded upon a decided and guaranteed presence, one that has passed beyond the time when identification was still a task to be accomplished and where the horizon of each individual was still a problem. This image of the magic world implies a radical recasting of our cultural 'Einstellung' and, above all, a widening of our concept of reality as one of the categories of examination and judgment. In order to measure the extent of this recasting, let us repeat certain questions in the light of our extended historical horizon: first, the question 'do spirits exist?' The reply accepted is 'there are no spirits and there have never been any. They are the result of superstition, of arbitrary beliefs, belonging to a long-buried historical universe or else to morbid psychological states'. Of course, there are no spirits if we consider as the only form of reality that which holds on to a *fixed and guaranteed* presence within a given world—the attitude of our own civilization. But if we consider not only the question of spirits, but also the question of our own concept of reality, then spirits do become a possibility, and we can no longer give so simplistic an answer. In a cultural order where the unity of the world and its objects is problematic, and still in the throes of being established, there can really be a 'beyond' that is made up of 'forces', 'energies' or 'demons' and 'spirits'. We could also translate such phenomena into our own language and say, for example, that spirits are second existences, or projections and personifications of feeling. But in the historical universe to which they belong, the spirits are every bit as real as the beliefs' of those who know and depict them; only a polemical misunderstanding could debase them to the level of 'arbitrary imaginings'.

There is still a problem. We have drawn a picture of magic in which the actors of the magical drama itself would be quite incapable of recognizing themselves; obviously, they would know nothing about a 'threatened presence', nor 'a system of guarantees or compromises, formed to redeem oneself from the risk of not being here'; nor 'a presence that is in the throes of making a decision about itself and the world'. All of these are worlds apart from the actual magic consciousness. The contention lies in the fact that we consider as the *problem* of magic something that is quite apart from the preoccupations of the actors in the magic drama. But this difficulty arises from a defect in historical method; namely, from the unreasonable insistence upon our notion of what magic is for the men who practise it. We can only attain a proper historical notion of magic through the opening-up of our *own* awareness to new perspectives; it is only *within us,* within our own awareness, that we shall arrive at an exact notion of magic. The meaning of an historical epoch is found within the movement of historic consciousness, and its problems exist only for posterity. Historical truth is not lost in chronological depths, but emerges in the present, creating both problems and a certain historical awareness.

PART III

The Problem of Magical Powers in the History of Ethnology

What was the attitude of ethnology towards the problem of magical powers during its developmental period as a young science? The answer to this question gives us an opportunity to amplify and confirm our basic thesis, by again emphasizing the limitations of our own historical and cultural horizons. One cannot stress too strongly that a sharp awareness of the effects of our own cultural orientation upon the object of study is probably far more important than any close examination of ethnological documents, more important than the organization of expeditions to the actual scenes and places concerned; the main problem for the historian is less to see, read and hear, than to know *how* to see, read and hear. The reaction of our cultural structure becomes more marked according to its sensitivity towards a particular sore-point. The stronger its reactions, the easier it is to see the limitations of our own civilization, its persistent cultural presumptions, its thinly-disguised hostility to the presumptions of the world of magic.

In our researches, we must be prepared to discard, or at least suspend, the ordinary assumptions with which we face our own rational world.

The history of the attitude of ethnology to magic is also the history of the relationship between ethnology and paranormal psychology. This link was made when ethnology was established as the natural science concerned with so-called 'primitive' civilizations. In Edward Burnett Tylor's work, *Primitive Culture, Researches Into the Development of Mythology, Philosophy, Religion, Language, Art and Custom,* the new science of ethnology faces the problem of what to call 'spiritual manifestations'. In 1871, when this work was published, the positive study of paranormal phenomena had hardly taken its first steps: it was the same year that saw the publication of the *Report on Spiritualism of the Committee of the London Dialectical Society,* and the *Experimental Investigations on the Psychic Forces,* by Sir William Crookes.

During the same period, the enthusiasm for spiritualism was spreading over Europe, in ideological forms that were in many ways similar to those of the new ethnological science. Tylor did not have 'positively verified' facts at his disposal, but dealt with rather crude material concerned with 'spiritual manifestations', in which belief and positive research, faith and psychology were all intermingled more or less indiscriminately. Tyler did object to this lack of discrimination, and pointed out the necessity to distinguish between the separate domains of faith and science.[1] But as an author, he did not always maintain this distinction.

Due to the absence of a 'scientifically' verified paranormal phenomenology, Tylor had to limit himself to making a collection of magical and animistic beliefs and opinions, disregarding the problem of their reality. It seems, at first, that Tylor was aware of this problem and he does mention the question of the truth or falseness of various claims and phenomena, setting aside the debate to discuss the history of belief in spirits.[2] However, he soon begins to pass judgments upon all animistic and magical ideology, calling it 'subjective', 'superstitious' and 'savage', and then proceeds to discredit modern spiritualistic ideology, saying that it is merely a derivation of the former. His whole attitude seems to indicate that the reality of paranormal phenomenology has already been disproved. He forgets that he is dealing with facts, undisputed at the level of reality, but only half verified insofar as they have to do with ideology and belief. He proclaims that many so-called magical phenomena are, in fact, simply the work of nature, or of pure chance.[3] He claims that 'magicians' cover up their failures with ambiguous replies, by calling upon some violated taboo or by blaming the more powerful opposition of some other magician. Then, unaware that a theory cannot be founded upon half-verified facts, Tylor sets out a series of 'explanations' of magic in which he affirms that magical procedures are based upon the *subjective* association of ideas that has been mistaken for an objective relationship between things and events.[4] This thesis presupposes at least one thing: that magical practices are *all* subjective and that the verification of their subjectivity is already an acknowledged fact of ethnological science. But such verification was totally lacking in Tylor's time, and even

1. E. B. Tylor: *Primitive Culture*, London 1871, 5th edit. 1913, I, p. 134.
2. Tylor: Op. cit., I, p. 137.
3. Ibid., pp. 115 ff.
4. Ibid., p. 133.

today there is nothing like any definitive ethnological research on this subject. Tylor's thesis is founded on assumptions and dogmatism because it excludes, without any examination, the possibility that magical practices are sometimes based on the actual paranormal powers of the magician excluding, a priori, the possibility that successful divination, for instance, could be due to real metagnomic powers such as clairvoyance, telepathy, precognition and retrocognition; hence, the careful distinction that we found in the beginning, between belief and the basis for belief, has been completely obliterated.[5]

At this point one wonders how Tylor, who showed such respect for 'facts', believed that a verification, one that had never even been broached, had been carried to its 'logical' end; one also wonders why he began by placing a limit on his research and then completely effaced this limit. Indeed, an emotional and polemical theme does run through Tylor's work, and in no way contributes to his reasoning; we see a struggle against superstition and the necessity to explain the existence of spirits. Tylor has plunged once more into antimagical polemics which Western civilisation has taken as their own throughout the centuries and shown himself to lack the calm and detachment that are necessary if one is to search for an adequate solution to the problem of 'spiritual manifestations'.

It appears that he recognizes the problem, but in reality he is not even disposed to approach it with the elementary purpose of verifying the facts. It is true that, in his time, there was not the least positive demonstration of the reality of magical powers; but the systematic verification of their illusory character was also absent. When documentation is lacking, then emotion takes its place and pretends that the documents would coincide with the ideas that emotion would wish to see expressed.

Tyler begins by mentioning the possibility of a fresh approach to magic and animism which involves giving a scientific consideration to the 'spiritual manifestations' (that is, to paranormal phenomenology), but, in fact, he takes a path diametrically opposed and tries to discredit the claims of modern magicians ('spiritualists') by setting out a tableau

5. Tyler: Op. cit., p. 133.

of the superstitious and barbarous world where such claims were originally manifest. The study of spiritualism and its comparison with ethnological documents shows, according to Tylor, that in the former, there is a resurgence of ideological forms that belong mainly to the philosophy of primitive ages and to traditions of folk lore.[6] Elsewhere he says that the history of belief in spirits shows us that it is in primitive science that we must search for the explanation of phenomena that are related to the intervention of spirits.[7] The polemical bias becomes even more obvious when he writes that, in order to find an example of the direct influence of antiquity and barbarity on our modern way of life, it suffices to see the relationship between the spiritualism of savages and the beliefs that, in his time, had so profoundly penetrated our civilization.[8]

Tylor's attitude towards the problem of 'magical powers' set a precedent. More than seventy years after the publication of his famous work,[9] the dominating tendency of religious ethnology had undergone very little change or modification. Ethnologists working in this field continued to obtain only a semi-verification of magical facts, derived from occasional and sporadic observations. Their starting point was the 'pretensions' or 'claims' of the magicians, and they took them, a priori, as 'unfounded' and 'subjective'. Using these, they tried to explain the psychological mechanism that gives rise to 'illusory' beliefs. Very little attention has been paid to the other thesis that attempts to make a systematic explanation of what true and real elements can be found in magical powers, and any result that have been achieved have been of rather poor quality.

The newly-developed European psychology of the second half of the 19th century, the studies on hypnotism, suggestion, and dual personality—and above all the material collected by the Society of Psychical Research—could not remain immune to the influence of religious ethnology in general, and to the ethnological problem of magic in particular. The first person to place this abundant research at the disposal

6. Tyler: Op. cit., I, p. 142.
7. Ibid., p. 155.
8. Ibid., p. 159.
9. Op. cit.

of ethnology was an English anthropologist and man of letters, Andrew Lang. He was a man of great erudition and insatiable curiosity, a non-conformist with a certain romantic propensity towards everything that could disturb, even momentarily, the rational order of things. So, for him, it was a point of honor to fight against the current ideas of evolution and materialism, and he chose as his battleground the area of fact. He set about doing this in two ways: firstly, by discovering autochthonal origins of the 'supreme beings' of primitive races, and secondly, by indicating paranormal facts which could be at the basis of animistic and magical beliefs. In the first case, his obvious intention was to show the inconsistencies in the 'dogma of evolution'; in the second case, he was attempting to endorse the hypothesis of the origins of religion, based on facts that are perhaps not entirely in agreement with materialism in its present dogmatic form.[10] It is nevertheless necessary to underline the limits of this basically 'naturalistic' position. Lang takes as his starting point a belief that was reported by Hearne in his *Journey*, published in 1795. Among the Indian tribes of North America, the aurora borealis was depicted as a herd of reindeer that crossed the sky causing the sparkles to appear. This image is based on a sound observation, that is, that if a reindeer's fur is rubbed at night-time this causes sparks to appear. As, in this case, an arbitrary notion has been based on a sound observation, one can suppose, generally, that other sound observations lie at the base of numerous other arbitrary notions held by primitive races. Thus the series of positive facts that motivated the animistic ideology may not necessarily be limited to those facts that are 'normal' and 'acceptable to the community'—sleep, dream, shadow, ecstasy, death—but may be based on other facts that are rejected by modern science, such as clairvoyance, telepathy, etc. And as science recognizes the soundness of the observation upon which the Indians based their absurd notion, it could also find itself obliged to take into account the various primitive observations related to paragnostic, and more generally, 'paranormal' facts.

Among the vast quantity of information concerning para-

10. A. Lang: *The Making of Religion*, 1900, 2nd Edit., p. 43.

normal phenomena among the primitive races, Lang refers, in particular, to Tylor's work *Primitive Culture*. Lang states that Tylor apparently considers it outside the limits of his thesis to examine the actual reality of the phenomena, both in the primitive and civilized worlds. Similar to the works of other anthropologists, such as Huxley and Spencer, Tylor bases a theory of the origins of religion on ethnological foundations. This is explained as being the result of crude and false reasoning about certain biological and psychological facts, whether normal, or (in the minds of primitive people), supernatural. This sort of reasoning leads to belief in souls and spirits. If supernatural phenomena such as clairvoyance, telepathy, ghosts of the dead and dying are actually experienced, then it is possible that the conclusions drawn by primitive people after such experiences are quite erroneous. However, conclusions drawn by the materialists, who reject supernatural phenomena, are also probably incomplete.[11]

Lang considers paranormal facts as 'natural facts' that may be observed and employed in experiment by modern science, just as they were the object of observation and deduction of primitive science. He envisages the possibility of a collaboration between paranormal psychology and religious ethnology which would open up the way to a more complete understanding of the natural causes of magical-animistic ideology. It would also widen the outlook of modern scientific materialism through the recognition of an order of positive facts that 'science' had, until now, completely neglected. It is convenient to stop at this point in Lang's thought, because he has provided an example of that offshoot of ethnological studies which is identified by an interest in the problem of 'magical powers'. It is certainly possible to consider paranormal facts *as if* they were natural facts. It is even useful to consider them as such to examine more closely the problem of their reality. It is wrong to presume that they are to be completely understood by considering them through the eyes of a naturalist, forgetting that they are *cultural facts* and that, as such, they belong to a special historical universe in which they are the expression of an *existential drama*. Instead of remembering this drama (the

11. Lang: *The Making of Religion.*

presence that wants to be within the world), and instead of seeing these powers as part of its development, we introduce our various scientific considerations into the magic world, and imagine that the man belonging to this world has *observed* the paranormal phenomena exactly as we ourselves would observe some phenomenon in nature, and that he has then taken them as the basis for his erroneous notions. Instead of reconstructing the magical link between the presence and the world, as is expressed in paranormal reality, we endow the magical age with our own decided and guaranteed presence and a *given* world; we lose sight of the fact that the real problem is not created by the man of the magic world who *observes* the paranormal phenomena, but rather by the presence which, engaged in the characteristic drama of magic, *produces, conditions and regulates* these phenomena by expressing the drama through them. The error lies in the dogmatic supposition that, because of the constant efficiency of the realistic attitude, there is a *given* nature that is either normal or paranormal, usual or unusual, and that there is the presence, determined in a univocal fashion, according to the model offered by Western civilization. The presence is seen as sometimes observing paranormal facts (as in the case of magic) and sometimes—it is not known why—either ignoring them or observing them insufficiently or badly, as in the case of the cultured man. However, the magic world has this one main characteristic— neither the presence nor the world are yet *given facts*.[12]

Although Lang remained within the limits imposed by a purely naturalistic methodology, he did at least underline the links between the ethnological document and the paranormal document, and attempt to integrate them. As an ethnologist, Lang emphasized the value of ethnological proof of the actual *beliefs* in paranormal phenomena that are held by primitive peoples. As a psychologist, he asserted the value of parapsychological proof in the establishment of the *reality* of these phenomena. Finally, as both ethnologist and psychologist, he

12. The scientists' idea that paranormal facts were observed by primitive peoples, while being neglected or denied-by modern science, leads to the false problem of a barbarous wisdom that, on this subject, is superior to our own knowledge; this gave rise to the romantic idea of the hermetic wisdom of the ancients, etc. Traces of this are found in Tylor's work, while Lang attempted to avoid it.

emphasized the fact that the ethnological uniformity of paranormal phenomenology, and its agreement with the corresponding cultivated phenomenology, forbids us to be content to establish a simple ideological analogy as Tylor had done. As far as the results of his research are concerned, Lang places psychic phenomena that engender animism together with paranormal facts: that is, metagnomic phenomena in general, telepathic hallucinations in particular, the mysterious movement of objects and so called evil spells, etc. Without giving any definite decision on the actual paranormal character of telekinetic phenomena, he advances the theory that such phenomena perhaps contributed towards the development of fetishism, or the belief that a spirit enters an object and acts, communicates or expresses itself through it. As we see, these are both very modest and very arguable points, at least, as expressed by Lang. He is unaware that it is essentially a question of the genesis of magical-animistic ideology, based on observed facts, and not a question of the spiritual and cultural conditions that make these facts possible and give them some meaning.

Lang does not exploit the possibilities of his line of thought with regard to the 'magical powers', holding to the thesis that magic is a collection of purely subjective phenomena. Like Tylor, he asserts that 'primitive' man, having associated two facts or objects in his mind, confuses this mental relationship with one that really exists. He then begins to explain events through procedures that we assess as purely subjective.[13]

We have already remarked that the 'naturalistic' examination of paranormal facts, when it goes beyond its limits, is tempted to endow the 'primitives' with our own attitudes as 'observers' and 'explorers', forgetting that the cultural conditions that encourage such phenomena are historically quite distinct from scientific attitudes. This weakness leads us to yet another arguable point: the claim that one can scientifically demonstrate the survival of the soul and communion between the living and the dead through observation and experiment, forgetting that animistic ideology, as an historical formation, may be 'reconstructed' only in the cultural milieu of which

13. Lang: *Magic and Religion*, 1901, passim.

it is a part. It is true that the Society for Psychical Research wished to restrict itself to the examination of facts, but it is also true that many of its members, Lodge, for example, were sooner or later tempted towards a sort of 'spiritualism', this was a remarkable hybrid product, part pseudo-science, part pseudo-magic and part pseudo-religion. This state of affairs did much to prevent a fruitful collaboration between paranormal psychology and ethnology. Ethnologists began to feel justified in considering 'animistic beliefs' and 'magical powers' as 'superstitions', and to hold the research of these men to be suspect. A discussion between Lang and Clodd, in 'Folk-Lore' provides an interesting and instructive document on this crisis in the relationships between the two young sciences. Clodd, in his presidential address to the meeting of 16th January, 1895, made particular mention of the problem of 'psychical research'.

The polemical argument against the Society's claims was the same as the one used by Tylor in his attack upon spiritualism. Clodd says that paranormal psychology, when analyzed in the light of ethnology, appears as nothing more than a duplication of barbarian spiritualistic philosophy. The old animistic elements are simply dressed up in vague and pompous words and expressions, such as 'subliminal consciousness', 'telepathic energy', the 'immortality of the psychic principle', the 'temporary materialization of supposed spirits' etc. He makes a bitterly ironic attack on various forms of propaganda used by the society which, admittedly, cannot be taken very seriously—for example, it offered crystal balls of varying diameters for sale. Of the members of the society, he says, 'We may bracket them all together, the vulgar materialists and the "psychists". The scientifically-orientated members, some of them quite respected, are blamed for giving up their dearest principles, once they step outside of their own domain, to become the most fervent advocates for the acceptance of "fact" on faith alone'.[14] It is nevertheless difficult to prove that Clodd's comments were completely just. The 'spiritualistic' side of some of the Society's members did justify the scorn that was directed at them by the men of science; those who were more faithful to the obligations and

14. 'Folk-Lore' VI, 1895, pp. 78-81.

limits of really serious scientific research. This does not
prevent Clodd's arguments from being tainted with the usual
basic error, the persistent and naive realism of the 'naturalist'.
Echoing the position taken up by Wundt some years previously,[15] Clodd wonders how men, for whom there is an
organized nature with fixed laws, can nevertheless believe in
the possibility of a systematic violation of these laws by
mediums and 'sensitives'. It is as if two natures exist side
by side—one belonging to science, the other subject to the
whims and caprices of individuals who are not only mediocre,
but frequently hysterical! This argument is obviously based
upon the dogmatic presupposition that nature has always
been a 'given fact', as it is in our own civilization, and that,
as seen or perceived by a fixed presence, no other nature is
possible. Clodd holds only to the relationship between
presence and world that belongs to our civilization; he does
not see it as developmental. This is the same presupposition
as held by Lang, and one that we have already criticized.
Clodd, however, pushes his emotional intransigence even
further than Lang, and goes so far as to consider man's
powers over nature exclusively within the framework of
possibilities related to the presence-world rapport of our own
civilization. But surely such an approach to the problem of
magical powers is strongly colored by cultural presumption?

Lang attempted to reply to the polemical arguments of
the presidential address. He admits that the specialists concerned had no authority as observers in the area of psychic
research. But who, then, would one consider as having
appropriate authority? Perhaps a trickster, or prestidigitator?
And if these were puzzled by some phenomena, to whom
would one turn? Clodd asserted that the 'phenomena' did not
demonstrate the existence of a spirit-world. Lang replies by
asking who is speaking of spirits. He points out that Oliver
Lodge spoke only of physical phenomena and certainly not
of any spirits. Unfortunately, Clodd was provided with some
justification for his scorn when Lodge did finally end up by
talking of 'spirits', as did many others, among them, the
famous physician E. Wallace, who 'communicated' with his

15. See Chapter I.

dead son during the first World War.[16] Lang also points out the distinction between paranormal phenomena and spiritualistic ideology. Clairvoyance using a crystal ball may be interpreted according to the doctrine of spirits: this does not alter the fact that, quite apart from the doctrine, the hallucination is effective, and that this phenomenon does merit some study, one that would also include the ethnological point-of-view. Even if it can be successfully demonstrated that all these 'so-called' paranormal phenomena were the result of bluff and trickery, the subject would still be of interest to the specialist in folk-lore. Supposing that the levitation carried out by Home, and observed by Crookes, was nothing more than a trick, then this would give the folklorist the opportunity to seize hold of the origins of a most important element in folkloric beliefs.

'But Mr. Crookes, a distinguished man of science, acted as a good folklorist. He went to see Mr. Home. I have rarely been more curiously impressed than when I heard Mr. Crookes very gravely aver that he had seen Mr. Homes rise in air, in full light in a drawing room, had felt all round his body, and had discovered no material supports. Here was a gentleman whose word science accepts to a millimetre for accuracy of observation, yet he tells us this! And he is only one out of dozens.

"Here," I said to myself, "is the explanation of the large folklorist and hagiological chapters about levitation. What was good enough for Mr. Crookes was good enough for Australian blacks, Presbyterians, Celts, Platonists, Peruvians, Catholics, Puritan divines, and all the other witnesses. They, or some of them, had received the impression which Mr. Crookes received; hence the stories."

Again, I presume that Mr. Clodd does not deny the possibility of inducing artificial slumber without the use of drugs, and of making suggestions which have the force of reality to the patient? If he denies it if he says with Lord Kelvin that hypnotism is all imposture and malobservation, I am silenced, except from bad words. But if he cannot carry scepticism to that pitch, then I think that the facts, as far as he admits them, account for much that occurs in folk-lore, namely for tales of "glamor", and for the behavior of the so-called "bewitched" patients. Thus

16. See his book, *Raymond*.

folklore and psychical research are again on common ground. Yet where comes in "the old animism"? Or will Mr. Clodd say, "There is nothing at all in hypnotism, nothing at all in the evidence of Mr. Crookes, except survival from the mental condition of savagery. Mr. Crookes, under that inherited stress, deceived himself, and thought he saw what he did not see. The countless French, German, and Italian savants who write on hypnotism are all in the same condition, all slaves of hereditary instincts, and victims of the survival of the unfittest ideas." It would be odd that the least "fit" of all ideas should "survive" with such vigor!

Conceivably, though not probably Mr. Clodd may explain, at least, Mr. Crookes's view of the floating Home in this way. Let it be so, is it not worth while to examine a survival, or inherited capacity, which can make a sane man of science tell such a tale, and be "in a tale" with savages and priests.

If we meet rustics who are treasures of traditional beliefs and observances, we do not discourage or laugh at, but cherish and fondly observe, them. They are survivals! In the same way, taking Mr. Lodge, F.R.S., the learned Professor Sidgwick, the poetic Mr. Myers, the healing genius of M. Richet as (on this ground) mere survivals of old animistic philosophy, why should we discourage them? If the censures of our President smote the conscience of these worthy but retrograde physicists, physicians, and so on if they ceased to carry on what Mr. Clodd thinks their foolish old business, I deem that we should be depriving ourselves of raw material.

Last year Mr. Basil Thomson sent me his "South Sea Yarns", with the tale of how he saw, in a religious ceremony, Fijians march unscorched through a trench filled with stones on which a great fire had been lighted. The stones were hot enough to scorch a handkerchief laid on them, but they neither harmed the Fijians nor even burned their ankle fillets of dry fern. That same day a Bulgarian gentleman told me of a similar rite in rural Bulgaria. Virgil, as you know, mentions an exactly parallel religious performance. Mr. Lang, from New Zealand, refers me to the Journal of the Polynesian Society, vols. ii and iii, with a photograph of the fire-walkers. Mr. Thomson, by the way, also sent me a photograph, which I exhibit, with the scorched handkerchief.

In these cases an animistic theory explains, among savages and Romans, the failure of fire to burn. I shall not trouble you with cases from saintly legend, from the Bible from missionary records, from mediæval ordeals, or from Iamblichus. These stories are surely within the province of folklore. But, as soon as they are told on the evidence of living and honorable men, psychical research also examines them. Now, what is the folklorist's attitude to be? Is he to refuse to listen to Mr. Thomson, Mr. Crookes (in Home's case), the writers in the Polynesian journal, Father Brebeuf, and others, merely because they say that they have seen phenomena of which savages and others give an animistic explanation? Here is on one side a folk-lore belief in certain phenomena. On the other side is the evidence, to the same phenomena, of cameras and of the eyes of living and distinguished men. Surely the cause which makes Mr. Thomson and the rest tell their story, is the cause which inspires folk-lore tradition to the same effect. And what is that cause? I do not think that folk-lore should be careless to know merely because psychical research is curious to know.

My conclusion is that certain obscure facts are, or may be, at the bottom of many folklore beliefs. Since psychical research investigates the alleged facts, as a folklorist I welcome in her an ally. Already, in my opinion, psychical research has explained the world-wide practice of "specularii", the tales of magic mirrors, by showing that as a matter of every-day fact, a proportion of persons can provoke hallucinations by looking into a clear deep. When Sir Walter Scott, a folklorist, intended to investigate this phenomenon in Egypt, he became, in intention, a psychical researcher. Are we to condemn him?

What I cannot understand is this: as long as a savage, mediæval, or classical belief (as in Fire-Walking) rests only on tradition it interests the Folklorist. As soon as contemporary evidence of honorable men avers that the belief reposes on a fact, Folklore drops the subject. Psychical Research then takes it up, because a "psychical" explanation of the phenomenon has been given by mystics. I can understand why Psychical Researchers become interested, but I cannot see why Folklorists cease to be interested. Whatever else the Fire-Walk may be, it is a piece of Folk-lore. When psychical students are accused, en masse, of approaching their subjects with a dominant prejudice, the charge, to me seems inaccurate (as a matter of fact) and, moreover, very capable of being retorted. Not the man who listens to evidence, but the man who refuses to listen (as if he were, at least negatively, omniscient) appears to me to suffer from a dominant prejudice.'17

Clodd's reply to Lang's 'protestation' contains the usual mixture of prudence, legitimate scorn and a priori polemical condemnations. He explains that what gives rise to suspicion and, to some extent, supports criticism, is not psychical research in itself, but rather the methods used by those involved in it. The committee set up for the examination of 'hallucinations' concluded that they possessed facts supporting 'the theory of the continuity of the psychic life and of the possibility of communicating with the dead'; they also decided, unanimously, that there was proof of a relationship between death and the appearance of the dying person that was not due to chance alone ('Report of the Committee' in 'Proc. Soc. R.P.', 26th part, p. 394). Clodd criticizes the committee's make-up, its working-methods and its conclusions which, in his opinion, were due to the persistent influence of old animistic themes. To Lang's argument that nobody had spoken of spirits, Clodd replied that, even if Crookes or Sidwick did not employ the term, it was nevertheless certainly in their thoughts. There is no denying that Clodd's comments on this matter are justified. But, once more, he begins to confuse the issues and rejects the actual object of psychic research; that is, he denies the existence of any paranormal phenomenology. He thinks that such 'phenomena' may be explained by hallucinations and trickery, and points out that the fallibility of human senses has been the source of much of man's error. On the subject of the Fijian firewalkers, Clodd is convinced that the whole performance is faked. He refers to the callosity of the natives' feet, which allows them to bear a degree of heat that we would be unable to tolerate, even in our shoes. He remarks that the native prestidigitators are just as skilful as the more cultured variety, and that the participants are probably just as aware of the hardening effect of sulfuric acid on the skin. Clodd argues against the possibility of an effective liaison between

17. 'Folk-Lore' VI, 1895, pp. 236-248.

psychical research and folklore, and he concludes: 'The psychical researcher represents a state of feeling, the folklorist represents an order of thought.'[18]

In the discussions between Lang and Clodd, the dispute between paranormal psychology and ethnology came to a deadlock. Paranormal phenomenology had still not furnished any really strictly-established results, and psychical research was in danger of becoming a science without any real aim, other than un-masking tricksters and charlatans. Even Lang himself was unable to quote one certain, acceptable result of psychic research, except 'visions in a crystal ball'—something which, in any case, is only indirectly related to the subject. It was precisely because of the problematic character of this young science that Lang had to resort, in order to support the collaboration between ethnology and metapsychics, to pointing out that the unmasking of tricks and the study of bizarre hallucinations could be of some value to the ethnologist and folklorist. This was an altogether unfortunate argument, because it almost pointed towards a denial of the existence of 'paranormal phenomena' as such. Also, the spiritualistic attitudes of many members of the Society further complicated the question and discredited the other more serious members. But Clodd himself may well be attacked for his assertion that the only possible universe is that of the naturalist.

However, there were deeper reasons for the crisis between ethnology and paranormal psychology. Even though the latter was eventually purified of its 'spiritualistic' under-tones, and made great efforts to transform itself into a pure science of observation and experimentation, leading to the establishment of the fact of paranormal phenomena; although it led many scientists to a more flexible attitude towards the possible and impossible, and helped to confirm certain 'strange' powers possessed by some sorcerers and Shamans—despite all this, there was no systematic integration of the two sources of documentation, no great change in ethnological study was brought about, nor was there introduced any new, fruitful approach to the problem of 'magical powers'. The two disciplines remained separated, either through the artificiality

18. 'Folk-Lore' VI, 1895, pp. 248-258.

of academic categorization or else through superficial naturalistic comparisons. Because of the absence of any real historical definition of the magic world, the problem of
magical powers remained caugnt in a web of difficulties and
contradictions. Two main paths were followed: those concerned either denied the existence of facts, limiting themselves
to the ideology alone, or else the facts were recognized,
giving rise to the insoluble problem of their possibility in
our physical world, with which they were basically in conflict.
The error lay in thinking that the natives observed them in
the same manner as Western man, with one difference—the
former drew erroneous conclusions. But there still remained
a question to be answered: How could the primitives have
observed these facts, whilst civilized man had missed them,
even to the point of denying their existence, despite the
observations of a 'civilized' witness? Then, to complicate
the question still further, there came the intervention of
tricks and frauds, either supposed or proven, to cast a shadow
of discredit over the whole subject. Then there were the
spiritualistic interpretations, based on paranormal facts, that
blossomed throughout Western civilization and seemed to
confirm the essentially superstitious nature of the study.
There were yet other difficulties: the magic world advanced
claims that were clearly subjective and in no way verifiable;
pure beliefs with no firm basis in reality—such as incredible
communications and completely illusory practices, etc. People
were unaware of the relationship between these obvious
superstitions and the reality, however tenuous, that appeared
to be included in certain communications. There was no
unifying principle that took into account the utter diversity
of magical manifestations, a principle that would open the
way to true understanding and fruitful results. Under such
conditions, it is not surprising that the ethnologist refused
to become completely involved in the question and that he
continued his work, paying no attention to Lang's objections.

One could give many examples of the inertia of 'paranormal phenomenology' within religious ethnology, and show
the failure of metaphysical facts to cause any deep, lasting
renewal of research within the area of 'magical powers'. We
shall limit ourselves to taking some examples from the

Encyclopaedia of Religion and Ethics, the most comprehensive modern work concerned with the 'science of religions'. In Lewis Spence's article on Amerindian divination,[19] one reads that there are numerous proofs of the American Indians' ability to predict events, that there is hardly any question of their not possessing gifts of clairvoyance. However, in the article that actually introduces the subject, J. H. Rose states that divination is a false and deceptive science.[20] Elsewhere,[21] we read a report of an apparently metagnomic exploit by a Cumana sorcerer, as witnessed by Antonio de Herrera, and references are made to similar exploits among Peruvian magicians, reported by Jose de Acosta; but the whole question is treated without depth. H. B. Alexander quotes David Leslie's experience (see our quote) but makes the observation that, if one believes this, then all the claims of the civilized world's clairvoyants become credible.[22] Lang, in his article 'Savage and Modern Dreams', writes of clairvoyant dreams etc., and in the article on crystal-gazing, he reports on metagnomic aptitudes that may become apparent through visions in a crystal ball; as a basis, he quotes the studies of Miss Goodich Freer that appeared in the 'Proceedings of the Society of Psychical Research', as well as his own observations.

Some progress was made by Otto Stoll in the study of magic powers.[23] Stoll applied the results of research into hypnotism and suggestion (carried out in the latter half of the nineteenth century) to ethnic psychology, and helped to make the idea of 'successful' magical practices acceptable, but he gave no credit to paranormal psychology which, in his opinion, was confused with 'spiritualism', 'theosophy' etc.[24] (this, of course, was partly due to the members of the

---

19. 'E.R.E.' IV, p. 782. On the subject of Amerindian prophecies concerning the coming of the white man, and also concerning the visions of Princess Papantzin, sister of Montezuma, see Spence's article in 'E.R.E.' X, p. 381.
20. 'E.R.E.' IV, p. 775.
21. 'E.R.E.' I, p. 434.
22. ibid. XI, pp. 7730 ff.
23. O. Stoll: *Suggestion und Hypnotismus in der Volkerpsychologie,* Leipzig 1894, 2nd edit. 1904.
24. Stoll mentions his surprise at discovering that a respected scientist-friend is involved in the mysticism of a Madame Blawatsky. He later blames this on the unfortunate effects of suggestion that led men like Crookes, Wallace, Zollner to take up spiritualism and damage their reputations as scientsts.

'Society') and he tried to reduce all paranormal phenomena to the effects of 'suggestion'. He therefore chooses to deny or at any rate ignore the beginning of paranormal elements that are sometimes found in certain phenomena of suggestion. Thus, when one says that someone may die, be cured or become insensitive to pain through the effects of suggestion, one admits, implicitly, an extension of the powers of the will into an area that is 'normally' inaccessible to them; but the whole accent is placed upon the suggestion process, and the fact of the extension of power is minimized. It is nevertheless true that Stoll's studies did draw attention to the real efficacy of certain magical practices. Ethnological science eventually admits that the violation of some taboo may have a fatal result, that the sorcerer's therapeutic magical practices may have a positive effect, and that hoodoo can actually kill. On this last point, Wundt wrote: 'The enemy whose effigy is pierced does not suffer symbolically, but actually, even if the instrument that goes through his image cannot touch his real body. But it is able to touch his soul or spirit, and, in this way, it may cause sickness and death to his body. It is correct to insist that suggestion plays a very important role in such instances. It can help to consolidate all sorts of magical beliefs, because the conviction that one has been the object of hoodoo can, in the end, make one sick and paralyze onces resistance to such a danger, thus producing the actual intended effects.'[25]

Alfred Lehmann's work, *Aberglaube und Zauberei von den altesten Zeiten an bis in die Gegenwart*,[26] does not really make any significant contribution to the subject. Lehmann was the product of a scientifically-orientated cultural climate; a student of the Copenhagen polytechnical school, he was influenced by Wundt's *Grundzuge der physiologischen Psychologie* (Elements of Physiological Psychology) and became interested in psychophysiological studies. In Leipzig, he was Wundt's student. Perhaps the best expression of his thought

25. W. Wundt: 'Volkerpsychologie' IV, 2nd edit. 1910, p. 278. On this subject, Wundt quotes Stoll, op. cit. Documentation on the subject will be found in Frazer: *Taboo and the Perils of the Soul*, 3rd edit. 1911, pp. 134 ff.
26. 'Superstition and Magic from Ancient Times to Present Day' Translated from the Danish by Petersen. Stuttgart (Enke) 1925, 3rd edit; original, 1896.

is found in *Die elementare Aesthetik der Farbe* (The Elementary Aesthetics of Color) in which he tries to determine the physical conditions that render a combination of colors 'pleasing'. So it is not surprising if he outlines the psychology of 'superstition' and 'magic' in the following manner: 'As everything in this world, magic cannot be without its *causes*. When a man thinks he has seen a ghost, there is no doubt that·he has seen something. This could be a curtain floating near an open window and reflecting the moonlight, or else it could be the product of a morbid state of mind; in either case, something is definitely perceived; only the explanation of the perception is erroneous. So, behind all superstitious imaginings there are certain observations, the meaning of which have been simply misunderstood. Superstition is certainly formed by errors. Just as it is interesting to show the error and false explanation of certain observations, it is equally interesting to identify the physical and psychic phenomena that caused these errors . . . In fact, it is legitimate to designate certain concepts as erroneous and superstitious only if one can demonstrate that these concepts are created as a result of the erroneous explanation of certain facts which, upon subsequent reflection, should be understood in a quite different manner. This is why, throughout my work, I place such importance upon this definitive research.'[27] Instead of carrying out some positive research into the actual extent of paranormal phenomenology, and instead of making an historical judgment of the cultural aspect of magical powers and the existential drama that produces them, Lehmann tends to deny the reality of all paranormal phenomenology; he suggests a scientific analysis of the *causes* of superstition. These 'errors of observation' that the author considers to be the cause of superstition and magic could be of use as an example. An unusual octopus was at the roots of the legend of the giant 'kraken', and a rhinoceros gave rise to the legend of the unicorn. Regarding the origins of the art of divining and of belief in prophecies, Lehmann reminds us of the hyperaesthesia, hypermnesia and cryptomnesia that are often found in the 'prophet',[28] and of the suggestibility

27. A. Lehmann: *Aberglaube und Zauberei*, p. 14.
28. Lehmann: op. cit., pp. 541 ff., 546, 643.

of the person to whom the prophecy is made.[29] The movements of the divining rod, the so-called turning tables,
and automatic writing are all 'unconscious movements' that
appear through the influence of certain agencies and certain
emotions. When one attributes such movements to 'magical
force' or to the actions of 'spirits', etc., there is, in fact, a
real and positive phenomenon behind this explanation, but
as one is unaware of the actual cause, ignorance and
weaknesses in our reasoning powers make us search for the
solution in a product of our own imagination.[30] Magic
therapeutics may have successful results, hence it has a
certain positive basis; but when a cure is attributed to the
'power' of the magician, or to the help of some spirit, and
when the sickness is seen as the result of an evil spell, there
is once more evidence of a lack of critical approach: it is
all a question of suggestion, and this is the only real cause.[31]
Suggestion also explains the successes of 'black magic'.[32] On
the subject of telepathy, Lehmann admits that 'There are
certain facts that are difficult to explain without accepting
the hypothesis that telepathy does exist, because the actual
conditions surrounding the phenomenon are still unknown'.[33]
But immediately after (apparently afraid that this concession
may undermine the absolute nature of the scientific concept
of nature), he explains that the hypothesis of telepathy does
not violate the laws of nature, because the phenomenon is so
remarkably similar to the wireless, telephone, etc. The only
problem would be how to demonstrate scientifically the
manner in which the telepathic transmission takes place.
In the use of the divining rod, one could put forward the
hypothesis—until a more positive demonstration is possible
—that the human brain might be influenced by the presence
of certain radiations.[34] Lehmann rejects the possibility of
clairvoyance.[35]

Because of the insufficient experimental basis, and the

29. ibid. p. 630.
30. ibid. pp. 478 ff.
31. ibid. p. 633.
32. ibid. p. 636.
33. ibid. p. 594.
34. Lehmann: op. cit., p. 594 ff. He generally admits the reality of so-
called geopsychic phenomena, such as water divining, etc., and also the
agitation of animals before an earthquake, volcanic eruption, etc.
35. ibid. p. 595.

'naturalistic' manner of considering the problem, it is not surprising that Lehmann retains the current concept of magic as a 'superstition'. According to him, it was the lack of the technical means of mastering nature, and the strength of certain human desires, that led to the birth and development of magical practices; they were used to satisfy these desires because nothing better was offered.[36] The laws that regulate the association of ideas and images—association by contiguity and by resemblance—form the psychological foundation of magical operations.[37] The author nevertheless concedes that the sorcerer is not a vulgar charlatan who knowingly uses tricks in order to retain his position and power within the community; he is rather the son of his race and of his era, and is firmly convinced that his skills are effective. To admit the absurdity of his beliefs, he would have to possess knowledge that he does not have, and above all, he would have to know how to avoid making errors of observation as did modern specialists such as Crookes and Lodge who, because of this, caused 'magic and superstition to be born a second time in their laboratories.'[38] The magician is prisoner of the beliefs that tradition has passed on to him and which are easily maintained within the milieu in which he lives; he is as much mistaken as his own spectators. Even when he fails, belief in him is not lessened because his failure is explained away by saying that a more powerful agency had interfered. Briefly, magical methods are *absurd,* and magic is a false technique, founded on insufficient or misinterpreted observation.[39]

Lehmann's statements concerning the problems of magic and magical powers are clearly tainted by the usual basic error. He judges magic according to our concept of reality as a 'natural given fact' or a 'decided and guaranteed phenomenon', and dogmatically presupposes that this form of reality is applicable and valid in all civilizations. Lehmann depicts an 'observer' of nature, one who sometimes 'observed' badly (from whence magic and superstition), and sometimes observed precisely (science and truth). He tries to give

36. ibid. p. 25.
37. ibid. II, p. 27.
38. ibid. pp. 36, 463 ff.
39. Lehmann: op. cit., p. 37.

psychological explanations for the bad observations, accounts which supposedly explain the establishment of the more or less arbitrary forms of superstition. Thus, magic takes on the appearance and character of a false science, one that should be corrected by true science. The curtain that floats near the open window is transfigured into a ghost by a magic and 'visionary' mentality; according to Lehmann, it was such errors of interpretation that led to the fundamental formation of the magic ideology. But the criteria adopted by Lehmann lead him into serious difficulty. Reality is not so indifferent to the various so-called correct or erroneous, superstitious or scientific interpretations, that superstition cannot introduce a new element into reality, as in the cases of therapeutic magic and telepathy. Lehmann attempts to rescue his criteria, either by trying to minimize the extent of effective magical powers (he seems to recognize only telepathy and so-called geopsychic phenomena), or by trying to make it understood that telepathy may be part of the framework of known phenomena, such as the wireless and telephone. But we have already seen what problems are created by the attempt to assimilate paranormal reality into the natural order of the positive sciences. Even if the magical claims are shown to be unjustified, except in the case of telepathy, then, at least in this case, the magical methods cannot be considered absurd; nor is the related magical technique founded on insufficient or misinterpreted observations. In this particular case, magic shows itself to be more respectful of reality than the positive sciences, because the latter still hesitate to recognize a phenomenon that magical observation, as imperfect as it may be, has recognized for what it is. The author's treatment of the problem of magic and magical powers has led to numerous difficulties and contradictions. All of them derive from his ignorance of the methodological principle involved in the historical and cultural conditioning of magic reality, and his failure to accept the magical forms of reality in their relationship to the magic existential drama.

One finds no solution to the problem of magical powers by reverting to uncontrolled irrationality. Our following section deals with the treatment of the problem by those who hope to overcome the 'naturalistic separation' by calling upon the support of magic and religious 'life'.

A suitable starting-point is the work of J. W. Hauer: *Die Religionen, ihr Werden, ihr Sinn, ihre Wahrheit,* of which the first book, *Das religiose Erlebnis auf den unteren Stufen,*[40] is of particular interest to us. According to Hauer, the science and history of religions is primarily concerned with the objective examination of religious and magical facts, with the diversity of beliefs and practices, and does not show sufficient interest in how these things were 'lived' or 'felt'. The author, along with R. Otto and F. Heiler, affirms the necessity of penetrating the 'Erlebnis' (the religious experience), and of facing up to the truths surrounding the inner experience of the supernatural. Hauer writes that until now, ethnological and historical research into religions has 'collected, with exemplary zeal, an infinite amount of material and have set out . . . the classifications of magic; however, it would be difficult to find a specialist who has turned his attention towards what is actually experienced during these magical acts. And yet, it is here that the basic and most important problem lies, the problem of the internal reality of all these extraordinary actions. It is too facile to consider the various forms of magic and its basic beliefs as illusory, the question of truth has been largely ignored; not once has serious thought been given to the problem of the reality of the observed experiences. If the task of the history of religions is to examine not only the forms, but also the evolution of religious life, then this situation must change. There is nevertheless a new orientation in Wundt's works: his 'Volkerpsychologie' deals in depth with the more intimate aspects. Otto Stoll has tried to open up magical phenomena to psychological examination and in this he has certainly taken the right direction. But what is lacking is awareness of the religious aspect of these phenomena . . . His rationalism tends to 'flatten' the question.'[41] Hauer wishes to analyse the religious (and magical) experience or 'Erlebnis', not only in by describing, from a psychological viewpoint, the experiences that the magician *believes* he is having, but

40. 'Religions, their development, thought and truth'; 'The religious experience in its initial stages'.
41. Hauer: op. cit. p. 121.

also by verifying if real powers are manifested in these experiences and beliefs. 'Stoll's examples, taken from older literature about Australia, point to the probability that magical practices cause definite psychic reactions. Many documents show that magical actions often lead to the curing of sickness. Our own knowledge of the effectiveness of suggestion affirms the reality of such experiences. "Miracles", in the sense of extraordinary experiences, received through subconscious psychic forces, are very frequent among primitive peoples. Any cure that results from a magical action is a miracle of this type. The cause of such miracles is related to a basic belief in the supernatural. In other words, it is linked to "powers". The magical act provokes a kind of "sacred" emotion in the magician, and this is communicated to those on whose behalf he is acting. One could say that a flux of magical forces is put in motion and becomes evident in the shape of emotion and excitement. One feels the presence of the "force": it operates through subconscious psychic laws. The miracle takes place: the wound no longer hurts and is healed; a new vigor spreads through the weakened body; the magical instrument, charged with "mana", hardly touches the coward and he becomes brave. The supernatural has once more been present, plunging the believer's soul into faith . . .'[42] After dealing with practices in which the crystal ball is used, Hauer broaches the problem of the origin of images that enter the subconscious during the visions seen in the crystal ball: besides the normal explanations (images that have previously been presented to the consciousness, or images that have never been conscious and which belong entirely to the subconscious), he also mentions the possibility that metagnomic knowledge is involved. He wonders whether 'clairvoyance takes place, that is, the vision of what is far away in space and time, the contemplation of future events, the supersensitive perception of far-away places and happenings. This is a problem that has existed . . . ever since the wide-spread doubt that such experiences exist; but no satisfying solution has been found . . . there is still a conflict of opinions. Today however, even among those who are gifted with a great deal of

42. Hauer: op. cit. p. 122.

critical sense, there is a tendency to admit at least the vision of what is far away in space, and this has been strengthened by affinity with the past.'[43] Hauer remains doubtful about the existence of paragnostic facts, even though he is inclined to consider them likely. He believes that the history of religions would profit considerably from a solution to the problem: 'If such experiences, or even part of them, were proved to be real, we would obviously appreciate much more their value for the history of religions . . . We would then find ourselves in front of facts that prove the existence of extrasensory perception, which the primitive can only explain as a relationship between man and the extrasensory world that hides the knowledge and all the powers to which man may have access. These aptitudes are, for the primitive, the proof of an extrasensory world, a superior world, that excites veneration.'[44] Further on, he say 'According to whether or not this problem shall be solved, so shall the specialist approach with more or less enthusiasm the study of primitive religious life. If clairvoyance and precognition are confirmed, not only shall we see the extent of the influence of the primitive prophets on their milieu, on the destiny of their peoples, on the social and religious structure of primitive society, but we shall also have proof of the existence of ·aptitudes beyond what is normal and of a link between these visionaries and the background of many events, which leads us to suppose that within their souls . . . they have accumulated intuitions that rise up from unknowable depths.'[45] In regard to precognition, Hauer refers to the 'metaphysical consequences' if its reality was proved,[46] and he maintains that the *possibility* of its existence should not be the subject of a priori rejection.[47] On the subject of Polynesian and Amerindian prophecies, he writes: 'It would not be without interest to make one comprehensive collection of all the prophecies concerning the advent of the white man and compare them with one another. Perhaps it would decide, once and for all, whether or not it is possible to see into

43. ibid. pp. 280 ff.
44. Hauer: op. cit., p. 281.
45. ibid. p. 286.
46. ibid. pp. 280 ff.
47. ibid. p. 281.

the future . . . If this is the case, then one could say that the Amerindian prophets were (through clairvoyance or through telepathy?) aware of imminent events: a tense, mental state was established and this was manifested by different "visions" . . . It is up to historical and philological research to prepare the way for the examination of pure facts on the basis of a careful comparison. Only after this may we approach the documents with the idea of finding a solution to the problem.'48

To obtain camphor, the Bataks of Sumatra, after suitable preparation, go to sleep in a sacred place; they do this so that a dream shall reveal where they will find the plant. If the dream appears, they go and search in the place indicated. Hauer comments on this: 'Unfortunately, when one relates such facts, one never tries to establish if a real clairvoyance has taken place in these dreams . . . It seems unlikely that pure chance has so frequently appeared to support this belief in dreams, to the point that they remain, even when no real experience was at the basis of the dreams: whilst saying this, it must not be forgotten that beliefs of this type persist, despite the most frequent disillusionments. On this subject, it is up to the ethnologists to do some psychologically-orientated research.'49 Hauer also quotes some cases of clairvoyance taken from the works of Livingstone, John Tanner, and John James Brown. He remarks that, even if they do not demonstrate the actual reality of clairvoyance, they still 'make the reality of the phenomenon quite credible'.50 He reports on the Tombo custom in which the new prophet must 'discover' the symbol of prophetic dignity that the old prophet has hidden in a crack in the rocks; he puts forward the opinion that, in this particular case, it is 'perhaps a question of real clairvoyance, as shown at times in paranormal psychology'.51

Hauer does not place as much credence in 'physical' paranormal phenomena as in 'mental'. He describes the psychic state in which the subject feels that he is possessed by the

48. Hauer: op. cit. pp. 286 ff., 289.
49. ibid., p. 258. On the subject of dreams that excite an almost 'sacred' emotion, see p. 232.
50. ibid. p. 285.
51. Hauer: op. cit., p. 465.

supernatural and he distinguishes subconscious impulses and possession within this experience. He analyses the type of 'possession' that is expressed in unconscious impulses, and sees two different forms: divination through automatic movements and, secondly, through ordeal. Hauer might have taken up and discussed the problem of telekinetics and the possibility that objects may move without being influenced by any unconscious physical impulse. But he says nothing about this, considering, probably, that the related documentation is too ambiguous. His theories concerning ordeal are of greater interest than the question of actual magical powers. Of course, modern specialists are inclined to regard ordeal as iniquitous, or, at least, pointless, *even* in the magic milieu. But Hauer is aware that such an attitude is far too simplistic: 'Even if mistakes and cheating can be revealed in ordeal, it cannot be *basically erroneous* (otherwise it would not have held on so tenaciously through the German Middle Ages), and if we are to accept that it was trickery, then we must also assume that all the judges that presided at such trials were men without any conscience whatever. Here again, we have the action of unconscious forces that helped the innocent and indicated the guilty. But this could only happen so long as the strength of the suggestion was effective. The innocent person who was not prone to suggestion simply had to suffer. Whenever the effectiveness of the suggestion was weakened, then the truthful aspect of the ordeal also declined'.[52] According to Hauer, two conditions are necessary if the ordeal is to be effective: a definite susceptibility to suggestion and a sense of law. Among the Amerindians, for example, the practice was never developed because they lacked a sense of law, and the civilized Europeans abandoned it because 'they are no longer sufficiently prone to suggestion'.[53] Ordeal succeeds only when unconscious impulses are allowed to act: the guilty person absorbs the poison and dies, whereas the innocent's body rejects it; sometimes a harmless potion can cause the guilty one to die. In the same way, ordeals by chance, duel, or by immersion in water, are not 'completely without foundation, *within their*

52. Hauer: op. cit., pp. 364 ff.
53. ibid. p. 365.

surroundings, because the test can excite and activate psychic forces that save the innocent . . .'[54] Hauer feels that modern psychology's interpretation of suggestion cannot cover all types of ordeal, particularly ordeal by divination and ordeal founded on a resistance to heat and fire: 'As far as ordeal by divination is concerned, in the discovery of the guilty person, one may avoid difficulties by putting forward the hypothesis of the hyperaesthesia of the medium, which has been demonstrated by hypnotic experiments concerned with the subconscious psyche. The most imperceptible changes in the guilty person's behavior or appearance are observed by the sorcerer and subconsciously condensed into stimuli. During an ordeal in a native village, for example, nobody would risk staying at home: the guilty one will therefore almost always be present. I am not concerned, here, with the widely-discussed problem of "clairvoyance" . . . The fire-walking test may be considered as the presence of god and his power within the individual who is unharmed. . . . I do not offer my opinion on the reality of such experiences, even though the related documentation is so comprehensive that it is difficult to ascribe it all to tricks, chance or illusion. . . . The present state of research makes it difficult to establish the *possible* extent of suggestion in ordeal. My own opinion is that the limits should be pushed further back, in consideration of the primitive people's susceptibility to suggestion'.[55] Ordeal must be examined within its own surroundings: . . . we have no right to consider this magical practice, in its own milieu, as iniquitous and baseless. 'In such cases, the history of religions should turn to the school of parapsychology'.[56] In other words, it is a question of an institution that is linked organically to the psychic structure of the primitive individual: once this structure has disappeared, then the institutions also fade away. The disappearance of susceptibility to suggestion is replaced by 'a development of the human soul, the evolution from a subconscious experience to one that is conscious, rational and considered'.[57] Hauer has called the attention of religious ethnologists and religious

54. ibid. p. 371.
55. Hauer: op. cit., pp. 366 ff., 371, 373.
56. ibid. p. 374.
57. ibid. loc. cit.

historians to the problem of the 'reality' of magical powers. But the possibility or probability of these powers still had no effect on *historical* awareness. If Hauer insists upon the importance of establishing the actual extent of paranormal phenomenology, it is because this is necessary if research is to be more precise. On the subject of prophets, Hauer says: 'Whatever our decision is to be on the reality of precognition, the opinion of the prophets is quite clear: man . . . through the grace of God . . . is able to listen to the far-away steps of events that are approaching, and the shadow that they cast in front of them fills his soul with a mysterious thrill. . . . This is what forms the divine nature of clairvoyance, and the *religious* value of such experiences. For this reason, they belong to the history of religions'.[58]

On ordeal through divination, he writes further on: 'The religious significance of ordeal does not depend upon the solving of this problem (of clairvoyance). . . . It is expressed in the German term "Gottesurteil"—judgment of God—and it is also illustrated by the religious practices that accompany the ordeal . . .'[59] It must be pointed out that a history of *magic* cannot separate the reality of clairvoyance from the reality of magical powers in general. But the historiographic lack of concern for the problem of magical powers becomes most obvious when Hauer speaks of the structure of the primitive mentality: 'The religious consciousness of the primitive individual has a quite different resonance from that of the man who has reached a superior degree of culture. The primitive man's typical experience of the sacred is determined . . . by his entire psychic structure. He is inclined to lose his individuality in the object. His ego is not yet entirely autonomous in its relationships to the world around it; his consciousness is complex and his concepts synoptic. At the most primitive stages of spiritual evolution, this psychic structure implies a magical and somewhat lethargic yielding to the world and to the forces hidden in it. . . . Wherever emotions related to the sacred touch a soul that is at this stage of evolution, then the world of magical forms is established'.[60] Hauer does not see the close link between

58. ibid. p. 291.
59. Hauer: Op. cit., pp. 365, 367.
60. Ibid., pp. 489 ff.

the problem of magical powers and this magical 'koinonia' of beings and things; consequently, all the previous references to 'paranormal phenomena' remain barren, and contribute almost nothing towards a better understanding. Besides this, for Hauer, the 'koinonia' is a type of mentality, and not a stage in the existential magic drama. When detached from this drama, the feeling of belonging to the universe is understood negatively, as in 'inability to distinguish', as a 'defective delimitation between the ego and the milieu', as a psychic state 'where subjective visions and voices' rise up from the subconscious.[61] What is lacking is the historiographical designation of a 'koinonia' as a threat to a presence that wishes to 'be here'. The magic world is not understood as the movement of a presence and a world that are still making decisions. Hauer does not refer to historical reason, for which he sees no real problem. In his desire to recapture the 'thrill of the divine', he entrusts himself almost entirely to feelings.[62]

As we have already pointed out, the study of magical practice and ideology usually proceeds as if no problem exists, or as if it has already been negated. Frazer's famous collection, *The Golden Bough*, is a typical example. We quote the following passage:

'This belief in the sympathetic influence exerted on each other by persons or things at a distance is of the essence of magic. Whatever doubts science may entertain as to the possibility of action at a distance, magic has none; faith in telepathy is one of its first principles. A modern advocate of the influence of mind upon mind at a distance would have no difficulty in convincing a savage; the savage believed it long ago and, what is more, he acted on his belief with a logical consistency such as his civilized brother in the faith has not yet, so far as I am aware, exhibited in his conduct. For the savage is convinced not only that magical ceremonies affect persons and things afar off, but that the simplest acts of daily life may do so too'.[63]

61. Hauer: Op. cit., p. 490.
62. The link between the magical 'koinonia' and paranormal powers was affirmed explicitly by Edgar Dacqué. But instead of making it part of a history that would have introduced magic into a widened self-awareness within our civilization, he related it to romantic ideals, as a kind of lost paradise, as an eschatalogical ideal. Magic was not included in the perspective of historical reason—it became just an archaism.
63. Frazer, J. G.: *The Golden Bough*, The Magic Art 1913, 3rd edit. I, p. 119.

Everything points to an avoidance of the question surrounding the actual existence of telepathy; the author limits himself to the ideological aspect of the magical belief. It is certainly a quite legitimate attitude, but on one condition: that the half-verified nature of the facts is recognized and that, before various beliefs are discussed, some *theory* concerning the origins or value of magic is propounded. Frazer considers magic as 'a spurious system of natural laws as well as a fallacious guide of conduct', as 'a false science as well as an abortive art',[64] more exactly, as an ideological formation and mode of conduct that has engendered false associations through resemblances (from which comes homeopathic or imitative magic) or through contiguity (contagious magic). He declares also that not one claim, nor one declaration from a magician, is based on the *least* factual foundation, that not one is devoid of fraud, be it conscious or unconscious.[65] It must be pointed out that if paranormal phenomenology is real, then the magicians' claims may have *some* basis; and that if science *doubts* the existence of telepathy . . . it is wiser to make no judgment in the light of primitive beliefs in the distant communication between individuals and in the effectiveness of various practices related to this belief. Frazer does recognize, however, that hoodoo can prove fatal, as may the violation of taboo; so, at least in these cases, the claims are not without foundation. Writing on the origins of totemism, Frazer takes into consideration the possibility of the effect of the mother's magical actions on the foetus,[66] which shows just how premature was his statement that magical powers are non-existent. The avoidance of the problem of magical powers is accompanied by the association of magic with a sort of delirium, by attempts to examine the logic behind this delirium and to reconstruct the type of mentality involved. According to Levy-Bruhl, the primitive mentality is *impervious to experimentation* because it is so dominated by supernatural influences that it is incapable of seeing how things really are. In a society that is dominated by the 'law of participation,' the primitive man would be tempted to introduce attributes and substances into the inter-

64. Frazer: Op. cit., p. 53.
65. Ibid., p. 215.
66. Frazer: *Totemism and Exogamy* IV, 1910, pp. 61-64.

relationships that are, *in reality*, either independent or distinct from them. It is a question of a mental function that has diminished in the more cultured man; a function through which everything takes place as if a veil of fantasy has been cast over the objective links between worldly realities.[67] It is obvious that this 'theory' (ignoring the objections that one could make to it on purely ethnological and methodological grounds) has been thought out as if paranormal phenomenology did not exist, and as if the related problem of magical powers had already been negated. The fact remains that all magical *participation* is real (as shown in the previous chapter), and that the sympathetic 'koinonia' of beings and objects does produce, in some cases, an historical form of reality that is 'paranormality'; so it is not a question of the primitives being 'impervious to experimentation' but rather a question of a magical experience that makes possible forms of *reality* which are not typical of *our* cultural experience.

Levy-Bruhl, in his book *Le surnaturel et la nature dans la mentalite primitive*,[68] mentions some paragnostic 'beliefs' among the primitives, and then makes the following comment: 'These facts, which are very similar to those that have been collected by the Society for Psychical Research, or that are reported in the Phantasms of the Living, are not as mysterious for the primitive mentality as they are for our own. . . . From the primitive outlook, these facts need no special explanation. They are no more surprising than metamorphoses or miracles. The primitive mentality sees in them the participation of invisible powers. At the same time, the emotion that the primitive individual experiences indicates that these elements belong to the affective category of the supernatural'.[69] Here, as in the quote from Frazer's work, we see that the author is avoiding any definite statement on the subject of magical powers, and he also expresses his intention to limit himself to the examination of ideology and beliefs. But why does he express a theory that is based on the presupposition that these powers are non-existent, and that calls upon the 'law of participation' and the 'affective category of the supernatural' in order to justify the assump-

67. See Levy-Bruhl: Op. cit.
68. The supernatural and nature in the primitive mentality.
69. Levy-Bruhl: Op. cit., p. 40.

tion that magic is impervious to experimentation? Basically, this theory does not interpret and explain the magic world, but is rather a typical reaction of the Western mentality, still imprisoned by its limited historical outlook.

Levy-Bruhl's historical limitations are expressed in the following passage, which reveals why the author rejects the question of the reality of magic: '. . . the image that the individual has of himself, both in the primitive society and our own, must be distinguished from the subjective feeling that he has of the various states of his consciousness, his emotions, thoughts, actions and reactions, etc., as he depicts them for himself. He is, for himself, an individual who is quite separate from all others, who is in opposition to them, and who considers himself in a manner that is quite different from the way in which he considers the individuals and objects around him. But this immediate perception, however strong and continuous it may be, is only a small part of the perception that he has of his entire person'.[70] Here we discover an extremely instructive dogmatic statement. Levy-Bruhl makes the a priori comment that the experience of the individual, as a unity, is common both to the magic world and to us, and the only difference between the two is in the actual *image* that we have of it: whilst we have an image of our individuality exactly as it is, that is, as a unity, the individual of the magic world, a prisoner of traditional, collective portrayals, would not recognize his own reality. He would abandon himself to his wild imagination, seeing himself as the meeting-ground of mystical participations and sympathetic links, as a unity that is unsteady and fragile in its relationships to the rest of the world, and not incompatible with the duality and plurality of existence. Whilst, for us, the individual as a unified presence is a given fact, one that accompanies us, largely unendangered, in our daily life, and because it is a given fact and not part of a cultural problem or a historical drama, Levy-Bruhl assumes that this is also so in the magic world. It is just such a misunder-

---

70. Levy-Bruhl: *L'âme primitive*, p. 70. Cf. pp. 1 ff. 'In our eyes, the individual, no matter how complex, has the basic and essential trait of being one. If this were not so, he would no longer be an individual, but a composition of several. But the primitive's concept of himself does not involve such a strict insistence upon the "oneness" of the individual'. (Op. cit., p. 250.)

standing of the nature of the personality of primitive people that stands in the way of a proper analysis of the problem of magic. Again, it is our own cultural presumption which raises our historical mode of being present-in-the-world to the dignity of metaphysics.[71]

Olivier Leroy, in his work *La raison primitive*, shows relatively few of the prejudices we have encountered regarding the possibility of paranormal phenomena. Following the experiments of Fere and Reichenbach, the author points out the possibility that primitive symbolism, generally, and the symbolism of colors in particular, correspond to a psychological reality, that is, to phenomena that are related to synaesthesia; and he puts forward the hypothesis that our habit of thinking abstractly has made us 'incapable of reacting, as nature intended, to certain subtle impressions'.[72] In a discussion with Levy-Bruhl, who uses collective images as the 'deus ex machina' in his attempt to explain belief in dreams, Leroy observes that this belief is more likely to have originated in certain individual experiences, such as dreams that reveal some particular somatic state, or those that waken latent memories within the 'subconscious memory', and give a basis to suspicions that have occurred in waking thought, etc. In other places he mentions the use of the divining-rod, and the ability to sense subterranean stretches of water. He accepts telepathy, together with precognition, as probable: 'I fail to see why people refuse to admit that the universal belief in clairvoyance and, more particularly, in its judiciary effectiveness, may not have had as its point of departure facts of this type, which seem to be more frequent among the uncivilized than in our countries, and have helped to destroy, in primitive minds, the notion that time unfolds in a unilinear series of successive moments, a concept upon which Mister Levy-Bruhl bases his philosophy.'[72] The pheno-

71. Pierre Janet commented on the facts collected by Levy-Bruhl in *L'âme primitive*: '. . . A man . . . grants himself the quality of unity, as also does he grant it to his children and to the men around him. Therefore, it is said, there must be an entity within metaphysical reality, a unity of this type, and our idea of the individual is only a copy of this real and deeper individuality. Today we are losing some of our pride, and we tell ourselves that these ideas have been fabricated by men, slowly, after much error and effort, and that the individual is our own invention . . .'' J. Janet: *L'evolution psychologique de la personnalité*, Paris, Chanine.
72. Leroy: Op. cit., p. 160.

mena related to telekinesis, among the Fans, the rapports between the 'nagual' and its owner, the effectiveness of therapeutic magic, the danger of spells, meterological crypt-aesthesia and the problem of rain-making—all these 'puzzling' subjects are dealt with by the author.[73] He reports, without comment,[74] on various exploits of sorcerers that were described to him by Father Trilles.

Leroy thinks that it is legitimate to conclude from this probable existence of a paranormal phenomenology that magic has certain 'bases in experience': 'Some facts, however few they are, and however much they have been generalized through an excess of imagination and desire for power, nevertheless provide sufficient basis, and I believe that only the deliberate rebuttal of individual experience and the assimilation of primitive by civilized thought . . . can cause my theory to be rejected'.[75] Further on, he writes: 'With this point of view, one must insist upon the experimental (or pseudoexperimental) legitimacy of the spiritualistic beliefs of the primitives, who have in their midst mediums equally as skilful or, if you prefer, as powerful, as any of the famous European mediums. The seances held in any poor Aboriginal camp are the same as any metapsychic seances held in Paris, London or Berlin. Everything is found in the primitive setting—raps, or strange noises, the displacement of objects without any obvious contact, the interrogation and replies of spirits, and levitation phenomena, with the difference that the Kurnai or Wotjobaluk medium, instead of rising a few centimeters, may be found, after the seance, perched high up in a tree, where he claims to have been placed by the "mrarts" or spirits. According to Leroy, the

73. Ibid., p. 181 ff.
74. Some of the facts mentioned are a) The sorcerer placed a stick, chosen at random, in a balancing position in the fork of a branch that had been stuck in the ground; placing his hand about ten centimeters above one end of the stick, he forced it, just by moving his hand, to make a circular movement, causing either the branch or the stick to break, even though they were both of hard wood, and the stick was as thick as a man's hand; b) another sorcerer plunged his finger into a vessel full of water and the water seemed to flee in front of his hand, forming a cone of about twenty centimeters around his finger; c) the sorcerer took a vase full of water, then took his hands away from the sides of the vase and it remained suspended in the air for a certain time before falling to the ground. During these phenomena, Trilles suspected that he was the victim of suggestion and used various mental exercises to ensure that this was not so.
75. Leroy: p. 147.

same thing sometimes happens to certain 'possessed' Africans who leave their abode at night and are found, in the morning, attached to the highest point of some tree. Father Papetard, of Nice, head of the African missions, told Dr Imbert-Gourbeyre that he had seen sorcerers rise up two or three feet in the air and walk on the tips of the blades of grass'.[76] According to Leroy, Levy-Bruhl's main error was to have underlined the grotesque and sensational side of magical ceremonies, thus giving the wrong impression to uninformed readers who are 'ignorant of the effective and, in a sense, strictly experimental side of these practices'.[77]

Once more we are faced with a false setting-out of the problem of magical powers, with all the consequent contradictions, difficulties and insufficiencies. Once more, we see the polemical reaction of our own cultural 'Einstellung' to the 'scandal' of paranormal phenomena. In the first place, it is hard to know if Leroy takes certain magical powers as proved, or only as probable, or even as just possible. There is definite uncertainty on this point: at one stage, the author admits that, even if the powers have no basis in reality, it is sufficient, for the thesis to be invalidated, that the illusion of their reality be unavoidable even for a 'normal' intelligence.[78] It is obvious, however, that if one does not decide in what sense magical powers are 'real', one cannot speak of an experimental basis of magic, because this can never be provided by an illusion, however 'unavoidable'. Before setting out his experimental theory of magic, the author should decide if the magical powers are real, in this sense— that a normal intelligence, a civilized man (for example, Crookes, Lodge or Richet) cannot escape the illusion of their reality; otherwise he must decide if they could be real in some different sense. Although the author seems to accept the probability of paranormal phenomena and even, in some cases, chooses to say that they are real, he does not entirely reject the thesis of 'unavoidable illusion'. He speaks of the 'effective and, in one sense (which?), strictly experimental side of magic practices' and of their experimental, or pseudo-

76. Ibid: p. 175 ff.
77. Ibid., p. 190.
78. Leroy: Op. cit., p. 148.

experimental legitimacy[79]; he then mentions the over-generalization of certain facts. Leroy has other difficulties. Paranormal facts do not form the only basis of magic: the Shaman's psychic voyage to the sky or to the depths, the 'ngwel' level of reality, actions carried out in dreams and perceived as real, etc., all of this cannot come into the framework of experimental magic, in the sense that one can positively prove facts and events that are held to be real. From this point of view, the concept of magic becomes both composite and contradictory: on one side, magic would be founded upon positive facts (clairvoyance, telepathy, etc.) and, on the other, rather large side, it would have no foundation whatever. According to this, the man of the magic world is able to observe some facts better than the civilized person to the point of admitting phenomena that our science, despite the refinement of research techniques, has allowed to be overlooked; at the same time, he would be a kind of visionary, plunged into a sort of dream world, subject to delirium and 'impervious to experimentation'. The difficulties and contradictions arise from the fact that Leroy has not previously analysed the various forms of magical reality and that he employs the term 'reality' uncritically. It is worthwhile to examine this basic fault in his work more closely. Given the dogmatic presupposition of a 'fixed and guaranteed world' as the only possible world, and given that *what has taken place* is the only form of reality that may be the object of the presence's experience, there are two possible basic attitudes towards the problem of magic powers: either one denies the existence of these powers (or refuses completely to even consider them), or else one more or less admits their existence, but on the condition that they may be integrated within the framework of *our own nature* and considered as given phenomena, having their place within the order of scientific laws. In the first case, ethnological research turns towards a psychological explanation of the errors, illusions and hallucinations of magic, or else it tries to reveal a particular 'mental structure' that may explain the so-called imperviousness of magic to experimentation. In the second case, ethnological research sets out an experimental theory

79. Ibid., p. 281.

of magic and an examination of the legitimate deductions that magic has made from the 'observation' of paranormal phenomena. In the first case, it is because *we* are impervious to the magical experience and to its historical forms of reality that magic becomes the imperviousness to experimentation that is implied by the reality of our world. In the second case, we impose, dogmatically, what our nature considers has taken place upon magic powers, and transpose our historical way of being present and of being able to observe the world into the magic civilization. Either way, we are doing violence to the historical realities of the world of magic, by presupposing that the fixed and guaranteed world is the only possible one, that the unthreatened presence is the only real one, that our concept of what has taken place is the only form of reality that the presence can possibly experience.

This basic error is most obvious in Vierkandt's analysis of the problem of the 'success' of magic activities. He points out various cases where the magic action may be successful, particularly the following:

a) The success is based upon the choice of an opportune moment. When the Dakota dance in order to make the bison appear, they may succeed because the beasts will eventually appear anyway; similarly, the magician will not practise meteorological magic except with extreme prudence, that is, only when his long experience shall permit him to be more or less certain that a change in the weather will appear.

b) The natural effectiveness of threat; the threatening or cursing traits of some magic rites may have real effects. For example, fright can paralyse the enemy, cries and noises can obviously affect wild animals. Before a battle, a warrior-dance may discourage the enemy and facilitate victory. People endowed with the 'evil eye' can have real effects upon others.

c) Predictions that come true: the examination of dreams to see if a plan should be abandoned or continued may have some basis 'because dreams can reflect a sort of self-knowledge, an unconscious estimation of the for and against, a concentration and unification through which one may satisfy various hopes; a favorable attitude contributes towards success'. Predictions can also influence conduct through suggestion.

d) Suggestion: one's disposition may influence conduct, particularly an optimistic disposition and a firm belief in the success of the magic action—these will create the best circumstances for actual success (which explains the effectiveness of the sorcerers' suggestion-therapy); a pessimistic disposition may have a real paralysing effect (this explains the death of someone who has been the object of hoodoo, or who has transgressed some taboo).[80]

It is obvious that Vierkandt, in this list of cases where the magical action seems to be successful, does not take the paranormal form of reality into account, nor does he mention the successes that may take place at the 'ngwel' level of reality, i.e. at a level of reality that no longer plays a part in our culture. His judgments and interpretations are based on his defining the success of an action solely as the success that is obtained at *our* historically-determined level of reality. All of them must conform to the Western concept of a successful action. The interpretations that are based on the theory of suggestion express the opinion that the person who is the object of suggestion is acting within an utterly false framework of reality. This implies that the person who is not acting through suggestion is acting within an absolutely valid framework of reality. There results a continuous distortion of the concrete magical adventure; it is incessantly manipulated to satisfy the latent polemical requirements. On one hand, the problem of paranormal reality is intentionally avoided; on the other we are supposed to accept the conscious artifices of the operator—choice of an opportune moment, skilful exploitation of normal experiences, psychological effects of threats, etc. Such distortions and manipulations help to disguise the insufficiencies and contradictions of the research; the polemical requirements are usually satisfied, but a closer look indicates the necessity to revise our own cultural 'Einstellung'.

Vierkandt makes the following observation on a warrior-dance in the Fijian islands: 'If this dance had had some

---

80. A. Vierkandt in 'Archiv fur die gesamte Psychologie' XCVIII, 1937, pp. 484-487.

warrior-magical meaning, directed against a neighboring tribe that intended to attack, and if this tribe, by means of witnesses' reports, experienced the feeling of terror that the dance excited, perhaps it would have hesitated to carry out the planned attack. In the majority of cases, the small distances and the tendency for information to spread quickly would ensure that the object of the threat would hear of what had taken place, even if he was not present'. Vierkandt does not even consider the possibility that paragnostic phenomena could play a part in this case, and his theory pays no heed to the possibility of 'influence from a distance'. Nevertheless, this paragnostic 'suggestion' is something that the ethnologist must take into account. For Vierkandt, magic remains, basically, an ensemble of illusory beliefs. Accepting this premise, he wonders how the conviction that magical powers are effective came about. He cannot conceive that magic may have originated as the expression of a presence-world relationship that is quite different from the one we know.

Ethnological research into this matter is not much better. The work carried out in paranormal psychology has had but little influence, and Lang's wish that specialists in paranormal psychology be included in ethnological expeditions has met with little support.[81] Whenever explorers, missionaries, colonial officials or members of ethnological expeditions have had the opportunity to witness apparently paranormal phenomena, they have been content to report them in a fragmentary manner, fearful of their reputations if they make any explicit affirmation. Others have considered the whole matter as trickery, or as the product of individual or collective hallucination; sometimes the whole subject was completely repressed, as if unworthy of attention, or as being outside the interests of their work. It is only in very rare

81. Specialists in paranormal psychology make quite frequent, and explicit, references to the paranormal aptitudes of certain primitive peoples. In 1928, the Society for Psychical Research in London published a list of all information received in its 'Journal' and in its 'Proceedings'—information dealing with supposed paranormal phenomena among more or less primitive populations. In 1936-37 the society began enquiries among the missionaries of the Belgian Congo to see if they knew of sorcery-phenomena . . . their efforts were rewarded with just two replies. For more recent efforts in this field, see Betty M. Humphrey: *Paranormal Occurrences Among Preliterate Peoples*, in 'Journal of Parapsychology', vol. VIII, 1944, no. 3, pp. 214-229.

cases that descriptions in any detail have been written; there
has never been any systematic research. We shall look at
some examples. On the subject of the intense dream-
experiences of the Yamanas, Gusinde writes the following:
'The thing that most encourages the Indians in their belief
in dreams is the fact that, from time to time, the presenti-
ment that arises from the dream sometimes comes true'.[82]
And concerning the Selk'nam, he says 'If a native saw a
sick relative in a dream, he would send a messenger the next
day to make enquiries'.[83] Of the Selk'nam magician Tenenesk,
we are told: 'He sometimes spoke to us of future events
that he had seen in his dreams'.[84] Tenenesk is also said to
enter a psychic state at night, during which he contacted
his 'guide': 'It was almost always concerning future events,
ones that formed some sort of threat to the Selk'nam'.[85]
Gusinde makes no deeper, no more systematic enquiry, and
his information is useless if one is trying to establish the
reality of paragnomic phenomena; the documentation is too
fragmentary and vague. Elsewhere, Gusinde declares, in a
most prudent manner, that he is *unable to decide* if the
sorcerers used knowledge based on experience and exact
observations;[86] but he is a little less prudent in a reference
to the Selk'nam: 'when the sorcerers announce that bad
weather is approaching, one cannot reject the presumption
that they are making unconscious use of their natural observations'.[87] The inadequacies of both expression and judgment
are obvious.

In Trille's work on the Pygmies of Equatorial Africa, we
find some haphazard observations that cause one to regret
the lost opportunities to make some form of systematic
examination of magical powers. There is no detailed description, even though the author exclaims 'And how many other
cases we could quote!'[88] Similarly, Schebesta, in his work,
*Der Urwald ruft wieder,** describes a magical procedure
used to catch a thief (the text does not tell us if the persons

82. Gusinde: *Die Feuerland-Indianer II*, p. 1297.
83. Ibid. I, p. 716.
84. Ibid., p. 727.
85. Ibid., p. 728.
86. Ibid. II, p. 1422.
87. Ibid. I, p. 772.
88. Trilles: Op. cit., p. 181.
* The Virgin Forest Calls Again.

indicated by the witch-doctor were really the thieves) and then he concludes rather sceptically by saying that, upon hearing such things, he could only 'shake his head in disbelief'. He considers that it was a question of hallucinations 'despite all the assurances given by the informers'.[89] The specialist in paranormal psychology would be aware of the unsuitability of such a priori scepticism. In another similar case, Knud Rasmussen, after reporting the story of the Shaman Ingjugarjwuk, makes the following comment:

'I never attempted to contradict him, even if some of his accounts seemed quite improbable to me. For instance, I could not understand that a man could survive thirty to fifty degrees of cold, sitting in a tiny snow hut without taking any nourishment simply a little tepid water twice during the whole period. I was afraid of making him cautious by doubting or asking him questions, and after all what I wanted to get to know, here as elsewhere, was these people's own beliefs. And there is not the slightest doubt that they themselves believed that the holy art itself, which consisted in being able to see into the riddles of life, imparted to novices and practitioners some special power that enabled them to go through what ordinary mortals would not be able to survive'.[90]

Rasmussen remains faithful to his methodological principle of examining *beliefs,* and sees no need to conduct a systematic enquiry into the actuality of metagnomic phenomena among the Eskimos that he was studying. He considers it sufficient to know that the Shaman *thought* he was capable of 'second sight' and that the others called him 'The one who has eyes'. The artificial separation between magic ideology and magical powers is fully revealed in this example. Given the present state of affairs in ethnological research into this subject— the reality of paranormal phenomenology among primitives— one should not be surprised that Ohlmark's richly-documented work on shamanism treats only the areas of experience and ideology, and makes only a fleeting reference to the powers that seem to appear during certain seances.[91]

The analysis of the problem of magical powers within the

89. Schebesta: Op. cit., p. 45.
90. Rasmussen: *The Intellectual Culture of the Cariboo Eskimos,* Copen. 1930, p. 55.
91. Rasmussen: *The Intellectual Culture of the Copper Eskimos,* p. 27.

history of ethnology has once more revealed the extreme limitations of our historical outlook and the circumscribed nature of our particular humanism. The association of magic with the inexact or false sciences, with an abortive technique, the reduction of magic to its ideological aspect, the rejection of the possibility of a paranormal sphere of magic reality, the attempt to place 'paranormal facts' within the framework of our own nature, the uncertainty and contradictions in research, and the utter sterility of some ventures into the subject—all of this is a result of the polemical error that attempts to make a universal application of the presence-world situation that is typical of *our* civilization. The analysis of the problem of magical powers in the history of ethnology makes us aware that what we consider as a theoretical examination of the magic world is nothing more than a practical attitude, and that what we take as understanding is still nothing more than a polemical negation. Once we are aware of this, we have at least reached a higher historical perspective and we are on the way towards a richer humanism.

In order to measure the extent of our limitations in this subject, one has only to examine the philosophy of which Hegel was prisoner, even though some of his comments show signs of a potential mastery of this limitation. Whilst the Romantics quoted dreams, ecstatic states, somnambulism and clairvoyance as gateways to the understanding of 'superior truths' and to the 'elevation of the spirit', Hegel opened up a different perspective: 'There has been a lot of discussion on man's cosmic, sideral and telluric life. Animals live in such an essentially sympathetic relationship with their surroundings; their particular nature and evolution depend upon it. . . . In man, such connections lose their importance as he becomes more civilized, and the conditions of his life depend more and more upon a basis of liberty and spirituality. . . . Among the superstitions of some peoples and the abnormalities of feeble minds, among those people who have made less progress along the way of spiritual liberty and who consequently live in a closer communion with nature, one finds certain real rapports, certain visions (founded upon these) of marvellous situations and events. But when the mind is liberated, and when the mind has a deeper understanding of itself, these mediocre attitudes, founded on the relationship between man and nature, disappear. On the other hand, the animal, like the plant, remains subject to them'.[92] Hegel does not only attack this Romantic idealization of the archaic, but also the wariness of men of 'good sense' for whom proofs and guarantees are never adequate when they are obliged to make certain concessions to 'magic reality'. On the subject of 'somnambulistic states' and the paranormal aptitudes that appear in them, Hegel observes that, if these facts must be guaranteed, this would be superfluous for those who require the proof, because they could much more easily pass them off as illusions or frauds, however reliable their source. 'In this field, if one is to believe what one sees and, moreover, understands it, then there is a fundamental condition—that one is not hampered by intellectualistic categories.[93] He goes on to state that such phenomena, and the related psychic states, cannot be understood 'so long as one retains the presupposition of personalities that are independent of one another, and independent of content, and the presupposition that temporal and spatial divisioning is absolute'.[94]

And yet, as we have said, the traditional limitation is also to be found in Hegel himself. He constructs an opposition between 'liberty of mind' and the indiscriminate union of man and nature, and he relates paranormal aptitudes to the latter servile state. Magic is still seen as something negative, as a non-culture. Hegel is unaware of the problem of the magic world, unaware of the freedom for which it is struggling, and unaware of the culture that it is trying to establish. He does not see that magical powers must be understood within the framework of the drama of a threatened presence, one that is in danger of not being here and is defending itself against this danger; it is an historically-determined existential situation that gives rise to forms of reality that are foreign to an historical situation in which the presence is guaranteed in its relationship to a 'distance' world that is

92. Hegel: *Enzyklopadie der philosophischen Wissenschaften im Grundrisse,*
   392.
93. Ibid., §406.
94. Ibid., §406.

experienced as a *given fact*. For Hegel, magic is still within the area of 'superstitions' and 'abnormalities of weak minds'. But this artificial antithesis between 'culture' and 'magic' has its origins in the persisting limitations of an historical outlook that makes culture, liberty and history the only areas in which one may find the traditional values of the 'Mind'. Hegel does not see that even the simple, humble presence that accompanies our daily acts can become a cultural problem, part of history, and the scene of a struggle for liberty. There is no doubt that the liberation that is made possible through magic is of an elementary kind, but if primitive humanity had not achieved this, we would not now be striving so vigorously for a final and complete liberation of the 'Mind'. And this modern struggle against all forms of *alienation* presupposes, as an historical condition, man's effort to save and conserve the elementary foundation of this struggle—*a presence that is guaranteed in its relationship to and within the world.*

FURTHER READING

The following books are recommended texts on magic and shamanism.

Bharati, A. (ed.), *The Realm of the Extra-Human*, Mouton, The Hague, 1976

Castaneda, C., *The Eagle's Gift*, Simon and Schuster, New York, 1981

Drury, N., *The Shaman and the Magician*, Arkana, London, 1987

Eliade, M., *Shamanism*, Princeton University Press, 1972

Elkin, A.P., *Aboriginal Men of High Degree*, University of Queensland Press, Brisbane, 1977

Halifax, J., *Shamanic Voices*, Dutton, New York, 1979

Harner, M., *Hallucinogens and Shamanism*, Oxford University Press, 1973

Harner, M., *The Way of the Shaman*, Harper & Row, San Francisco, 1980

Larsen, S., *The Shaman's Doorway*, Harper & Row, New York, 1976

Lewis, I.M., *Ecstatic Religion*, Penguin, Harmondsworth, 1971

Oesterreich, T., *Possession*, University Books, New York, 1966

Shirokogoroff, S., *The Psychomental Complex of the Tungus*, Routledge & Kegan Paul, London, 1935